AROUND THE WORLD IN MANY WAYS

AROUND THE WORLD IN MANY WAYS

Travels with a
Typewriter by
JOAN MOONEY

COLLINS AUSTRALIA

© text and photographs Joan Mooney, 1987

First published by William Collins Pty Ltd, Sydney, 1987.

Typeset by Post Typesetters, Brisbane
Printed by The Book Printer, Victoria

National Library of Australia
Cataloguing-in-Publication entry:

Mooney, Joan (Joan Veronica).
    Around the world in many ways.

    ISBN 0 00 217550 9.

    1. Voyages and travels. 2. Travelers. 3. Mooney,
    Joan (Joan Veronica)—Journeys. I. Title.

910.4

CONTENTS

People

Mysteries

Places 2

Hotels

INTRODUCTION

I first caught the travel bug when I was six as my mother regaled her family with tales from *The Arabian Nights* and the fairy stories of far-away lands.

My most treasured illustration was of an old-fashioned grocer complete with wrap-around apron magically flying through the air to the rescue of children locked in a tower by a wicked witch.

Their heads poked up through the chimney, mouths agape in astonishment at seeing their unlikely hero flying like Superman to the rescue.

It was the first intimation of a life-long affair of the heart with the romance of travel. Like the children in the tower, I still experience that vaguely unreal feeling when the big jet drops me in some exotic corner of the world.

By the age of eight, I was setting off, haversack packed with a picnic, through the suburban streets on voyages of discovery.

'I'm off to the Amazon,' I'd tell my mother, who would reply, 'Be sure to be back for tea.' My sisters and I would eat our Sao biscuits and Vegemite by the banks of some industrially polluted river. Or we would sail a leaky old tin boat, bailing furiously with a jam tin, on a small water-filled hollow in the wasteland beside the local abattoir, cheering as the sheep-filled freight trains chugged by. The smell of sheep sweat and dung was as exotic as the perfumes of faraway Araby.

By fourteen the adventure travel books of Richard Halliburton held me enthralled. He had crossed the Sahara to Timbuktu, 'bought' two Negro children in the slave market, lived with the tough soldiers of the French Foreign Legion, fallen in love with an Arab dancing girl. He had explored Baghdad, been arrested in Teheran, visited Siam and Malaya, lived with a tribe of headhunters in Borneo, swum the Hellespont. He died in a storm, crossing the Pacific in a Chinese junk.

My brothers and sisters all became infected with wanderlust. Perhaps something stirred in us from our Irish forebears who had adventured to the Antipodes to settle (one trying his luck on the Western Australian goldfields), or from their Norman ancestors who had conquered and colonized wild Ireland in the eleventh century.

Great-great aunts had travelled—Sister Marie Bernard as a missionary nun to India and Sister Laetitia to Algeria. An Aunt, Sister Eileen, was a missionary in Tonga. Grandmother sailed to America to collect a fortune which did not materialize. In any event, my brother, Justin, by the age of four was off on his dinkie peddling furious miles beside the railway track to distant suburbs until captured by alerted policemen who brought him home, screaming and protesting and still clutching his bike.

Later, he lived in New Zealand, doing what jobs he could find, worked in mines in South Africa, made cars in the industrial north of England.

Jim, a merchandise controller, went to London to study in his twenties, journeyed widely thereafter on business, including a trip to China to buy silk, when only a few foreigners were being allowed in.

Monica went off to live in London at twenty and married an Englishman she met there, who later became a foreign correspondent. They were equally at home in Singapore, Bangkok, Delhi and London, until her husband, Tony, was killed on assignment. She and her young son Daniel still travel abroad from Australia most years, in school holidays.

Kathie became a lawyer and seemed set to stay at home, while her husband, a senior public servant, travelled the world on business. But, once her children were grown or nearly grown, she journeyed with him to South America, Canada, Europe and South East Asia, and holidayed with the children in Bali and China.

But it was my sister, Pat, who took off with me, both of us in our early twenties, to see the world, setting out excitedly on a tramp cargo boat across the Pacific to live and work in Canada, while we saved for the Grand Tour of Europe.

The following year, in London, we worked and lived on sausages and fish and chips, shivering over the two-shillings-in-the-slot gas meter, to save our pennies. We queued on stools to see some of the best theatre in the world from the 'gods' and pinched ourselves to be sure it was really happening when Charles Laughton and Elsa Lanchester threw money in the hat of performing buskers.

Our hearts were young and gay and the world was our oyster.

Years later I returned to live and work in London, the base of my travels.

Pat settled down and married a pharmacist, hanging up her travel shoes for the time being at least.

Not to be outdone, my mother, once her family had grown up, took herself off on a world tour. As for me, after a nursing career, fifteen years ago I became a journalist, specializing in travel writing. At first I worked as a feature writer on the *Daily Telegraph* and *Sunday Telegraph*. I remember when first offered my big chance, a job on the *Daily Telegraph*, I told my future boss, Ita Buttrose, 'I can't start straight away, I'm off to India for two months.' She grinned and acquiesced: 'But write some stories for us.'

Five years later I began freelancing as a travel and feature writer, becoming, in turn, travel editor of the *Australian Women's Weekly*, *Leisurelife* and *Better Homes and Gardens*. I also wrote about travel for numerous magazines and newspapers including the *Australian*, *Sun-Herald*, *Sydney Morning Herald* and the Adelaide *Advertiser*. And so to my first travel book.

This is not your typical guide book but one for the armchair traveller—a kind of 'magic carpet', a book for a cold rainy day, or that half hour before you turn out the light and dream. You'll meet the people I've met, see the places I've seen, stay in the hotels I've stayed in, adventure with me. You may even decide to travel to some of the places.

As one wise man said: 'Travel is a good way to spend your money, because it buys experience.'

This is also a book for my old age when I can only travel in memory.

ITHAKA

As you set out for Ithaka
hope your road is a long one,
full of adventure, full of discovery,
Laistrygonians, Cyclops,
angry Poseidon—don't be afraid of them:
you'll never find things like that on your way
as long as you keep your thoughts raised high,
as long as a rare excitement
stirs your spirit and your body.
Laistrygonians, Cyclops,
wild Poseidon—you won't encounter them
unless you bring them along inside your soul,
unless your soul sets them up in front of you.

Hope your road is a long one.
May there be many summer mornings when,
with what pleasure, what joy,
you enter harbours you're seeing for the first time;
may you stop at Phoenician trading stations
to buy fine things,
mother of pearl and coral, amber and ebony,
sensual perfume of every kind—
as many sensual perfumes as you can;
and may you visit many Egyptian cities
to learn and go on learning from their scholars.

Keep Ithaka always in your mind.
Arriving there is what you're destined for.
But don't hurry the journey at all.
Better if it lasts for years,
so you're old by the time you reach the island,
wealthy with all you've gained on the way,
not expecting Ithaka to make you rich.

Ithaka gave you the marvellous journey.
Without her you wouldn't have set out.
She has nothing left to give you now.
And if you find her poor, Ithaka won't have fooled you.
Wise as you will have become, so full of experience,
you'll have understood by then what these Ithakas mean.

C.P. Cavafy

The poem, 'Ithaka', is from *Collected Poems* by C.P. Cavafy, translated
by Edmund Keeley and Philip Sherrard, published by Chatto and
Windus, London.

JOURNEYS

OVERLAND BY BUS FROM ENGLAND TO INDIA

THE craving of the travel addict to set out on yet another journey is never satisfied.

The lure is not simply exotic scenery or the chance to acquire rare and beautiful objects. It is also the strange encounter, the exciting adventure which draws the traveller, for a time, into an entirely different life.

The non-traveller exclaims: 'Why are you wasting all your money on trips?' The traveller says: 'I am buying experience and that is beyond price.'

My journey from England overland to India was packed with rare experiences, especially in remote areas.

South of the Great Salt Desert and the Great Sand Desert lies the desolate waste of Baluchistan. A province of Iran, it borders Pakistan. By bus we journeyed to the border at Mirjaveh. All day we had bumped over rutted tracks, been jolted through dry river beds and inhaled the fine dust which enveloped us, despite the scarves wound around our mouths and noses.

At night the wind swept across the desert, temperatures fell rapidly and there was no protection in our tents against the biting cold.

Once we stopped to look at a fire tower in the desert. Like a lighthouse, it acted as a beacon for travellers. A tall round tower, at night its fires guide the camel trains across the sea of desert.

Bands of camels passed our bus. The occasional mud village came into sight and the encampment tents of nomads, their women dressed in brilliant red and pink dresses with lots of gold jewellery.

Once the terrible yet fascinating monotony of the desert was broken by the beautiful blue and green domes and minarets of a village mosque.

At night we pitched our tents where we found firm ground, if possible near a stream. This particular night we had come to a strange formation of tall, eroded rock pillars. They looked like enormous termite columns and at night cast weird and mysterious shadows. Between two such columns I spread out my camp stretcher. The moon came up, quite enormous, then suddenly disappeared behind a bank of clouds.

In a moment of revelation I knew why the desert held such fascination for the hermits, desert fathers and mystics who had retreated here over the centuries.

After a week of travelling through such desert, my skin was a fine mixture of mud, sweat and dust. Carefully I had hoarded enough water to heat for a bath. So, when dinner was over and the portable gas cookers free, I boiled the water, then, with my round plastic bowl, retired behind the largest rock column I could find for the luxury of a sponge with hot water.

Afterwards I joined my fellow passengers huddled in the bus, consuming vast quantities of 'anti-freeze', an aromatic brew of cheap red wine, spices and any fruit we could manage to collect boiled together with sugar. With the illusion of warmth this concoction gave us, we had the courage to brave the cold desert night air in our tent encampment.

Every passenger was secretly polishing up an item to entertain at our forthcoming bus concert. So I crept away from the bus to practise a song I had written for the occasion. I told myself the desert held no terrors for me.

Behind a dry, withered bush, by the light of a candle, I crouched learning my surprise item song. The desert stretched to the rim of the world. I seemed the only person in existence.

But suddenly I became aware of what looked like a glow on the horizon. A shooting star perhaps? A fire in the desert? An encampment of nomads? The glow rapidly became larger. I was caught in the beam of a strong dazzling yellow light which was closing in. I realized it was truck headlights!

I felt like a dazed rabbit. I did not know which way to run. My candle went out. I could not see the road because the terrain was flat to the horizon, so I had no means of knowing where the road lay or which way to run to avoid the truck.

In those few seconds I knew if I made the wrong decision and ran into the pathway of the truck I would be killed. I ducked to the right. The truck was almost upon me. With one last effort I threw myself to the left. The truck almost grazed me, then sped off into the distance and disappeared. It must have been the only truck through the desert that night.

From afar the sound of singing came from the bus where the wine was still passing freely. I lay on the cold sand, my heart still pounding with fear. The truck's yellow light quickly disappeared. I knew then that the driver had not even seen me.

Another night-time incident took place in a Persian garden.

The Caspian Sea lay on our left as our bus sped along the highway through the dark Persian night. On our right the hidden mountains were full of bears and other wild animals.

The night air was humid, soft and enervating. Rice, tobacco, and bamboo grew in profusion. Malaria flourished in the damp swampy areas. There were rumours of opium takers and attacks by wolves. It was something of a surprise then to come to the huge luxury hotels, gambling casinos and bathing sheds of a Riviera-like coastal resort. The town of Ramsar was a popular spa with sulphur baths.

The lights of a huge golden hotel-cum-casino twinkled in the moist electrically charged air, but it was too expensive for our slender resources. Our bus driver searched diligently for a camping site as the night grew late.

We had been warned of the dangers of sleeping out away from the towns. In despair we approached the local police station for help. Complete with police escort on motor cycle with red light flashing and siren screaming, we sped on our way to the botanical gardens where we had permission to sleep.

The ground was too hard to pitch our tents, so we put our canvas stretchers on the well-kept gravel paths around the fountain. A gentle breeze had sprung up carrying the scent of the garden's roses, orange blossom and jasmine. Exhausted, I soon fell asleep.

It must have been about 2 a.m. when I woke suddenly, with the uneasy feeling that something was wrong. I lay quite still. Yes, someone was marching up and down through the lines of stretchers. I listened to him tramp to the end of the line, stop, turn, and retrace his steps. Carefully I opened one eye and caught a glimpse of a rifle. The man passed the head of my stretcher.

I lay for some time in that state half way between sleeping and waking, not quite sure whether I was dreaming the whole thing. Then, realizing I could not do anything if a brigand had us under guard, I somehow managed to drift off to sleep.

About 5 a.m. I woke to the sound of marching feet as our guard was changed. Were we prisoners? Had some opium fiend come down from the wild mountains to hold us to ransom? I raised my head. We were surrounded by exotic shrubbery from which peered curious faces. One of the local people, armed with a stick, kept the gaping villagers at a distance. They stood silently in rows staring at the strange gypsies camped in their gardens.

A kindly policeman, our armed guard of the night hours, handed out roses to all the ladies as he gently woke us. The smell of frying eggs rose into a cloudless blue sky. I washed in the garden fountain which the rising sun bathed in rose pink and pinned my rose on my blouse.

Ramsar by day looked far from the desolate place of my fears the previous night. Misty blue mountains, rice fields, thatched roofed barns on stilts where rice was stored and holiday cottages bordered a flat, grey sea. We drove to the large attractive hospital to contribute our collective donation as thanks for hospitality, but staff would not accept it.

So, to the sounds of flute and drums of a band posed on an outdoor dais, and to tooting horns and waves from passing buses, we sped away.

Pakistan was the country of my next adventure. In Lahore I met the incredible Fakir of Lahore.

Hidden deep in the city's teeming markets near the Bhati Gate lay his treasure house. In the surrounding crowded bazaar, copper artisans beat into shape huge pots and pans in front of an audience of village belles.

They had come to Lahore from a small village to help one of their number, a bride, select her trousseau for her wedding day on the morrow. Thousands of rupees were spent ($A1 is worth about nine rupees) on a bride's 'box' and since family pride was at stake and the dowry goes on public display in the village, families often go into lifetime debt to provide an extravagant wedding display.

But it was the Fakir I had come to visit. He welcomed us—a portly man with a straight army carriage and courteous smile—in the gateway. We proceeded through a dim cool courtyard and mounted a flight of steps, continuing through a series of drawing rooms. Like an Aladdin's Cave, they were crammed with art treasures—paintings, carvings, historical books and letters, and jewels in old carved boxes. There were Chinese carpets, precious manuscripts, heirlooms and souvenirs of life in the Mogul courts.

The house, with all its treasures, was a private museum of the Fakir, who opened it to the public.

It was my first meeting with a Fakir, a title given to a holy man. Long ago, the founder of his family settled in Lahore in the service of the Governor and quickly rose to become minister. This ancestor had been interested in medicine and mysticism, becoming a disciple of the local 'saint' and, in turn, receiving the title of Fakir, which passed on to his descendants.

In 1799 his eldest son, a physician, treated the Conqueror of Lahore, Maharaja Ranjit Singh, for an eye infection. The Maharaja liked the witty, charming young man and took him and his brother into service.

The two brothers advised on diplomatic matters and the British government, knowing they had the Maharaja's ear, sent them many gifts. Queen Victoria presented the family with a gold-framed portrait, a chiming clock and a state coach and horses which remained in the family for seventy years, although not used much because the roads were so bad. Finally the coach was sold to a blacksmith.

The present Fakir's father was honorary magistrate and the Fakir himself a retired major.

When two small children, a boy of four and a girl of two, appeared, the Fakir swung them high in the air.

'Your grandchildren?' a tall British lady enquired of the elderly Fakir.

'My children,' he replied. 'I have ten and we hope to make it a round dozen. After all, my wife is a young woman.'

'Oh, the lovely things—are they for sale?' exclaimed a gushy American lady, not over the children but over the sparkling jewels.

'Perhaps you would like to choose one,' replied the Fakir.

She hesitated and was lost as her husband quickly interjected: 'You've got enough, honey.'

Defeated, she murmured: 'I'll bet you love your jewels, sir!'

'These are my jewels,' replied the Fakir, hugging his children.

Among the delicate embroideries, the paintings and fine silver, a tea tray appeared and the bearer served delicious flower-scented tea and small sweet biscuits.

While we ate, the Fakir told the story of his family's Holy Koran. It was hand-written by a poor peasant who spent a lifetime writing in large letters adorned with coloured designs, for all the world like a medieval monk.

The book became so large that he hired a cart to take it to the local nawab or ruler. But, as he was passing Lahore Fort, the Maharaja saw him wheeling his cart and called him in. On hearing his story, the Maharaja paid the peasant a fabulous sum for the book. Later he gave it to his favourite physician, the present Fakir's ancestor.

During the British Raj the Fakir was asked to bring some of his treasures to the vice-regal lodge at Simla to show the Governor and his wife.

Four o'clock chimed on the Queen Victoria clock. The American lady began again:

'I bet I know what you think of first thing in the morning.'

The Fakir raised his eyebrows: 'Indeed?'

'Why, your beautiful treasures, of course.'

'Madame,' the Fakir replied sternly, 'the first thing I think of in the morning is my God!' Then, to soften his apparent rebuke, he added: 'Like most Christians.'

We lingered for a last look through the treasure house. The Fakir bowed and took his leave. Finally, we recrossed the courtyard where the laughing children played. As we came to the gate, I glanced back into a room opening off the courtyard.

Inside was the Fakir, head bowed to the ground in the direction of Mecca, kneeling on his prayer mat.

The sound of his intoned prayers followed me: 'Allah is Good. Allah is Merciful. There is no God but Allah.'

And so we journeyed to India where I encountered the Vegetarian Congress in Delhi.

The city was festooned with banners which entreated in English and Hindi: 'Do not eat your friends the animals.'

We emerged through the gateway of the Red Fort, still dazzled by the magnificent Sound and Light spectacle, our heads full of stories of cruel Mogul emperors, slaves, barbarian invasions, massacres, beautiful weeping harem women and the might of the British Raj.

Crowds streamed along the road and taxis were scarce. Then a gentle Indian voice at my elbow offered assistance.

'You will come with me please, miss. The lady with you is elderly. Our bus will carry you.'

My new-found acquaintance seated himself beside me.

'And what do you think of the Congress?' he asked enigmatically.

Baffled, I fenced for time: 'A good idea.'

'But what did you think of the American speaker?'

'Interesting,' I replied. I could not keep this up indefinitely. I had not the remotest idea what he was talking about.

'But I do not think he should have said what he did!'

'Oh?'

'Yes, when he said he thought the food was good and he hoped there was more coming from the same direction!'

It was then I sighted the banners. We had managed to become involved with the Vegetarian Congress.

I asked the bus driver to let us off at the Moti Mohal restaurant in the Old City where we intended to dine.

'Oh, are you going?' exclaimed my new friend regretfully.

'I'm afraid so.'

The Moti Mohal is famed for its chicken *tandoori*, so feeling

like traitors to our new-found animal-lover friends, we tucked
into delicious spicy chicken, accompanied by *chapatis*. There
was no rice since it was one of Delhi's rice-free days. The
idea was not only to conserve rice but to accustom Indians
to eating rice-free meals.

We were munching the bones when to my horror my
vegetarian friend reappeared. Hastily, we pushed our plates
with the telltale bones under the table.

'Oh, I have found you!' he exclaimed. 'May I join you?'

'Please do.'

He gave a little chuckle.

'I thought you were with the Congress, so I was surprised
when you got off the bus.'

Looking at our bare table, he said: 'Now I will order sweets.'
And on his instructions a motley array of rich, milky desserts
appeared. Highly flavoured and wrapped in edible silver paper,
they were exotic, sweet and perfumed.

'Try one of each,' our host insisted.

When we commented that riceless days seemed a good idea
given the then shortage of rice, our friend said:

'India can feed itself, it is just poor distribution which causes
famine,' and he discoursed on Indian economics. We learned
that he was an economist from Bombay.

'Would you like to meet Mrs Gandhi?' he asked suddenly.

'We would love to but our bus leaves tomorrow.'

'No, you must stay,' he insisted. 'I will also introduce you
to the President.'

Was he just being polite or saying what he thought would
please us, I wondered. In any case, we never found out. It
was time to go.

Outside the restaurant, the markets had closed. The night
had grown quiet. A few beggars slept in the streets. A flower
seller walked by and quickly our Indian friend hailed her.
Garlands of jasmine exchanged hands. He took our wrists
and entwined them with jasmine. Clutching balloons pur-
chased from another street seller, we were ceremoniously
ushered into a small taxi. Our friend bowed.

'I hope you like India,' he said and stood motionless, watching our taxi disappear.

My companion smiled. We had the same thought. 'They
say India gets into your blood,' she said.

It was the feast day of the founder of the Sikh religion.

All day the faithful had gathered at the Golden Temple in Amritsar in the Punjab area north of Delhi. Clad in rainbow-hued saris, the men wearing intricately folded brilliantly coloured turbans, the pilgrims gathered, garlanded with ropes of the auspicious flower, the orange marigold.

The Sikhs don't cut their hair. The little boys wore it tied in a small topknot encased in a knotted white handkerchief. Their father's long hair was turbanned, beards greased and encased in fine hairnets tied under the chin.

Wild-looking holy men with matted hair and staring eyes carried tridents, the symbol of the god of destruction, Shiva. Priests wandered among the crowds doling out handfuls of a sweet porridge-like substance which I accepted and ate in one gulp. It was not polite to refuse *prasad* (holy food).

Every Sikh wishes to visit the Golden Temple at least once during his life. Lord Buddha is believed to have rested here. The 'tank' or 'pool' was built in the sixteenth century and the temple is situated in the centre of the Tank. It has had a chequered history, the temple being desecrated and destroyed many times by Mogul rulers. It has been used as a dancing hall and as stables. Now it is once more the centre of the Sikh religion.

A two-storeyed marble building, built on a twenty-metre square platform in the centre of the tank, it is called 'golden' because its dome and upper walls are covered with gold-plated copper sheets. Its four doors open east, west, north and south, symbolizing that the temple is open to all, irrespective of caste or creed.

Inside the temple, on a platform under a jewel-studded canopy, rested the Sikh bible, which is carried in a golden palanquin from the 'Divine Throne' to the Golden Temple, at 5 a.m. in winter, 4 a.m. in summer, and returned at 10 p.m. in winter, 11 p.m. in summer.

Without ceasing, songs from the Holy Book were sung by the *ragis* (musicians). Upstairs in the marble Hall of Mirrors the priests recited the Sikh bible from cover to cover. Hymns were inscribed in letters of gold on the walls.

The rules of the temple are simple and apply to all visitors. Tobacco, narcotics and intoxicants are not to be brought into temple precincts. Shoes, used socks, sticks and umbrellas must

be left outside. Temple employees guard them free of charge.
A visitor may wear unused socks, but failing this, must wash
his or her feet at the taps by the entrance to the grounds.
Visitors, including men, must keep their heads covered while
on the holy premises.

The Sikhs are renowned for their hospitality. Cooked food
is distributed in the free kitchen twice daily to all visitors.
A free hostel is maintained for pilgrims and, not surprisingly,
is used by many young people travelling on a shoestring,
who can stay up to four days. The hostel has 156 rooms
and eight large halls, and lodgers are obliged not to teach
anything contrary to Sikhism.

I knew of the Sikhs' kind welcome to visitors, as friends
had stayed there to rest and meditate, using the extensive
library and sitting quietly by the Tank at night. Today the
House of Hospitality was full. I was staying at a nearby
inexpensive lodging place with other travellers on our overland bus from Europe.

The Golden Temple was reflected in the still waters of
the Tank and tiny candles in holders surrounded the water.
At night the myriad flickering lights would be reflected in
the dark water, while overhead fireworks would explode in
showers of colour against the black velvet sky. The smell
of incense drifted on a wave of sound as the blind musicians
played their plaintive hymns and sang in high-pitched voices.

Inside the temple an altar covered with a beautiful cloth
was heaped with gifts of jewels, silverware, money and flowers.
The officiating priest solemnly garlanded me with marigolds.

Upstairs, the holy men read the Sikh bible unceasingly—
three shifts of men taking eight hours each over the twenty
four hours. Lights, colourful crowds, incense and singing, and
children holding balloons, added to the gaiety.

Outside the holy compound, stalls sold souvenirs—wooden
combs used to tidy the long hair of Sikhs and kept tucked
in turbans, bangles of friendship worn by Sikhs, swords with
which they gird themselves.

Despite the crowds, there was a still centre to the celebrations—an air of tranquillity. I wanted to stay on and enjoy
the peaceful atmosphere but had to leave.

Slowly I threw a marigold into the water. It floated off
as the candles were being lit one by one around the pool.

A soft voice issued from a figure clad in a pink and silver sari: 'You have ensured your return to India,' said the oracle.

The orange marigold, like a small flame, floated across the Tank and came to rest against the Golden Temple.

(Note: On a later visit to India troubled times had come to the temple, with Sikh uprisings and an invasion by Indian troops to clear the temple of arms and ammunition, which later led to the assassination of Prime Minister, Mrs Indira Gandhi by her Sikh bodyguards.)

BY BOAT TO CHIANG RAI THROUGH OPIUM WARLORD COUNTRY

IT was at Fang, a little Thai town near the Burmese border, 900 kilometres north of Bangkok, that one of our party narrowly avoided disaster.

Convinced he was born a trishaw driver, he borrowed a rickety-looking vehicle from an astonished local. To his horror, it had a mind of its own and went careering off towards a canal.

A swift 'about wheel' averted a dunking, but overturned the trishaw. The result: a speedy pay-up for the damaged hood.

Fang was also memorable as the place where we acquired an assortment of headgear, conical coolie hats, army-type tropical helmets, Charlie Chan models, baseball hats and wide-brimmed peasant straws.

We may have looked like a lot of Charlies but the hats plus long shirts and slacks were to be our only protection against the scorching sun on a five-hour trip down the broad Mae Kok River in an open, long-tailed motor boat.

Our destination was Chiang Rai, an ancient town and centre for treks into tribal country where more than 50,000 colourful hill tribe people live in small villages.

Chiang Rai is the nearest Thai town to the notorious opium-growing Golden Triangle, the area where Burma, Laos and Thailand meet.

A two-day trip from the capital city of Northern Thailand

Chiang Mai, to Chiang Rai, taking in the elephant training school at Mae Sa, the river trip and an overnight stay at Chaing Rai cost about $200 per person in 1982. We could also have taken a raft trip which takes several days. After negotiating the rapids, we were glad we hadn't.

We could also have taken a bus from Chiang Mai to Fang, hired a trishaw to Tha Ton where we boarded the river boat. It took ten people and cost us about eight dollars each.

It's a fascinating trip, well worth any minor discomfort such as sunburn.

Along the way we gave a lift to two armed soldiers who made us feel secure against the odd marauding opium smuggler who might appear out of the jungle. Villagers also hitched rides with us.

As monsoon clouds scattered across the sky, we passed big bamboo fishing platforms, thick jungle, corn fields, kids swimming naked in the river, water buffalo and army checkpoints.

We went ashore for lunch, clambering up muddy banks into a jungle alive with insects and butterflies. We enjoyed our sandwiches, fruit, beer and fruit juice, despite the strong smell of sulphur from a nearby stream.

Thus fortified we continued our journey, trying to appear nonchalant as fierce swelling rapids seemed to threaten to swamp the boat. Having safely negotiated the rapids, we passed a strange, tree-covered mountain, where steps led from the bank to a cave inhabited by a solitary monk who meditated in front of a statue of Buddha.

As we neared Chiang Rai, huge wooden water wheels came into view. We disembarked into the riverside Natural Cafe. Menus featured such exotic dishes as 'chicken gratification' and drinks weirdly named 'cream-curdled raspberry whisky sour', 'kiss kiss' and 'bartender'. I stuck to cold beer.

The Natural Cafe also advertised Turkish baths, although how anyone would want a Turkish bath in the steamy jungle heat was hard to fathom.

The pile of business cards on the cafe counter advertised the Porn House. They read: 'When you arrive in Chiang Rai, don't hesitate! Porn House welcomes you. It's a great experience!'

It was not, however, what it seemed. The Porn House is the original house for Westeners in Chiang Rai. It boasts:

'Cheap rates, good food and milkshakes... backgammon, chess and Master Mind... or if you prefer badminton or table tennis.'

At that time (1982) a dormitory cost one dollar, a private double room two dollars. Another guest house, the Chiang Rai, sounded a safe refuge, boasting it was 'safe, clean, quiet, comfortable', and continuing 'we will be your friend through thick and thin'. A single room cost one dollar fifty.

This guest house runs Chiang Rai Tribal Trekking Tours, travelling, it advertised, by 'bees, mini-bus and foot'. I've tried many strange forms of transport but never bees.

Chiang Rai is the starting point for many hikes through beautiful country and remote tribal villages, including those of the Yao, Lahu, Akha and Lesu tribes. A trek into the 'Poppy Field' for December to February sounded adventurous, especially if you happened to meet an opium warlord. Trekkers can eat meals in the villages. Costs then (1984) were about twenty-five dollars for three days to about fifty dollars for seven days. Your personal porter was an additional cost.

Day tours of Chiang Rai itself included a trip to Maesai to shop for jewellery and jade, visits to a hill tribe shop, to the Fish and Crab Caves and to the monkeys in the forest.

Less adventurously, we took trishaws to the Western-style Wiang Inn Hotel, the only first-class hotel in town. Its brochure boasted that its Hill Club offered 'romantic and exciting atmosphere of technical and colourful lights with music'. It also enthused about a local sightseeing trip to 'Chiang Saen of historical and archaeological fame—hill tribe settlements, breathtakingly beautiful waterfalls, monasteries ornately decorated in the traditional architectural style and the Phra That Doi Tung Temple, pride of the Chiang Rai People'.

Chiang Rai was a pleasant little town for a peaceful evening stroll. Locals enjoyed dinner at sidewalk stalls and small backyard industries included a shop which recycled tin cans into buckets.

That night I tried the Hill Club, which turned out to be the hotel's nightclub. The 'romantic music' was loud rock, the 'exciting atmosphere of technical and colourful lights' was the torches used by waiters to light their way in almost total darkness.

Next morning we returned to the delightful Chiang Mai, back on the beaten tourist track.

But no tourist delights could beat the unique flavour of the Chiang Rai experience. Some day I'll return and take that tribal trek travelling by bees.

THE THAMES—
WIND IN THE WILLOWS
COUNTRY

'NOTHING seems to matter. That's the charm of it. Whether you arrive at your destination or whether you reach somewhere else,' said Ratty in *Wind in the Willows*.

It is a perfect philosophy for boating on the Thames. And that's not surprising since author, Kenneth Grahame, wrote his delightful book about riverside life in the little Thames-side village of Pangbourne.

For centuries, the Thames has been celebrated in poetry and song.

'Sweet Thames, run softly, till I end my song', wrote Edmund Spenser in the sixteenth century.

And when Sir Walter Raleigh wrote: 'There are two things scarce matched in the Universe; the sun in heaven and the Thames on earth', it must surely have been after boating on the river on a fine summer day.

Thames country has some wonderful characters, such as the Vicar of Bray, and actor Garrick, who built a villa and Ionic Shakespeare temple here in the eighteenth century.

As for the pageant of history, the Thames boasts a cast of thousands including Julius Caesar, Alfred the Great—whose sons guarded its crossings—and William the Conqueror, who held England through his chain of great castles along its course at Windsor, Wallingford and Oxford.

Henry VIII moved into Thames country when the out-of-favour Cardinal Wolsey gave him Hampton Court—a gesture meant to save his head from the block, but a fruitless one.

You can dawdle along the Thames by steamer from Windsor to Oxford, stopping off at riverside towns along the way. The steamers also provide a service for most of the 146 kilometres between Kingston and Oxford. You can hire a motor cruiser, punt, skiff or sailing boat. Or you can do it in luxury on a holiday package deal aboard a motor boat.

It's a delightful way to spend a holiday—watching the river craft, the picturesque Thames villages, and the working of the locks as boats proceed up and down river.

From Teddington, near Kingston, the Thames comes under the care of the Thames Conservancy, a government body which looks after its forty-four locks, weirs and overfalls on the 217 kilometre stretch from Teddington to Cricklade, 112 kilometres beyond Oxford.

The Conservancy also removes sunken vessels and obstructions from river and towpaths, regulates water levels, grants licences for river works, registers river craft and prevents pollution from vessels.

Kingston, an old market place, now a bustling town, boasts the coronation stone of the Anglo-Saxon kings, which gave the town its name. It lies outside Kingston's Guildhall.

The ghost of Henry VIII's fifth wife, Catherine Howard, is said to haunt the galleries of Hampton Court, where she was executed. Hampton Court, on the Thames, has many tourist attractions including the state apartments, banqueting hall, the Great Vine (planted in 1769) and the maze where tourists often get lost. (In 1986 one of the wings was gutted by fire. A multi million dollar restoration is planned.)

Runnymede and Magna Carta Island bring back memories of 'bad' King John and the barons. There is also a modern memorial to President John F. Kennedy.

Magnificent Windsor Castle was begun by William The Conqueror and added to by Henry I. State apartments and the chapel of the Knights of the Garter, with its banners and helmets of knights, are open to the public when the court is not in residence.

Eton College, across the river, was founded in 1440 by Henry VI. Visitors to its school rooms will find the initials of many famous men carved in the desks.

The Thames at Windsor is a tangle of ducks, swans, barges and steamers. People lounge under gay umbrellas in riverside gardens or sip wine in riverside restaurants with flowered patios, ideal vantage places for viewing life on the great river.

The panorama of river life continues to unfold. Fishermen squat patiently on river banks. Swimmers bathe gently in its shallows. Families picnic in fields of yellow buttercups.

Luxurious mansions, including that of Michael Caine, are glimpsed behind thickets of trees.

Past Windsor, Datchet village is famous for its mead (stream) where Falstaff was ducked by the merry wives of Windsor.

At Black Polts that dedicated fisherman, Izaak Walton, and his friend, Sir Henry Wootton, came fishing. Walton was inspired to write his *The Compleat Angler*, the fisherman's 'bible'.

Kids splashing in the Thames obviously had not read the notices warning that it was unsuitable for bathing. Pollution was not, however, a patch on New York judging by the comment of an American couple: 'You can't swim the Hudson River, you'd be dead before you reached the other side!'

Maidenhead is a beautiful town which received its charter in the time of Elizabeth I and still boasts old alms-houses. Its river lock, Boulters' Lock, has very beautiful flower gardens.

Cookham Village, with its picturesque churches and houses, was the home of painter Stanley Spencer, who did his visionary modern village Christ and the Apostles paintings here.

The scene is quite a contrast to the magnificent mansion, 'Cliveden', once linked to the notorious Profumo scandal. In 1963 Cabinet Minister Profumo was involved in nude midnight romps in and around 'Cliveden's' swimming pool. Its former owner, Viscount Astor, gave it to the National Trust and it is now open to the public.

Bourne End, a long straight reach of the Thames, is much loved by yachtsmen. A little way upstream, the colourful detective writer Edgar Wallace is buried in Little Marlow churchyard. Australia's own Dame Nellie Melba stayed in Quarry Cottage in the near-by Quarry Wood.

Marlow, with its long graceful suspension bridge and old churches, is a favourite spot for lunch in the gardens. The poet Shelley lived here and wrote *The Revolt of Islam*. So did the woman who later became his wife, Mary Godwin, author of the spine-chiller, *Frankenstein*.

The steamer proceeds upstream past Bisham Abbey, a Tudor house haunted by a most unpleasant lady, the cruel Lady Hoby, who beat her child to death for blotting his copy book.

At the thirteenth-century Medmenham Abbey, The Hell Fire Club with notorious Sir Francis Dashwood and his wicked rakes, known as the Monks of St Francis, staged their lavish orgies.

The river becomes a narrow, sun-dappled stream with leaning willow and lime trees, quacking 'up tails all' ducks and graceful swans.

The Thames swans belong to the Queen and to the Vintners' and Dyers' companies. Each of the three groups of swans has it own 'swan master'.

Every year the colourful ceremony of 'swan upping' is held. 'Upping' involves cutting nicks in the beaks to mark the birds. Vintners' birds have two nicks. Dyers' have one and royal birds have not been marked since 1910. Swan upping takes place in July or August and is done by officials in six boats. The two companies received the privilege of owning and marking swans in the time of Edward IV.

The swan population is kept at 610—500 grown birds and 110 cygnets. Of these, sixty-three birds belong to the Dyers, forty-five to the Vintners and the rest to the Queen.

The river's ever-changing scene is now composed of quaint thatched cottages, sunburnt kids, canvas camps, couples walking dreamily along towpaths, and brown and white cows knee-deep in green pastures.

Boats come in every shape, size and name. There are *Toad II, Running Wild, Starfish, Sunburnt* and *Just in the Nick of Time* (bought before inflation perhaps).

Henley-on-Thames is the famous sailing regatta town. Its other claims to fame are a fine old church and ancient inns. Charles I slept at one, the Red Lion, in 1632.

Houseboats and pretty riverfront restaurants testify to the town's popularity.

There are many towns along the Thames where you can stay overnight. I stayed at Reading, an industrial town famous for its university, biscuit factory and the fact that Oscar Wilde wrote *The Ballad of Reading Gaol* while a prisoner in its Victorian Gothic prison.

Next day the climate had changed dramatically from mid-summer sunshine to autumn grey mist. Old ladies briskly walked dogs along towpaths. Graceful riders pranced by on jet black horses. Ducks abandoned the chilly water for the grassy verge. It was an even more beautiful Thames, with just a touch of mystery.

From Reading to Oxford we passed many beautiful old timber houses, smothered in flowers, stone churches and picturesque villages.

Mapleduram House, which dates from the time of Richard II, was rebuilt during the Civil War and is now open to the public. The Thames here is marked by rushing weirs and small islands covered in green trees.

Pangbourne, where Kenneth Grahame wrote *Wind in the Willows*, is linked by a bridge across the river to the pretty village of Whitchurch.

The river journey is leisurely and there are dozens of locks to negotiate, each with its own character. Some are famous for flower gardens. Others have notices advertising for sale anything from animal drawings to home-grown watercress. All the locks have quaint stone cottages where the lock keepers live. Tiny Bell Weir Lock has pink hollyhocks and trellised roses.

The lock gates open, the craft from another river level emerge, then our boat enters the lock. The water level rises and the boat, steadied by guy ropes, rises as smoothly as an elevator.

Descending to a lower level of the river, there's a white roaring, frothing and spraying of ebbing water, as the lock empties and the overflow swells the distant roar of the weir.

At Goring, the Chiltern Hills, with their thick woods, crowd the river. We stopped at the ancient market town of Wallingford for lunch and to take a look at its interesting churches and picturesque buildings. William the Conqueror granted it the privilege of sounding the nightly curfew an hour later than anywhere else. The nightly curfew has been tolled proudly ever since.

I lunched at a little cottage restaurant on family-style roast dinner with three vegetables, followed by home-made raspberry pie and custard.

Shillingford and Benson are pretty villages. Nearby Ewelme has a church with some of the best brasses for brass-rubbing enthusiasts. It also boasts the tomb of Alice, Duchess of Suffolk, grand-daughter of Geoffrey Chaucer of *Canterbury Tales* fame.

Jerome K. Jerome wrote the Thames classic, *Three Men in a Boat*, at the riverside pub, the Barley Mow, in the delightful village of Clifton Hampden.

The lovely old town of Abingdon has a stone quay, swans, interesting old churches and alms-houses, including one by the extraordinary name of Twitty's Almshouse.

At nearby Hawthorne, Queen Victoria spent part of her honeymoon.

The last two locks before Oxford are Sandford, with its large paper mill, and Iffley, which has one of the finest small Norman churches in England.

Just a kilometre or so along and Oxford's 'dreaming spires' come into view.

You can either take a fast train (one hour) back to London or linger on to explore the beautiful colleges and chapels, meadows and gardens of this famous university city.

That's unless you're so charmed with the journey that you decide to do the two-day voyage of discovery in reverse.

EXPERIENCES

A TRADITIONAL ENGLISH CHRISTMAS AT BOXLEY ABBEY

CHRISTMAS in London means cold, damp days of drifting mist, sometimes a light frosting of snow as temperatures plunge and water freezes hard in puddles and ponds.

At night crowds wander along Oxford and Regent streets viewing the spectacle of gold, silver and brilliant scarlet illuminations festooning the streets. Food bars do a roaring trade with hamburgers and hot coffee.

Hordes of children up late as a special treat press cold noses to brilliantly lit shop windows and sigh for enormous dolls, bicycles and cowboy suits.

The large department stores abound with 'Santas', reindeer, silver-frosted sleighs, Christmas fairies and nativity scenes.

In Trafalgar Square the golden spire of the Christmas tree, a gift from the Scandinavian people, soars toward Nelson's Column. At its base, carollers gather each evening to send splinters of song shattering the frosty air, and cascades of coloured water explode in the fountains, deluging pigeons and the lions which guard Nelson's Column.

I was quite happy to enjoy Christmas in London with its ballet, pantomime and round of concerts and plays, until an invitation arrived.

'Come to Boxley Abbey for Christmas', it read and, with visions of ruins of a medieval monastery and the ghosts of chanting monks and pilgrims enlivening a 'real English Christmas', I left London for a quiet country village in Kent, with my sister, Monica.

An hour's journey by train from the smoky cavern of Victoria Station takes you deep into beautiful Kent—in winter, the scene is of gaunt trees with smoke rising from small cottages; in spring, a mass of flowering blossom and, in autumn, a quilt of hopfields with hop pickers stalking on long stilts, like cranes, among the vines. Conical oasthouses dot the fields.

Sir John Best-Shaw, a beaming Falstaffian figure in plus fours and round tweed hat, met our train at Maidstone and, wound into a cocoon of rugs, we piled into the family station-wagon. The invitation was really from Julia, a daughter of the house, who worked with Monica in London.

Rounding a bend in the long driveway, we sighted a tall, three-storey, 'squared-off' house—Boxley Abbey. The old house was destroyed by fire and the present one dated from the nineteenth century, but the ruined Cistercian abbey in the grounds was twelfth century.

Lying on the road to Canterbury, Boxley Abbey was a famous place on the pilgrims' way in the Middle Ages, renowned in its own right for 'miracles'.

Kings, including Edward II, princes, peasants, wealthy merchants, the simple and the pious were drawn by tales of the 'miraculous' statue of Boxley. The 'miracle' was managed by a monk, hidden in the hollow statue, who manipulated the arms.

For a suitable donation the 'oracle' would 'speak'. But woe betide the wife who didn't open her purse wide enough! Then the oracle would denounce her as an unvirtuous wife.

All that now remains of the wealth and fame of Boxley Abbey is ruined walls, with the outline of some excavated rooms. Like other abbeys in England, it was dissolved during the Reformation.

Henry VIII cast greedy eyes on its treasures and stripped it of its wealth. The monks and nuns were dispersed or imprisoned, and the abbot executed in London.

Neglected and despoiled, the abbey fell into ruin.

Its last violent struggles are forgotten now. Peace reigns

in the little chapel which had been restored by Sir John. An altar had been built from its ancient stones and, on the wall, a blue della Robbia Madonna smiled gently above an inscription craving pardon for the persecution and destruction of the abbey.

The first Mass since the abbey's dissolution during the Reformation had been celebrated there by a Catholic priest friend of Sir John.

Near the ruined abbey stood the second largest tithe barn in England, where the monks stored tithes paid by the local farmers. It was perfectly preserved, maintained by the National Trust.

In the walled rose garden, the summerhouse held memories of Tennyson, who came to Boxley Abbey as house guest, and retired to the summerhouse when he felt the urge to write.

Speaking of visitors and writing reminded Lady Elizabeth, Sir John's wife, of the Commonwealth troops on leave at Boxley Abbey during the Second World War.

After their visits, she wrote to their families with the latest news. Her visitors' book was full of signatures of Canadians, New Zealanders, South Africans and Australians.

Sir John, who was fascinated with High Church liturgy, regaled us with details of feast days, vestments and ceremonials.

Author Rose Macaulay based the character of the commander in *The Towers of Trebizond* on Sir John, and the delightful Father Chantry-Pigg on a clerical friend.

By four o'clock on Christmas Eve the holly and the mistletoe were hung and the balloons blown up with the aid of a bicycle pump.

Tea was served on a silver tray—thin cucumber sandwiches, fruit cake and perfumed jasmine tea.

It was hard to leave the roaring log fire, but Evensong in the little twelfth-century Norman church summoned us.

The village congregation waited for Sir John, the squire, and his family to enter, and all stood as he went to the lectern to read the lesson.

A delicious pungent smell of fir trees, mingled with the musty smell of the old stone pillars against which they stood, filled the church. Holly and ivy festooned the walls.

We joined the procession to carry the statue of the Christ

Child to the crib, where it was placed on the straw.

Dinner that night, around an enormous oak table, was a hearty roast-beef meal accompanied by cider in heavy silver mugs.

Portraits of ancestors stared in serried ranks from the walls. The first Sir John, a wealthy merchant, was knighted by King Charles II for his 'loyalty and service'.

The present Sir John, with a twinkle in his eye, explained that 'service' meant providing men and money.

Mercenary troops were raised in the Lowlands and Spain and paid by Sir John to fight for the Stuart cause.

Once a year the portrait of Charles II was crowned with oak leaves to commemorate his escape, hidden in an oak tree, from his enemies. (The old soldiers at the Chelsea Pensioners' Hospital in London, founded by Charles, also crown his statue with oak leaves on Founder's Day.)

Nanny, a gentle old lady who brought up the children (all now adults), ruled over the kitchen, where a Siamese kitten was curled up on the window seat. She was busy stuffing the turkey.

The huge stove glistened with polish and one wall was covered with postcards from family holidays abroad.

Christmas Eve ended with our going to Midnight Mass, with its ancient ceremonial, familiar carols, candles and the Christmas blessing.

The cold drive through black countryside, lit with frosty stars, brought us back to Boxley and a hot toddy before bed.

Christmas morning dawned crisp and chilly with a pale blue sky. Breakfast was served from a side table laden with bacon and eggs, cold meats, kidneys, toast, marmalade and coffee. All the breakfast places were piled with gifts.

Hardly were the flowers arranged and the table decorated, than the vicar and his family arrived and champagne was served in the white and gold drawing room.

Christmas dinner was traditional—roast turkey with chestnut stuffing, plum pudding with brandy sauce, sweets, wines and liqueurs.

Around the Christmas tree, shining with gold and silver balls reflecting hundreds of flickering candles decking the branches, we sang 'Good King Wenceslas' and 'It Came Upon the Midnight Clear'.

The grandchildren were wide-eyed with excitement as Charlie, their uncle, thinly disguised as Santa Claus, opened his sack of gifts, after enquiring of each child if he or she had been 'good'.

Parlour games and the telling of favourite stories occupied the afternoon. The children had their 'nursery tea' in the kitchen with Nanny.

Full of mince pies, cold meats, fruit and nuts, we stretched out before the fire and became as sleepy as the Siamese cat.

'Dickens,' I thought. 'This is pure Dickens.'

Our host had planned a surprise for his guests—something traditionally English—for the following day.

Boxing Day. The sky looked clear and crisp, seen through windowpanes crackling with ice.

'We're going beagling,' called Sir John gleefully.

On seeing our puzzled expressions, he explained: 'Beagling is hunting a hare on foot with a pack of hunting dogs called beagles. They're specially trained to follow the scent.'

Nanny packed mountains of sandwiches and fruit, and we piled into the car to race across a wintry Breughel landscape.

We came on the hunters dressed in sensible tweeds, although the more sartorially correct sported black cap and jacket, white breeches, long socks, and riding crops.

The Master sounded the horn, calling the milling pack of excited, snuffling hounds to order.

'The dogs seem keen!' I exclaimed. 'They're all waving their tails.'

Sir John, as an enthusiast of the sport, was horrified at my blunder. 'The hounds are waving their sterns!' he corrected, knowing that I wasn't familiar with traditional terms.

Across fallow fields, the beagles bounded through mud puddles, cracking the caked ice. Mud everywhere! That's why the hunters wore old clothes. A pale sun tried to shine.

'If you see the hare, lie down,' warned Sir John.

'What! Down in the mud?'

'Certainly! And stay completely still.'

Suddenly the hare raced past so close we could almost have touched it. Far off the hounds were sniffing among the hop fields.

'They've lost the scent!' I whispered.

The horn blew.

'Gone to earth,' said Sir John.

Again the Master called the dogs to order, as another hare started up among the hop vines.

Secretly, my sympathies were with the hare.

'Run, rabbit, run!'

Lunch was a welcome break. Huge piles of meat sandwiches and slabs of fruit cake were washed down with red wine poured from travelling flasks. Port, coffee, and crème de menthe, and Turkish delight rounded off the meal.

'A wonderful *bonne bouche*,' muttered Sir John, munching the Turkish delight and looking very much the squire in tweeds, plus fours and muffler.

The conversation was of hunting, country meets, village fairs, country dances and parish matters, of antique shops, prep. schools, Eton and Cambridge, and 'old country families'.

For a moment the hounds, strung out in a thin line, were silhouetted against the horizon on the crest of the hill. The breeze carried the faint sound of the horn, then hounds and hunters disappeared.

The day grew chillier and we left the hunters still pursuing their quarry. Gypsies, camped on Sir John's property, waved.

'Cheeky devils,' Sir John laughed. 'I ordered them off the property two weeks ago.'

Reluctantly, we left Boxley Abbey for London and, in an hour, were back in a different world, a different century, even.

My 'typical English Christmas' was a far cry from my usual Australian Christmas, with heat, surfing, bush picnics and the drumming of cicadas drowning out talk of sporting fixtures and the Sydney to Hobart yacht race.

The ghosts of Boxley Abbey's medieval monks, kings, poets and peasants made it one of my most memorable Christmases.

FANTASY WORLD OF
BEVERLY HILLS

THE rich scent of the moneyed classes wafts along Rodeo Drive as carefully coiffured and perfumed, elegantly dressed ladies walk their poodles past gleaming shop windows.

Rodeo Drive is Beverly Hills' answer to London's Bond

Street, Rome's Via Condotti and the rue de la Paix of Paris. You can spend a fortune in the fashionable boutiques of famed couturiers.

I arrived in style in an air-conditioned chauffeur-driven Phantom V Rolls-Royce with bar, telephone and television. I hired it for the day for a mere $2200 plus fifteen per cent tip. I am sampling the rich life—all in the course of reporting the swank life of millionaires and film stars.

My chauffeur drives down the cobblestone driveway of the Rodeo Collection shopping complex, past the 250-year-old bronze statue encased behind glass in the brick wall to the Auto Reception Level where cars are parked. When money is no object, you don't have to worry about the free shuttle-bus service around Beverly Hills shops.

My first stop is at Giorgio, with its yellow and white striped awnings, matching flower boxes making it one of the most glamorous shops for the well-heeled.

Inside, they're playing an appropriate Sinatra song 'I've Got the World On a String'. The salesgirl sprays me with Giorgio perfume. Yes, I'll take an ounce—a steal at $150.

There is an elegant bar next to the fireplace. A notice reads: 'The bar is for customers and guests only.' I opt for the free glass of champagne, but I could have requested a frothy cappuccino. I glance at the complimentary magazines, watch two men play snooker on the pool table, note the signed photographs of stars who shop here.

But down to the serious business of shopping. I buy an exquisite Rizia Italian beaded jacket for $5735, a soft suede belt for $105, a Judith Lieber handbag (the best designer in the States) for $530. A classical Dior dinner dress sets me back $6000; an amusing Zandra Rhodes one a mere $2000. My least expensive buy is a simple $66 machine-washable wool sweater. Tax is added to my purchases which are wrapped in the distinctive yellow and white Giorgio paper and gift boxed.

The Gucci shop is my next port of call. As I walk there in the clear spring sunshine, I realize the world of the rich is coloured pink—pink and white blossoming fruit trees, window boxes of rose-coloured flowers, pink-painted buildings. The Gucci shop has a deep rose carpet. A sign reads: 'Quality is remembered long after price is forgotten.' How true! I buy a pair of Gucci shoes for $375, a silk shirt for $185, a day dress for $1600 and a gabardine business suit for $570.

My purchases are wrapped in embossed paper, sealed with a gold crest, popped into the distinctive green and red boxes and shopping bags and tied with silver ties.

I resist the tempting jewellery in the favourite shop of the Gabor sisters, Van Cleef and Arpels, bypass The Happy Millionaire, Cartier, Hermes, Vidal Sassoon and Yves St Laurent. It is time for a cappuccino at Pastel, a smart cafe in the Rodeo Collection, an elegant complex built of rosa aurora marble from Portugal, solid brass, bricks and cobblestones. It sports balconies, columns, balustrades, high arched windows, sprays of plants and flowers, cascading fountains.

And the boutiques! Nina Ricci, Louis Vuitton, Laurent, Rive Gauche, Emanuel Ungaro, Gianni Versace.

I sit on Pastel's patio enjoying the sweet-smelling jasmine, the splash of the tinkling fountain, the sheer pleasure of being rich.

Next stop is Robin Rose where I buy some hand-made chocolate truffles flavoured with Bailey's Irish Whisky, ignore the liqueur-flavoured icecreams but buy a book, *The Joy of Pigging Out—Say Goodbye to Food Guilt Forever*, by David Hoffman.

At Ylang Ylang I buy a little sterling silver heart for $150, note that the International News Stand sells *Figaro* (French) and *Il Giornale* (Italian) newspapers and that the Excelsior Restaurant advertises a champagne buffet.

I have a luncheon date at the famed Polo Lounge in the Beverly Hills Hotel on Sunset Boulevard. It is also known as the Pink Palace because of its colour and is the most likely place to spot celebrities. It is a favourite haunt of film stars, producers, television personalities, the rich and famous—the place to see and be seen.

The Polo Lounge got its name when Will Rogers and his movie-star friends used to drop by for drinks after a few chukkers of polo. Sure enough, I spot the trim figure of Ginger Rogers paying her bill. An autograph? Not bloody likely, as Eliza Doolittle would say. Autographs and the taking of photographs are strictly forbidden. It might embarrass an indiscreet patron there with a girlfriend, not a wife, or doing a business deal.

Is that Gore Vidal? Could that be Barbara Stanwyck? Surely I heard Lucille Ball being paged? To be summoned to the phone is worth a status point or two as dozens of eyes follow you. It is well worth the couple of dollars tip you slip the page 'boy'. Most of the calls are unanswered—were never meant to be answered. Whether you are a fading film star living in Mexico or a hot favourite for an Academy Award, it is good publicity to be paged in the Polo Lounge. And, who knows, there may be a film director, producer or backer around.

I order a pre-lunch Scotch and soda, which costs three dollars plus tip. Then I opt for the popular salad, McCarthy Salad, named for Neil McCarthy, polo player and a prominent lawyer to the movie stars in the thirties. A huge bowl of confettisized bits of chicken, tomato, bacon, egg, beetroot and cheese appears.

After lunch I book an appointment for a Miracle Morning at the Elizabeth Arden salon in North Rodeo Drive. I will dress in a pink robe, sit in a pink chair, under a pink towel, for a soothing massage, gentle facial, herbal mask and makeup. I will have a manicure, a hair wash, trim and blow dry—all for $100. Next time I'll try the Main Chance Day which costs $140 and adds a steam cabinet, pedicure, exercise class and light lunch.

On my way to Bijan, the most elegant shop in Beverly Hills, I stop at 'Fred' and buy an enamelled key ring for my Porsche.

Bijan is protected by armed guards twenty-four hours a day and open only by appointment. The showroom has luxurious Persian rugs and antique furniture and a waiter serves me a champagne cocktail on a silver platter.

The boutique clothes some of the world's most powerful men. My boyfriend will be pleased with my purchases. A soft silk shirt, a fine shirt of Egyptian cotton, styled in Florence, a vicuna sports coat and a suede jacket lined with chinchilla. For me—Bijan's perfume in a six-ounce handcut Baccarat crystal bottle (signed and numbered). The bill—a respectable $80,000.

Where else for afternoon tea than the elegant Zodiac Room in the millionaires' store, Neiman Marcus. At $6.50, it is the bargain of the day. I get a choice of teas—English Breakfast,

Darjeeling, Earl Grey or Spiced Twinings, assorted thin sandwiches, buttered scones with strawberry jam and whipped cream, a plate of *petits fours*.

Kings, queens, millionaires, heads of state, film stars shop here. Why not me? I buy a liqueur-flavoured toothpaste at $12, add a gold-plated key with Neiman Marcus initials at an extra $15, handy for squeezing out that last delicious squiggle. It is hard to choose between crème de café, peppermint, schnapps, or Irish cream toothpaste.

I can't resist a His and Hers set of Chinese Shar Pei dogs—each puppy costs $2000—but their pedigree dates back to the Han Dynasty in China—206 B.C. to A.D. 220.

Jewellery is next on my shopping list. I choose a gold, amethyst and citron necklace for $75,000. It is designed in Switzerland, has an Italian chain and stone from Bolivia. I add a $35,000 aquamarine set in eighteen carat gold, a $250,000 diamond ring, and pearl studs with diamonds for $550.

My fur ensemble is a grey broad-tailed lamb jacket trimmed with natural sable and matching leather slacks, which sets me back $28,500.

In the food department I buy a two-pound box of luscious Bachmann chocolates for $40, some Beluga caviar at $80 and the finest wild salmon from Norway at $70.

Purchases over $300 are gift wrapped free of charge. I end up with parcels wrapped in cream and gold butterfly-splashed Neiman Marcus paper and decorated with toy boats, wooden spoons, toy cats, flowers, bells and bows.

James chauffeurs me back to my hotel, the Beverly Hills. I could have stayed in a $155 a night room but I preferred a garden bungalow suite, price range from $340 to $1330 a night. My garden bungalow is the one occupied by honeymooning Liz Taylor and her husband (Senator Warner, I think).

Tomorrow I'll swim in the heated pool, lounge in a yellow and white striped cabana, take tennis lessons from former Wimbledon champion Alex Olmedo, the resident pro. I'll dine in at the Coterie restaurant starting with caviar, ending with Cherries Jubilee. With drinks, the bill should come to about $200. Then I'll have a private film showing for friends in the private screening room.

But tonight I dine at Trader Vic's. Entering through the

Beverly Hilton, I spot Nancy Reagan among a host of formally dressed guests, television cameras and press. The occasion? A Humanitarian Award for Nancy.

'There's Kirk Douglas,' exclaims my friend as we opt for a Passion Cocktail—gin, passionfruit nectar and lime juice. We avoid the powerful Zombie and the Missionary's Downfall.

After dinner, we head for the Shubert Theatre on the Avenue of the Stars to see the musical *Forty-Second Street.*

When I hear that every United States President since 1966 has stayed at the Century Plaza Hotel opposite, and that the Presidential suite is available for only $900 a night, I book it for the weekend. The ultra-luxury suite, the biggest in the world, is not yet finished, so I can't book it at $2500 a night.

But the next best thing has its compensations. How many can boast they've slept in President Reagan's bed?

Alas, midnight strikes and like Cinderella I return to the real world. It has been fun being a millionaire for a day— but I wouldn't want a lifetime of it.

THE LEPER COLONY

I don't know what I expected when I came to 'Raphael', a leper colony in the foothills of the Himalayas. Perhaps I had a little of the instinctive horror of lepers mixed with ideas from Graham Greene's *A Burnt Out Case*, whose hero journeyed to a far-off leper colony to bury himself alive. To expiate his sins, he devoted his life to caring for the 'burnt out' lepers whose disease had run its course, leaving them with permanent disfigurements.

When I read that book I certainly never imagined that one day I would be sitting pounding a typewriter in the midst of an Indian leper colony which a number of Australian women volunteers helped run.

The taxi reached the township in the middle of the night— it was a share-a-cab I had caught at one of Delhi's city gates for the long day's journey into night up into the Himalayan foothills. There were six passengers in the cab. I sat next to a bearded Sikh who told me of his parents' plans to arrange a marriage for him.

'Mummy knows best,' he said. 'I cannot trust my hot blood
to make a good choice.'

The driver having refused to budge further without payment
after letting off the other passengers in the town, I agreed.
He was right, the colony was some kilometres out of town
across the jolting Rispana River Causeway.

What emerged out of the night was a group of pristine
white square buildings with wide colonnaded verandas and
a neat garden.

The place was in darkness. The taxi driver honked his horn
and suddenly figures emerged—an old friend, Anne Young,
the sister in charge; Pam Holt, a children's nurse; Anne's
sister Pamela and her friend Christine, both holidaying with
Anne. I threw myself on them, half laughing, half crying:

'It's so wonderful to see people.'

This sent Anne into peals of laughter: 'What a comment
to make in India!'

But it was a breath of home after three months of lone
travel.

The colony consisted of a self-contained group of cottages
and a home industry for lepers and their families, a home
for sub-normal children, the Little White House for orphan
children, and a hospital for chronically sick patients and those
with tuberculosis.

At the time there were over 300 being cared for in the
colony by a staff of sixty, including Australians Anne Young;
Robyn Rankin, physiotherapist; Win McAlpin, Liaison Officer
and Adoptions Secretary; and Pam Holt, a children's nurse
in charge of the Little White House.

The colony is part of the International Centre for the Relief
of Suffering (supported by the Ryder Cheshire Foundation)
founded by Group-Captain Leonard Cheshire, the famous British wartime flying ace and one of the official observers at
the atomic bombing of Nagasaki, and his wife, Sue Ryder,
known for her work for Polish victims of the last world war.

Its chief executive was an Indian doctor, Colonel D. P. Puri,
its staff Indian, Australian, Irish, New Zealand and English—
volunteers from all over the world who worked for a small
living allowance, usually for a period of two years or more.

Australian volunteers had been associated with 'Raphael',
the International Centre for the Relief of Suffering in Dehra

Dun, since its inception, working as nurses, teachers, secretaries, physiotherapists and occupational therapists. Much of the money to run the home came from fund-raising activities in Australia.

So here I am typing on a rickety cane table surrounded by white cane chairs. The lounge room is high ceilinged with white walls, white whirling fans to combat the humidity and cool terrazzo floors. There are touches of home in copies of an Australian women's magazine, an Aussie calendar and a Scrabble set, which contrasts with the woven tapestry of Lord Krishna on hands and knees stalking a huge rabbit.

There is no such myth in Hindu mythology, but a patient in the TB Hospital made it and volunteers say it will create a new legend.

The table is set for tea—seven places, a neat green cloth and serviettes, fresh flowers from the garden.

The local military recently cleared and levelled the ground and a flower garden is blossoming. Colonel Puri, apart from being official administrator, is consulting physician. He ropes in the army for all kinds of assistance.

It was a different scene to my literary imaginings. I was to find courage and devotion, but not the flamboyant heroics.

The colony was bright, cheerful and well ordered, but the kind of crises, privations and disasters faced by staff were real enough. When the monsoon breaks, the causeway and the water pipes break. People are drowned trying to cross the angry waters of the swollen Rispana. Supplies are cut off—no food or water. The raging torrent can rise in half an hour to flood level; as rains pour down from the Himalayan foothills, streams become swift and dangerous.

Diseases are another danger. The area had endemic malaria and notices everywhere warn to be careful. Hepatitis abounds and nearly every foreign worker I knew in India had come down with it. Then there were worms—round worm, hook worm and thread worm. Anne just laughed it off and said that staff learned to regularly de-worm themselves.

Sometimes snakes came in from the jungle, their bite poisonous. And, before the monsoon breaks, scorpions may invade buildings. The previous year the lugubrious Indian cook, Sunny, was bitten on a finger and nearly died. The sting is very painful and the bite can kill a child.

In the heat, flying termites fly towards electric lights, shedding gossamer wings all over the carpet. Once there was a strike of local staff over necessary dismissals and threats of violence and burning down of buildings. The dismissed workers and their families camped outside the buildings, screaming abuse and threats. Lives were in danger before things were brought back to normal with the threat of a close-down of the entire establishment.

Great economy had to be observed as the colony was run on donations mainly from Australia. It was amazing what Sunny could do to ring the changes on a largely vegetable diet.

In summer the staff lived largely on eggplant (called *bringal*) because other vegetables are scarce. A curry made of cheese and peas called *mattar panir* was popular with staff. Usually there was lots of salad, potatoes and spinach, combined with rice and accompanied by *dahl* (ground lentils). Fruit included *chikous* (round little brown balls with skin like a Chinese gooseberry), loquats, apples, oranges, guavas, bananas, papaya (pawpaw), and pineapples.

Meat was on the menu about twice a week and Sunny prided himself on cooking 'European' meals—grills with mashed potatoes, liver, kidney and gravy, mutton chops, eggplant or tomatoes stuffed with mince, or potato.

My first dinner consisted of meat loaf, the remainder of which made stew with vegetable the next night. There were all sorts of delicious breads—puri, a little round puffed up fried wheat cake, *chapatis*, a flat dry cooked wheat cake, and *paratha*, a dough folded in three layers to form a triangle and fried.

Breakfast was usually porridge and a fried egg. Volunteers tried to eat an egg a day for the protein. If there were none, they fried tomato, chips or eggplant.

The big treat (Sunny's speciality) was called 'sugar basket'—a basket made of toffee containing fruit salad and custard. This was reserved for festive occasions.

The first morning I woke to a clatter like thousands of toothbrushes being stirred in metal cups. It seemed a lot of noise from a hundred patients or so. The explanation was more exotic. I came to know the sound as the cry of the brain fever bird. Its curious name described its irritatingly high-pitched sound, said to be so persistent and irritating

in the summer's heat that it brings on brain fever. Its sound,
'uh uh', is supposed to be saying 'pani pani' (water). It certainly
does get on your nerves. Other bird calls sound like 'chop
chop'.

But the birds are only one of many Indian calls heard around
'Raphael'. In any small village in India, there are many calls.
There is the biscuit wallah who carries a box of shortbread,
ginger biscuits and little round cakes on his head and calls,
'Caak, biscoot.'

On trains in the early morning the *chai wallah* or tea
attendant calls, 'Chai, chai.' In hotels the *dhobi* man makes
his round about six or seven in the morning calling plaintively,
'Dhobeee...' Then there is the '*Baksheesh*, mem-sahib' from
the beggars.

In Dehra Dun you can hear the jackals from the nearby mountains in the mornings. The icecream man calls 'Ice
ice', and the peanut vendor—the Moonphli man—calls 'Kachi',
and displays stacks of spiced nuts, and puffed rice, both sweet
and salted.

Last year the peanut man's box received a coat of bright
blue. The devout patients were painting the hospital lockers
blue—Lord Krishna's colour—and got carried away. Even the
mali's (gardener's) wheelbarrow became blue.

One day we visited the bazaar in Dehra Dun. In the crowded
narrow streets of the market sound, colour and movement
were inextricably woven. The old blind flute player played
a piercingly sweet tune. His carefully painted notice read:
'Namaste (thank you) to all. Please help this poor Blind. God
will help you. Thanks.' For a few cents Anne bought a bundle
of reed bamboo flutes for the orphan children.

Pan wallahs squatted over trays of sweet and spicy *pan*
(betel nut mixed with various flavours), said to freshen the
mouth. It is spattered all over Indian streets and looks as
if half the population are haemorrhaging.

There are bundles of gaudy coloured children's dresses, piles
of fruit and vegetables and, for the sweet-toothed (and most
Indians are), the sweetmaker stirs a huge pan of condensed
milk and sugar and concocts miracles of bright coloured can-
dies. I can't resist buying a big box of sweets for the staff.

From the minaret of the mosque the muezzin calls to prayer.
The call becomes lost as the local brass band parades in fire-

box red uniforms, belting out martial airs. Anne says they play at weddings and celebrations and usually get rather high on the local liquor before a performance. Of couse, there are bikes galore—India is chock full of bikes and sewing machines.

We take a horse-drawn carriage back to the colony. 'Raphael' is a world in itself. Just inside the entrance gate is the leper colony. Each family has a room with a veranda which serves as a kitchen—a kind of mini semi-detached villa with electricity.

In the first house Dhandoo and his wife, and Sharda, their two-year-old daughter, lived. Sharda was having tests to see if she too had leprosy.

Another couple, Phool Singh and Kamal Dei, had three children including a young daughter aged nine—Pratima—who had had polio. Pratima is a sweet little girl who was taken to Delhi by staff to have a calliper fitted on her crippled leg to help her walk.

When the home first opened all the children of lepers were put in the Little White House to separate them from their parents for fear they would catch leprosy. Now it is thought that the risk of contagion is not so great and children are left with parents.

The 'orphans', many of whom have parents too poor to keep them, face problems as they grow older. Parents return to claim them because they want to marry them off in the villages. They have a better education than most and some idea of hygiene, so are in great demand as wives. The children, used to a different life, don't want to return to the villages.

Employment opportunities were limited. The home hoped to set up a training centre to teach trades—plumbing, electrical work for boys and training for girls to become nursemaids or 'ayahs'. A few who showed academic promise would be sent for higher education. The three oldest children were in boarding school. By 1986 the training centre had not materialized—but children are sent to outside centres for job training.

I watched a group of men in the leper colony absorbed in playing with dice—a regular Saturday afternoon occupation. But, on week days, everyone who is able does four to eight hours' work spinning, weaving the linen for the home and hospital and for some clothing. A cobbler makes shoes for the leprosy patients. The barber does the haircuts. A carpenter does repairs and makes tables and benches. Some work in the vegetable gardens or tend the poultry. A couple work as dressers in the dispensary. The residents live an ordinary village life with their own head man.

Most show evidence of their disease with missing fingers, toes and limbs, collapsed bridges of noses, and many have poor eyesight. One little old lady lay blind and incapacitated. They have to keep constant guard against injury because nerves have been destroyed by the disease and they have no feeling. They can easily sustain burns or cuts. They have to be taught to handle their jobs with great care. Even a simple task like bathing their infected eyes with warm water is impossible. They can't feel how hot the water is so have to report to the hospital for treatment.

In the hospital the shrill cries of 'Aunty, aunty' echo as little Hem Lata practises her English. She is a spastic child, but very intelligent and is rapidly making progress in walking and talking with the help of Australian physiotherapist, Robyn Rankin. Her playmate, Sudeep, is never far behind. He is more severely spastic with speech difficulty, but he has proudly acquired a few words lately including 'bye bye'. The two can communicate without words, letting each other know what's going on with a kind of telephathy plus gestures.

They are great favourites with the staff and come in for a lot of cuddling.

In the home for retarded children there are sixty-seven mentally handicapped kids. The less handicapped help with household chores carrying water, feeding, dressing and bathing other children. They are paid a small allowance. They will always need care, but small gains have been made. Many can now dress and feed themselves, eating at table with plates and spoons.

Some, however, are untrainable and have to be fed and totally cared for. Many have been brought in off the street where they used to beg. Others are from families which could not cope with a mentally retarded child who can't be taught to work, or married off.

B. K. Grover (he always called himself B.K.) was a favourite of mine, perhaps because he had aspirations to be a writer, and enormous courage.

He is a spastic—his movements often uncontrollable, his speech difficult to understand. Yet he had learned to type, sitting with his legs strapped to a rubber tyre for stability.

Grover, determined to make his mark as a writer, had had forty stories published and wanted to write a novel.

He sits on the floor with the typewriter in front of him and hammers at the keys with a wooden peg. It's a slow process and he tires easily. He has read the story of the spastic Irish writer, Christy Brown, who wrote *My Left Foot* by typing with his toes, and was inspired to emulate him.

Grover often gets discouraged and feels sorry for himself but he has the courage to keep trying.

'Raphael' was not the place of despair I had imagined. Like the phoenix which rises renewed from the fire which destroyed it, these 'burnt out' ones had risen to new heights, creating a new life from despair.

CIPROVSKI — A FAIRYTALE VILLAGE IN BULGARIA

IT was like the Mad Hatter's Tea Party scene from *Alice in Wonderland*.

We sat under the blue plum trees in an orchard carpeted with wildflowers while Stalin (yes that was his name) poured fiery slivova rakia (plum brandy) from a china teapot and home-made wine from a coffee pot.

Elsa, his wife, presided over a table groaning with fresh farm food — nourishing vegetable soup, 'peasant' salad, egg-plants in yoghurt, veal schnitzel and bright pink watermelon.

Every few minutes the guests rose and clinked their china cups together, laughing and shouting what sounded like 'Nos-travi'. It meant, 'To life!'

Conversation flowed, but when they nodded it was to disagree and when they shook their heads it meant 'yes'.

This was breakfast in the Bulgarian village of Ciprovski, near the Yugoslavian border. Bulgaria has a fairytale quality. Peasants still danced in village squares on Sunday afternoons, little old men rode donkeys with paniers laden with hay, or jogged along country lanes in low wooden carts. Ikons gleamed in dim monasteries. And village wells with crystal clear spring water had metal dippers nearby for wayfarers to drink from.

While eastern European countries have modernized in many ways, life in many remote villages is still lived as it was in the eighteenth or nineteenth century, or even earlier.

Attracted by Ciprovski's fame as a weaving village, a friend, Rumiana Beck, a Bulgarian then married to Australian artist and sculptor, Lawrence Beck, had come to the village to have her designs woven into tapestries for her next Sydney exhibition.

Before I left for Europe, Rumiana had invited me to join her at the hospitable farmhouse of Stalin and Elsa, young relatives of one of her best weavers.

They were a handsome couple. Stalin, tall with brown curly hair and bright brown eyes, looked like the hero of *The Chocolate Soldier*. Elsa, with similar curly hair and humorous eyes, was a musician who taught in the village, while Stalin worked in the mines.

Their farmhouse looked out across a flower-strewn valley to fir-clad mountains. It was a peaceful place — white butterflies and bees among the pink hollyhocks, vineyards, fruit trees, a vegetable patch and beehives and a garden pump for washing before dinner. In the distance a tinkling stream, a donkey braying, chug of a tractor, a peasant woman pulling a cow by a rope.

On a nearby hill the ancient ruined monastery guarded its secret. Legend told of a fabulous gold treasure buried by the monks in a cave close by. They sealed the cave with beeswax.

The only man who had ever discovered its whereabouts, so the story went, was a partisan escaping from the police. He hid in a cave in the hills and woke to find it full of gold bars. Fleeing across the border, he took what gold he could carry. Years later, he wrote to the village authorities, but no one has been able to locate the monks' 'treasure'.

On my first evening in Ciprovski, two weavers came to the farm to tell us there was dancing in the village square. Although we were having a party in the farmhouse later, we couldn't resist joining the dancing.

Rumiana, Sabena (her friend from art-school days) and I linked arms and walked down the lane under a slice of golden moon and a star-filled sky, following the distant music.

We found the whole square in motion — everyone waltzing. Fathers with babies in arms, lovers, husbands with wives, brothers with sisters. The band, in Sunday-best suits and cloth caps, played drum, clarinet, trumpet and bassoon. Self-taught musicians who worked in the fields and mines during the day, they played at weekends for the sheer joy of making music.

Sabena asked them for a folk tune and the band took up a sinuous oriental melody, influenced by 400 years of Turkish occupation of Bulgaria.

Soon the square was a pattern of weaving circles. We three were seized by stalwart village men and arms linked, whirled into the leaps, small jumps and hesitations of a traditional village dance.

It was a fitting prelude to the party which got under way when the weaving co-operative boss arrived at the farmhouse. All the weavers and their husbands were there. Stalin's mother, Baba Mischa, wore a black head scarf and her eyes looked sad. Rumiana told me she was still in mourning for her recently dead husband.

The teapot of slivova rakia and the coffee pot of wine passed rapidly from hand to hand and clinking toasts were drunk to 'Bulgaria', 'Australia', 'Australian-Bulgarian friendship'. But the best toast was made by a humorous little man with twinkling eyes who kept leaping to his feet and shouting 'To life!'

We ate fiery peppers in tomato sauce, eggplants with dill and yoghurt, huge chunks of bread, salads and veal stew, the calf freshly killed that day and all the vegetables newly gathered. But the crowning dish was a tender, fragrant duckling stuffed with giblets, rice and mushrooms.

Its appearance caused a sensation. Only Rosko, the young son of weaver Sedevka, eyed it dolefully.

'He cried his eyes out over that pet duck, begged for its life to be spared if he gave Elsa two chickens in exchange,' said his mother. But when the savoury smell filled the air, even Rosko cheered up, accepted the inevitable and was soon crunching duck bones with relish.

Elsa brought out her accordion and we all sang. But Danche, of the silver voice, daughter of the weaver Raina, sang like an angel.

They were sad songs of Turkish occupation when the forests hid partisan secrets, songs about young boys snatched from their families to become Turkish Janissaries fighting against their own kin; nostalgic songs of flower-strewn plains, pretty girls with black silken hair, of trees and mountains, and the joys of love.

Then the company sang a song about Australia: 'Australia, Australia, how can you break up my family?' — a lament by a young wife whose husband had left her and her baby son to seek his fortune in far-off Australia.

Just when the atmosphere had become soaked in sadness, the humorous little man sprang to his feet and said he would play the guitar. Despite the fact that there was no guitar in sight, the audience sat up expectantly.

Liko was obviously the village humorist and, when he began plucking his long nose and humming through the vibrating nostrils, the audience laughed till they cried.

Then Liko changed to poetry — he recited Robbie Burns in Bulgarian, then his own composition about a fight between a wife and mother-in-law. It was a well-known village incident and had the audience in stitches.

By the time we had launched into sprightly Russian folk songs like 'Kalinka', everyone felt in the mood for dancing, so tables were pushed back, the men leapt to their feet and began to stamp, jump and twirl.

Rumiana, eyes glowing, handkerchief twirling, led the line, while everyone sang the folk song, 'Rumania', about a graceful maiden of that name who captured every heart.

My arm was seized and I was swept into the circle, leaping and hopping for hours to the insistent rhythm until I felt I would drop from exhaustion.

Half the company had taken off their shoes to be comfortable. The men's skin ran with sweat. A kind of joyful madness had seized the company as if their national Bulgarian hero, the legendary Orpheus, was plucking his lute unseen in the garden. Out into the orchard danced the line, answering the summons, leaping as though bewitched over a carpet of wildflowers by moonlight.

Then suddenly the thread of enchantment snapped. People began to realize the grass was wet to their bare feet and the air had grown chilly and the dancers melted away into the night.

The next day was a village feast day. Stalin took me to visit the little church which looked like a quaint house, its brown, toffee roof warm in the sun against its cool white walls. Churches were built like this to deceive the occupying Turks who had persecuted Christians.

Inside it was dim and cool, smelling faintly of incense from the early morning service and of the field flowers set before gleaming ikons. The floor, soft to the foot, was covered with carpets woven by the villagers.

Bent over his walking stick, an old man with two snaggled teeth hobbled over to ask in halting English why I had come to his village.

The weavers' co-operative was humming like a beehive. Nimble fingers flew like swallows in and out of brightly coloured wools stretched on looms.

Piles of wool — bold reds, greens, sky blues, browns and blacks — lay in corners ready to be woven into Ciprovski carpets with traditional abstract designs called 'Birds', 'King's Crown', '16 Things', and 'Cabbages'. Many were for export.

A seven-metre-square carpet cost about $400 and took three women a month to weave. Each day they started at 7.30 a.m. and finished at 4.30 p.m. with an hour off for lunch.

The weavers were dressed in beautiful, heavily embroidered costumes. Some had taken off their shoes for comfort and bare feet rested on plank footrests.

Some of the best weavers were working on Rumiana's tapestries — abstract designs based on the warm reds, pinks and oranges of the Australian outback, the orange, coral, yellow, white and black of fish among the coral of the Barrier Reef and the serene greens and blues of Australian sea and sky.

After work, I walked with Rumiana and Sabena in the village, while they searched for some special black wool for the tapestries. An old man rode past. His donkey wore a rose tucked over its forehead.

Roses are the symbol of Bulgaria. Every village grows rose bushes in its streets and the famous Valley of the Roses yields essence of rose which is exported to form the base of many expensive perfumes.

Old women held their baby grandchildren on their laps while they sat on street benches gossiping, illuminated by the pale gold of the setting sun like peasants in Old Master paintings. Children, riding home on top of donkey cart haystacks, shouted in glee.

Through open windows we saw huge looms with half-finished carpets sitting in living rooms. Carpet weaving started in Ciprovski in the eleventh century. Sheep were bred here, wool spun, carded, dyed with vegetable dyes and made into carpets to village designs. Mothers still taught their small daughters to weave so that the art was passed on in families.

One-third of the weavers worked in the co-operative, the rest at home where they could keep an eye on young children.

In one house we visited there was a barrel of home-made wine fermenting near the door and an apple tree hung with pots and pans.

The priest's wife, cheeks like red apples, hair tucked neatly in a peasant scarf, hailed us with an invitation to dinner to celebrate the feast day. The priest was still up on the hill surrounded by his flock, blessing bread and water.

All day the priest's house had flowed with food and wine for anyone who called. Rumiana protested politely, 'We are too many.' But the priest's wife replied: 'The Lord provides.'

Back to the farmhouse past a big walnut tree, hissing geese, lambs with neck bells ringing. At the farmhouse gate young Rosko triumphantly greeted us, cradling a bigger and better duck and with a grin from ear to ear. As he caressed and talked gently to it, he told us that Grandmother Mischa had found him a new pet.

Stalin, Elsa, Rumiana, Sabena and I set off for the priest's house for dinner. His aproned wife greeted us at the door and bustled us inside, where a long wooden refectory table seated twenty-four. The diners had peasant faces — strong, furrowed, full of humour and character, men in cloth caps, women in head scarves, children seated on laps, eyes bright with excitement and fatigue.

On the wall was a picture of the fiery prophet Elijah, his wooden chariot wheels aflame, two angels at the horses' heads. He was flanked by pictures of a calm Virgin and Child and a solemn crowned St Michael with book.

The priest was bearded and looked like Tolstoy. His saint-liness and devotion to the village had earned him a promotion in the church. The good news had been brought that day by the assistant patriarch and we congratulated the priest.

As we sat down, twenty-four pairs of eyes were fixed on us. One man said:'I hope you intellectuals don't feel uncom-fortable with us simple folk.' Rumiana smiled and replied: 'Who are you and who are we?' — meaning we were all simply recipients of the priest's hospitality.

The priest filled our glasses with plum brandy (about sev-enty per cent pure alcohol — it burned the whole way down) and straw-coloured wine.

His wife bustled around, encouraging us to eat from the groaning table, piled with chunky bread, strong garlic-flavoured green peppers, spicy tomato-onion mixture, peppery bean soup, plates of herb-flavoured cabbage, cold fish and chips, and honey-sweetened pastries.

The children, full of good food and sticky lemonade, had grown more round-eyed and, when urged by fond relatives to sing and recite, buried their heads shyly like birds under grown-up arms. One small boy had the courage to pipe up: 'Don't ask my little brother to sing. He doesn't know anything, he just copies me.'

'To your health', clinked the glasses. The priest, now for-mally dressed in long black coat and stovepipe hat, his long hair tucked into a bun on his neck, made his regretful farewell. He was off in answer to a summons to the bedside of a dying woman, who died later that night.

We left soon after. The priest's wife was still dispensing hospitality and protested: 'But you haven't eaten a thing!'

Outside, the stars whirled in a crisp sky as we strolled homeward arm in arm.

We rose early for the long journey back to Sofia next day. Our last meal under the apple trees consisted of white cheese, brown eggs, bread and honey, sweet meringues and cream cake. This unusual breakfast was washed down with slivova rakia from the teapot and home-made wine from the coffee pot.

The weavers called to say goodbye to Rumiana and me. Sedevka brought some fresh goat's milk for our breakfast.

Elsa gave me a beautiful tablecloth woven in the village and a silk handkerchief embroidered by her mother.

As we walked to the square the church bell began tolling for the dead woman. But, in the square itself, life bustled on. Women were drawing water from the well and a frieze of donkeys and farm workers with wooden rakes and forks wended its way to the fields.

Stefka, the pretty blonde weaver who liked to wear a rose in her hair, and Danche of the silver voice, were there to see us off. Danche pinned a badge with a scene of Ciprovski on my dress, so I would never forget the village.

As our car sped through the village, the ghost of a folk tune hung on the air. I could swear I saw a fiddler on the roof of the old church.

MY AUNT AND THE
MAGIC HORSE

I have two great-aunts buried in distant countries. Both were missionary nuns and spent a lifetime serving the poor.

Sister Marie Bernard, a combination of Irish humour and idealism, and straight Aussie practicality, had gone to Paris to learn humility and how to cope with poverty and serve the world's outcasts. She was only a teenager—tiny, high spirited, the belle of many a country ball. She died in 1947 in India at eighty-two after sixty-two years of living in poverty.

I never expected to find her grave or hear legends about her, but life is funny and unexpectedly one day I found myself a traveller in southern India.

Bangalore, where the Little Sisters have their home for the poor, ill and homeless, is a city with the feel of an English spa—a garden city, cooler than Madras, with wide streets and solid country-type homes, country clubs and grandiose buildings. It was a favourite retreat for sahibs and their memsahibs during the British Raj.

In search of my ancestor's grave, I caught a little scurrying beetle taxi scooter, was deposited at the wrong hospital, and setting out again, finally found the Home of the Little Sisters of the Poor.

Dry dusty ground was shaded with trees and shrubs. Verandas on both sides of the compound lead to the wards. A very old, gentle nun took me to the graveyard, to a plain grave surmounted by a cross, which stated simply that Sister Marie Bernard died in 1947, aged eighty-two.

We had tea in the polished wooden-floored parlour. Some nuns remembered my great-aunt, describing her as a sweet little old lady, only 1.5 metres high, in a bonnet, who looked after the postulants. She loved to make a fuss of the sick. One nun remembered that when she broke her arm, Sister Marie Bernard had asked if she would like a special treat— a cup of cocoa, and insisted she drink it. Shortly after another nun appeared and demanded to know what had happened to her cocoa.

The nuns were very poor, serving the poorest of the poor and begging for food in the market. The Hindu shopkeepers were generous.

The hospital rooms were neat, with fresh flowers and small possessions of patients. Sweet-natured old Sister Agnes was worried about Sarey and her five children—slum dwellers the Sisters visited. Sarey's husband beat her, she couldn't get a job because there was no one to mind the children, and they were all starving.

The Little Sisters regularly visited the slums. They rescued the ill and destitute from the streets and treated them with loving care. They were servants of the poorest—beggars for beggars.

One old lady with a bent back complained of backache.

'Why did you crouch to do the sweeping yesterday?' Sister Agnes asked.

'You do so much, Sister, I wanted to help.'

One old Indian lady had been married to a Scot in the Army Civil Service. When he became ill, she nursed him until he died, exhausting all their savings. After his death, his pension stopped and she had nowhere to go but to the Sisters.

Another old woman had elephantiasis—her legs were horrendously swollen.

As we entered each room, the old nuns gave loving greetings

and the patients gave the *namaste* sign, hands together, with smiles.

Sister Agnes comforted a bereaved son: 'He died very peacefully—I was with him—no suffering, he just closed his eyes.'

Today was a special celebration to welcome the new Mother Superior. The band played with gusto, sweets were distributed and the dining tables were set with festive food.

I left them to their celebrations.

Sister Marie Bernard would joke that India did not need beggars yet here the nuns were begging for daily food. It couldn't be helped. The Little Sisters looked after a hundred destitute old and sick people and had little money to feed them, let alone the long queue of tattered, hungry people who gathered silently at the kitchen door twice a day for their chapattis, rice and thin vegetable curry. The nuns ate the same fare, but their portions were often smaller, especially if the queue was longer than usual.

The market sellers didn't begrudge the Sisters old vegetables and slightly bruised and over-ripe fruit. Some stall owners actually saved some of their best produce. The nuns were Christian, but a devout Hindu could acquire merit from Brahma, the creator, by gifts to the poor. As well, nuns kept the beggars away from the market where they were bad for business.

Besides, who knew if the stall owners too might not end up one day in the Home for the Poor. Most of the people who were now the Sisters' guests had expected to die in their hovels or on the street. It was their *karma* (fate) for offence in a former life, and the merit they gained by accepting their lot without complaint would surely earn them a better deal in the next reincarnation. But they were still grateful to Lord Krishna for the chance to spend their last days in comfort on a string *charpoy* (bed) with food in their bellies. That was *karma* too.

From the nuns' remembrances of her a picture of Sister Marie Bernard's life emerged. She had never guessed as a young girl that she would spend her life in an alien country far from the small Australian country town where she was born. But she loved India, despite the heat, the daily problem of finding enough to eat, and the homesickness which could still assail her at times. The heat was hard to bear, especially in midsummer when the sun was like a ball of fire. And the poverty and squalor could still shock her, even after thirty years in India.

She remembered how she had entered the convent at eighteen, her friends taken completely by surprise. She had been one of the most popular dancers at woolshed hops and the first to get up a party for tennis or the picnic races. Everyone had thought she would be one of the first to marry. But, perhaps influenced by her older sister, a missionary nun, she had ended up in what her mother called that 'Godforsaken land'. But she never regretted the decision.

She had gone to the motherhouse of the order in Paris to take her final vows and, apart from one trip back to Paris to renew her vows, she never again left India.

A week after I arrived I met Victor, a charming Indian businessman whose aunt had been a nun in the order.

'We used to visit her regularly as children,' he said.

'Of course I remember Sister Marie Bernard—a tiny little thing of five feet with an Irish sense of humour—always joking.'

He told me the story of the Magic Horse and how Sister Marie Bernard had wrought a miracle.

It all started when the elderly horse which took the nuns to the market to beg, died. He was a bad-tempered old horse, not to say quixotic, with the irascible ways of the aged. But my great-aunt learned to pamper him with pats and sugar lumps and he got them to the market and back with the donated produce.

The day the convent horse collapsed and died on the way home from the market was a black day indeed. It was a big responsibility finding food for so many. The half-dozen nuns could manage on bread and soup or rice, but the thin, undernourished bodies of their charges needed something more substantial.

She cried, not understanding why the Good Lord had let the horse die. How were they to feed the convent household if they couldn't carry food home.

That night the nuns prayed hard for a solution to their problem. Sister Marie Bernard felt it was her responsibility to see that the horse was replaced because she was in charge of food collection. She decided to ask her favourite saint for help. After all, she reasoned, St Joseph had provided for his wife and baby. She didn't agree with Sister Agnes who said St Joseph was lazy and that's why he was always shown carrying the lily, while Mary carried the Child.

She remembered the advice the nuns had given her at school. If you wanted something, bury a medal of your favourite saint in the place where you want it to happen. The nuns had acquired two highly desirable properties by burying a medal in the grounds.

Sister Marie Bernard did not have a medal of St Joseph, so she did the next best thing. She had a model horse carved and buried it in front of St Joseph's statue in the convent grounds. She knew St Joseph was a powerful saint, but she hadn't realized what a fast worker he was.

The next morning when she opened the window, she was astonished to see a fine horse munching the marigolds in front of St Joseph's statue. It was even saddled ready to ride.

That day she rode to market with a light heart.

But next day, disaster struck in the form of a disturbing visitor, the adjutant from the nearby military barracks. He brought bad news. The Colonel was on his way to see the Sisters. His horse had been stolen and he had heard rumours that the sisters had a new horse which sounded very like his.

Sister Marie couldn't believe that St Joseph had let her down so badly. She was so upset that she found it hard to carry on her usual cheerful conversation as she washed and fed the old people.

It was late afternoon when Reverend Mother summoned her to the parlour. The Colonel, a tall man with luxuriant moustache, neatly confined in a fine net, and a white turban concealing his shoulder-length shiny black hair, sat stiffly in a straight-backed chair. Reverend Mother poured tea.

The Colonel looked severe:

'I can understand my horse straying into your garden, Reverend Mother, but I can't understand how you could keep it,' he said.

'Why didn't you have it returned to the barracks? You must have realized it belonged to us. We are the only people with horses in this area.'

Reverend Mother looked at my great-aunt for an explanation. Sister Marie Bernard felt very foolish but decided to be honest.

'I thought St Joseph had worked a miracle. Our poor old horse died yesterday and then a beautiful horse appeared in front of St Joseph's statue. It seemed an answer to our prayers.'

The Colonel, no doubt, thought the nuns as simple as children but he also sensed the heartbreak the loss of the horse had caused.

Next day he instructed his adjutant to buy an extra horse in top condition. When the beautiful animal appeared, the Colonel complained that it had a deformed leg and would have to be destroyed. He would do it himself first thing in the morning and remained adamant, despite his adjutant's surprised protests that the animal was perfect.

He rose before daybreak, saddled the horse and rode it to the convent where he tethered it to St Joseph's statue. To make sure there would be no mistake, he left a note on the saddle which read: 'To Sister Marie Bernard from St Joseph'.

Before she died, Sister Marie Bernard became too old to go to market, so the nuns gave her the job of convent door-keeper and she greeted every visitor with warm affection.

'A real character, your great-aunt,' they told me.

'She had a lot of faith and a lot of love,' and they laughed at the story of the wooden horse.

But I like to think that a little bit of Sister Marie Bernard lives on in that story. The legend of the nun and the magic wooden horse may even become part of India's rich mythology. Stranger things have happened.

ALCATRAZ— A DAY'S SENTENCE

THE clanging of the closing prison door had a terrible ring of finality to it.

I was locked into the totally dark and claustrophobic solitary confinement cell on the notorious island of Alcatraz, in San Francisco Bay, one of the punishment cells prisoners called 'dark holes' and guards called 'attitude adjustment cells' or 'treatment cells'.

It was only for forty seconds, our guide said. But it felt

like an eternity. I could feel panic rising as the time limit came and passed. What if... the door jammed, the guard forgot me.

I was never so glad to get out of any place, yet prisoners spent up to nineteen days officially—and more—here. There was no law limiting solitary. Inmates could be taken out for a day, then locked in again. One man spent 300 days in solitary.

Prisoners copped solitary for breaking rules—not keeping shirts buttoned to the top and areas clean, and not eating all the food on their plates, for example.

Once the most notorious prison in America, Alcatraz today is part of San Francisco Bay area's 16,000 hectare Golden Gate Recreation Area. 'The Rock', once home to some of the most vicious criminals in America, is now the most popular single tourist attraction in San Francisco.

Alcatraz was perhaps most known and feared during the Prohibition days of the 1930s, the Great Depression era. Alphonse 'Scarface' Capone was among the first group of fifty-three convicts transferred here from Atlanta prison in 1934. A notorious crime tsar with speakeasies, brothels and gambling enterprises, he rode in a seven-tonne armoured sedan and had a suite of fifty rooms in a Chicago hotel reached by private elevators.

The king of the underworld escaped murder charges but was nailed for tax evasion and given ten years. His first job on the Rock was in the laundry. Soldiers and sailors stationed around the Bay area wrote home boasting that notorious Al Capone did their laundry. Later, he cleaned latrines and shower rooms where he got into a fight with another convict and was stabbed. After that he asked to be moved from cell to cell for safety.

Capone did nineteen days in solitary for trying to bribe a guard to give him outside news. After a few years on the Rock his mind began to break and, rumoured to be insane, he spent two years in prison hospital. Released in 1939, he was promptly imprisoned in another federal penitentiary for an earlier sentence of a year not yet served.

He died seven years after his release, aged forty-eight.

George 'Machine Gun' Kelly, Arthur 'Doc' Barker, Alvin 'Creepy' Karpis, and Robert 'Birdman of Alcatraz' Stroud were other notorious inmates.

Stroud was not the gentle expert on bird disease portrayed by Burt Lancaster in the movie, *Birdman of Alcatraz*.

His first twelve-year term was for a murder committed in Alaska when he was nineteen. Two years later he injured a fellow inmate of McNeil Island Prison and was transferred to the notorious Leavenworth. There he stabbed a prison guard to death with an icepick. He was sentenced to death, but President Woodrow Wilson commuted his sentence to life imprisonment.

He spent the next thirty-nine years in solitary confinement, first at Leavenworth where he began studying bird diseases, and then at Alcatraz, when his fame caused authorities to transfer him there. He was fifty-two years old and had already spent thirty-three years in solitary confinement at Leavenworth.

At first a sympathetic warden let him continue his work, but later the new warden cut off his information supplies. He filed an appeal with the Federal Court begging to be allowed to continue his bird studies. It was denied.

His physical and mental health then deteriorated and he was put in the prison hospital. He died in 1963, aged seventy-two, the year Alcatraz prison was closed.

What was life like in Alcatraz? It was set up as 'the ultimate punishment society could inflict upon men short of killing them... the one place in the American penal system that made not even a pretence at rehabilitation, whose one avowed aim was to confine and to punish', according to a former United States Attorney-General, Homer Cummings. A writer called it 'the great garbage can of San Francisco Bay into which every federal prison dumped its most rotten apples'.

The daily routine began at 6.30 a.m. with the morning gong. Prisoners had twenty minutes for washing, dressing and tidying cells before the first head count.

At 6.55 a.m. they were released from the cells, marched single file into the mess hall past a metal detector, and given a steel tray with spoon and fork. Alcatraz served the best food of any prison and plenty of it. The reason, as for the hot showers, was security—to keep the men in a 'soft' condition, with bodies unfit to adjust to the icy waters of the bay should they attempt escape.

I read a framed menu of 21 March 1963—'assorted dry

cereals, steamed whole wheat, two scrambled eggs, fresh milk, stewed fruit, toast, bread and butter, coffee'.

The cafeteria was considered the most dangerous area of the prison because the inmates were all together. On outside window-ledges armed guards with shotguns and automatic weapons kept watch. Above, in the ceiling, tear gas could be released. During Alcatraz's twenty-nine years as a federal prison, the gas never had to be released. Twice, guards broke the window glass but inmates sat down before shots were fired.

The rest of the day consisted of head counts, work in prison factories, more meals, back to cells at 4.45 p.m. and lights out at 9.30 p.m. On Sundays prisoners were allowed an hour for chapel and two hours in the recreation yard, but only one hour for those who went to chapel. By 1940 they were allowed twenty minutes' exercise in the yard twice a week and sport on Sunday.

Prisoners were not allowed to talk except to ask and answer questions of guards.

On arrival, prisoners were placed in solitary until evaluated by guards and warden. They were not allowed to go to the cafeteria, but got meals puréed in one dixie cup and put through a slot in the door—two cold meals of 1200 calories total twice a day. Every few days they got a hot puréed meal.

The cells were steel boxes with steel floors, so cold that prisoners often crouched to keep warm. At night they got a mattress plus two blankets. If they caused trouble, they were taken to cell 14, stripped of their clothes at night, and given no mattress or blanket. The toilet was a hole flushed by the guard, who left it unflushed sometimes as extra punishment.

There was a solitary 'cop out sheet' which prisoners could sign, promising not to break rules if allowed out. But the rest of the prisoners took a dim view if they signed it.

Officially there were no escapes from the island federal prison. Swift tides, icy water and strict supervision saw to that. But there were five suicides (escape by death) and fifteen escape attempts.

Perhaps one of the last attempts was actually successful. No one knows for sure. Bank robbers, Frank Morris, and brothers Clarence and John Anglin, did escape in a plastic raft they had built and were never heard of again, presumed drowned. They were immortalized in a Clint Eastwood film entitled, *Escape from Alcatraz.* (I had dinner with Eastwood a week or so prior to my visit to Alcatraz. He turned out to be a courteous, gentle man, not at all like his violent screen person.)

Alcatraz had a long and interesting history before it became a federal prison. It was discovered in 1769 by Spanish explorer Don Gaspar de Portola and named 'Isla de Alcatraces', which means 'Island of Pelicans', because of the birds on the island.

The five-hectare island, which rises forty-one metres out of San Francisco Bay, was nicknamed 'Troublemaker Island' by early Russian sailors because of sailing hazards it caused.

It has been an island fortress, an American army citadel, a military prison and site of the first lighthouse on the West Coast.

In 1933, due to high operating costs, the army got rid of it to the federal prison authorities. It remained a federal penitentiary for the next twenty-nine years until mounting costs and the need for urgent repairs forced closure on 21 March 1963.

In March 1964 five Sioux Indians landed and staked a claim, but finally left. On Thanksgiving Day 1969, over 100 Indians landed and claimed it for the Indian nation. A year later, their attempt unsuccessful, they moved out, but many buildings had been destroyed by fire.

'Any ghosts?' I asked the ranger, as we walked to the ferry past the old warning sign, 'United States Penitentiary: Persons attempting to come inside buoys without permission do so at their own peril. Keep off!'

'I haven't seen one,' he smiled. 'But other rangers have heard the clanking of chains. There's no way I'd spend a night on the island.'

SUMATRA— GHOSTS, BARGAINS AND HONEYMOONERS

ONE of my most unusual holidays was a package tour to Sumatra with twenty-four Chinese-speaking Singaporean honeymoon couples. I was the only non-honeymooner and the only Australian—not exactly a recipe for a successful holiday.

Of course I had not planned to be a gooseberry on a honeymooners' special when I booked a six-day package tour to Sumatra with Singapore Airlines, while staying in Singapore. You could not book this tour in Australia, which was not surprising as things turned out.

I had expected an interesting mixture of expatriate European and Australian traders and government officials living in Singapore, a planter or two from Malaysia, perhaps even a diplomat on holiday (obviously I had read too much Somerset Maugham). So you can imagine how I felt when I got off the plane in Medan, capital of Sumatra, to find twenty-four smiling young Chinese holding hands and gazing into each others' eyes.

I mentally groaned as I boarded the bus and resigned myself to a week of silence more absolute than a retreat in a Carmelite convent. But it didn't work out that way. Far from being lonely, I never had a dull moment. Not only did the Singaporeans adopt me as a mascot, they also insisted on speaking English when I was around and treated me with a warmth of friendliness I would not have imagined.

I was included in mammoth Chinese meals for twenty-five (they would not touch Indonesian food, much to my disappointment). They showed me how to manipulate my chopsticks with dexterity and surreptitiously pushed all the daintiest morsels towards my plate. I felt part of a huge Chinese family listening to my young friends chatting about life in Singapore.

Touring was just as much fun. On free days, when we had no set programme and our bus stayed at our hotel, they squeezed me into ancient taxis with them, after beating down the price to an acceptable level. Singaporeans love to bargain. It didn't seem to matter that we all had to get out and push the cars uphill.

In convoys we proceeded to explore the countryside, hopping out at scenic spots for hundreds of honeymoon photos featuring me, mid-centre, the star of their wedding albums. There were going to be a lot of surprised relatives when the honeymooners returned home and showed their group photographs.

It was such an unusual holiday that I should not have been surprised when it became even more unlikely. Strange things happen in the primitive island of Sumatra, an Indonesian island. So the fact that ghosts kept popping up at various spots along our journey was not as surprising as it would have been in hometown Sydney. Besides, the supernatural is very real to many Singaporeans and no doubt the ghosts realized this.

The first ghost decided to call on me, knocking late one night on the window of my bungalow in the hotel garden on beautiful Lake Toba.

The sharp rat-a-tat-tat on the grass startled me awake from a deep sleep. I felt rather disconcerted after a day of hearing about black magic from our Sumatran guide. As the noise grew louder, I pulled the sheet over my head and prayed that whatever it was would go away. When it didn't, my rational mind came into play as I tried to solve the mystery. I made a swift foray to the window. No one was there.

The sound was so sharp that I decided the answer to the puzzle was a bird tapping its beak on the glass, however unlikely at that time of night, and I went back to sleep.

Next day, over breakfast, the hotel manager confirmed my guess. Birds peck at mosquitoes on the glass panes of windows, he said.

But the Singaporeans would have none of this explanation. It was a ghost for sure, they told me, urging me to take refuge with a honeymoon couple the following night. It looked as if they would draw straws for the honour of putting me up. I was touched, but reassured them I was fine on my own.

The next ghosts made their presence felt in Brastagi, a charming, tranquil hill resort, once much loved by Dutch colonials living in Medan. It was a cool place to escape from the searing summer heat. Its flowers and vegetables would have graced any English garden.

My Singaporean friends admired the beautiful golf course, the superb rose gardens, the tame donkeys for hire. They exclaimed over the lavish profusion of tasty tropical fruits in the markets and filled huge plastic bags full to take home to relatives. Cameras worked overtime on the magnificent pastoral views from hilltop lookouts.

But they had no time at all for the ghosts which they assured

me, after a night in the hotel, were about and would give
the place a bad name.

It was a fact that this peaceful place had been the scene
of a horrifying massacre of Dutch men, women and children
who had taken refuge there during a national uprising of
Sumatrans against the Dutch colonial rulers.

Something of their terror still seemed to cling to the place,
according to the Singaporeans. The place was cool and eerie
at night, they said. I did not like to admit that I had slept
like a top. It seemed insensitive. I listened but heard no ghosts.

But our party's most mystifying encounter with ghosts came
in the modern city hotel in Medan. It happened to 'Charlie
Chan', an affectionate nickname that his fellow Singaporeans
had bestowed on the boyish self-appointed leader who organized everything from splitting the lunch bill to hiring a fleet
of taxis to go downtown.

'Did you sleep well last night?' asked Charlie one morning.
It was obviously not a routine enquiry after my welfare. He
looked quite disappointed when I assured him I had.

'No one knocked at your door in the middle of the night?'
(He and his wife occupied the room next to mine.)

When I shook my head, Charlie insisted: 'You didn't hear
anything?'

I was almost tempted to joke and say yes. But Charlie,
normally a great humorist, even a prankster, was obviously
upset. He was also clearly dying to tell me why.

'A ghost came to our room last night,' he burst out.
'There was a knocking on the door and when I opened
it, no one was there.'

But that wasn't the worst of it. A mystified Charlie went
back to bed, but the ghostly prankster was still at work.

'I heard water running in the bathroom, but when I went
to turn off the tap, it was not turned on,' said Charlie.

'And there wasn't even water in the bath tub.'

A puzzled Charlie had become a terrified Charlie. He woke
his bride and they hastily moved in with another couple.

That was the end of our ghostly encounters, much to everyone's relief. My encounter had turned out to be non-
supernatural, although the Singaporeans clung to the ghost
theory, but none of the honeymooners knew what to make
of the other ghostly presences which had plagued them.

Shopping with Singaporeans was great fun. A nation of shopkeepers, they loved shopping.

'Shopping, shopping, what about shopping?' the girls would chant when another sightseeing trip was mooted.

And off we'd go on a mass shopping excursion. Some of our group spoke Malay, which was close enough to Indonesian to make themselves understood. They also came equipped with mini-computers on which they did rapid conversions of rupiah to Singaporean dollars. They bargained fiercely, but with good humour, though without success, at least in the villages we visited.

'In Singapore, we believe in making a little profit, but many sales—that's the way to get rich,' explained Charlie.

But, after a slow start with shopping in Lake Toba because the local shopkeepers did not understand the bargaining game, Medan proved a shopper's paradise.

We made for Pasar Ikan Lama for inexpensive batiks, then to Jalan A. Yani l, a street abounding in souvenirs, including handicrafts, delicate Javanese silverware, carvings, antiques, procelain, curios and woven straw goods. And, joy of joys, the shopkeepers understood what good bargaining was all about.

Bamboo lampshades, in the shape of the steeply gabled Sumatran houses, were the biggest hit with the honeymooners who were later to board the plane homeward bound with huge plastic bags full of them, destined as presents for admiring relatives.

Our only painful experience occurred in Medan, an overcrowded, poverty-stricken city. We were out walking one evening—a long crocodile consisting of twenty-four young Singaporeans and me, their precious mascot, gently shepherded out of harm's way, in the middle.

'Watch your handbag,' the girls kept warning me. We certainly seemed to attact a lot of attention from the locals. People literally stopped in mid-stride to gape, open-mouthed, at us. Tourists were still fairly uncommon in 1975 and we were a rather large and unusual group.

We ate at street stalls starting off, at Charlie Chan's insistence, with Chinese porridge—a rice gruel with pieces of chicken. We continued with delicious mild and spicy dishes ending with *murtabah*, a type of Indian pizza.

Then we got stuck into the real business of the evening—shopping. We were all enthusiastically trying on shirts, skirts, blouses and bathrobes in the batik shop, when a band of hideously deformed beggars invaded the shops. Lepers and maimed clutched at our sleeves and shook tin cups under our noses. Horror mingled with pity, as we fled from the shop—shopping forgotten—hellbent on returning to our hotel.

But, alas, there were no taxis and we had been warned against taking trishaws in ones or twos, because of possible robbery or attack. There was a lot of poverty in Medan and it was not safe to wander around at night looking prosperous.

The dauntless Charlie Chan did not give up. He flagged down an empty mini-bus and negotiated a price, while hostile trishaw drivers crowded around, angry at the loss of business.

All twenty-five panic-stricken tourists managed to cram inside the twelve-seater bus, Charlie crouched double in our midst, encouraging the driver to hurry. We zoomed off, but five minutes later hurriedly pulled over to the kerb. The driver and his offsider (every bus in the East has at least one) got out and had a long, involved argument, illustrated with wild arm movements, with the two motor-bike riders who had followed us.

The upshot of it all was that our driver told us we would have to pay 'protection money' ('squeeze' as the Singaporeans explained) to compensate the trishaw drivers for loss of business. If we refused, said our driver, he would be in peril—shot, even. We paid up promptly and urged our driver to take the shortest route to our hotel.

Despite our adventures and misadventures, Sumatra had proved a fascinating place with its villages of ancient tribes, its incredible beautiful 'sacred' Lake Toba, its tombs of the Toba Batak Kings and colourful red and black Batak houses with roofs shaped like buffalo horns. Its colourful markets, sweet Batak singers, tales of magic and strange primitive beliefs add to its fascination.

It was with real regret that I said goodbye to my twelve Singaporean couples and wished them long life and happiness. As far as I was concerned, Somerset Maugham could keep his planters. The Chinese were much more fun.

HEADHUNTING DAYS ARE OVER FOR THE WILD MEN OF BORNEO

ONCE the Dyaks of Borneo were pirates of the South China Sea. Today, their descendants take in paying guests.

It is only about fifteen years since the first tourists arrived in Sarawak (northern Borneo includes Sarawak, Brunei and Sabah, and all except Brunei are part of Malaysia now) and a day trip into the jungle to stay at a Dyak longhouse was an exciting and novel experience.

We shot down the rapids of the Skrang River in a long, flat, motor-powered canoe. Our native guide, crouched in the prow, stared intently into the turbulent brown water for shallows and snags. When our tortuous way led us too close to the river bank, he poled us off.

The jungle-clad banks were thick with creepers, bamboo forests, lianas, brilliant flowering red trees and banana trees. Occasionally a brilliant flash of colour caught the eye, as a bright-plumaged parrot alighted on an emerald branch.

We were a party of five—our guide Willy Choo; Marie Van Epp, an American tourist; her sixty-year-old mother, Susie; a Thai-Malay, Kamaruddin Abdullah; and me.

Our destination was the twenty-one door 'Mujan' longhouse ruled by Chief Minggat. Longhouses are called after the number of doors leading off the huge communal area to the private quarters of each family. The largest longhouse I heard of was a 200-door one on the Rejan River. Each door marked a family, so that particular longhouse was a 200-family affair.

In former times, the White Rajas, who ruled Sarawak until the Second World War, sent out expeditions along the same river we travelled, to pacify the Sea Dyaks. Sarawak was known as the Land of the White Rajas. An Englishman, James Brooke—a swashbuckling, handsome man who once worked for the East India Company—founded the dynasty.

The word Sarawak means 'I give to you' and commemorated the granting of land to Brooke by the ruling Sultan of Brunei in 1839, in thanks for subduing a Dyak revolt against Brunei authority.

We had left the strangely named capital, Kuching, early that morning. 'Kuching' means 'cat', and the city was named after a wild cat which sprang at the White Raja, just as he was trying to think of a name for the new capital.

We travelled the 200 kilometres by car, through Somerset Maugham country (he wrote 'The Yellow Streak', among other stories, here) past pepper plantations, rice paddies, roadside markets, cloud-covered mountains.

We lunched in the Rangers Park on barbecue chicken, cheese sandwiches, fruit and lemonade. Willy, our guide and cook, had even brought scented cold towels!

Then, shortly after, we loaded our provisions—food, cooking equipment, rubber mattresses, bed linen and bottled gas—into the flat canoe and spread our raincoats to give protection from the showers of water expected as we negotiated the rapids.

'No, we don't eat the Dyak food,' Willy explained. 'They boil everything up together and it is pretty tasteless.'

A spectacular welcome awaited us at the longhouse. Women dressed in glittering silver headdresses and colourful sarongs with overskirts of heavy silver coins, danced graceful welcoming dances.

Their arms were covered in silver bracelets and silver anklets graced their legs. The costumes are precious family heirlooms, passed down from mother to daughter and used for weddings and special festivals.

Then the men, armed with *parangs* (long knives) and shields, danced the traditional steps of defence and strike, once used to work up their fighting spirit before war expeditions. In slow movements, almost as if in a trance, they wove the sinuous movements for attack—dodging, weaving and lunging.

They wore feathered headdresses—the feathers and beak from the hornbill bird—richly woven loincloths, gold necklets and beads, and gold earrings so heavy they dragged huge holes in the ear lobes, which reached to their shoulders.

The Dyak men had elaborate blue tattoos covering shoulder, neck, arms and back. Most of the older men had been headhunters in their youth and each time they took a head they tattooed a joint of their hand.

Other tattoos sometimes commemorated a journey. The designs were of flowers, dragons, dogs, bamboo trees, hibiscus and traditional Dyak geometrical patterns.

The Dyaks first officially gave up their headhunting expeditions during the reign of the third White Rajah, but old habits died hard. When the British government took over Borneo after the Second World War, head hunting was again outlawed and became a capital offence.

When the head hunting expeditions returned to the longhouses, the women used to sing and dance, holding the skulls. Nowadays, during the big three-day Festival of the Devil, 'Gawai Antu', in honour of dead ancestors, the women still sing and dance but they use old skulls taken from the walls after a cock has been ceremoniously slaughtered. Much potent rice wine (*tuak*) is drunk and a good time had by all!

In the longhouse where we stayed there were white skulls lining the walls and a bunch of blackened skulls hanging over a fire in the centre of the long room. A small fire is lit every two weeks to smoke the skulls, which keeps their 'spirits' warm and friendly to the occupants.

The Dyaks believe the human skull has magical powers to bestow prosperity, health and virtue.

There are about 250,000 Sea Dyaks living in about twenty-five longhouses along the Skrang River. In the old days they were the fiercest tribe and other natives were terrified of them.

Dyaks built their longhouses on stilts and lived as a closely knit community as protection against enemies, floods, snakes and predatory animals.

Our longhouse was of bamboo and thatch, entered precariously up a steep log with notches cut in it for steps. A public area ran the length of the house and private quarters, kitchen and bedroom, for each family, ran off it. It was roofed with thatch, the walls were of bamboo and thatch and the floor of bamboo slats (some rotten).

Marie, intent on taking pictures, began to disappear with a scream through the floor as the rotten bamboo gave way. But, luckily, being a fair-sized person, she became stuck and was pulled out.

Scraps of food were pushed through gaps in the slats to the pigs and fowls, which competed below in the mud for food. Upstairs, a loft storeroom was stacked with rice, straw mats, baskets, fishing nets and firewood.

Inside the longhouse, the treasured fighting cocks (the

Dyaks love to gamble on the fights) were housed in rattan baskets and fowls wandered around—a few were tethered by twine to the floor.

Dogs fought and bare-breasted women in sarongs fed their babies or wove baskets or mats. Grandmothers rocked bare babies slung in cotton hammocks from the ceiling. Everyone smoked strong cigarettes wrapped in nipa palm leaves. Even three- and-four-year-old children smoked with casual aplomb. The tobacco was kept in ornately carved bamboo tobacco holders.

Children walked around completely naked except for silver anklets and circlets around their waists. The women had blood-red mouths from chewing betel nut, and gold teeth (a sign of wealth). The Dyaks work hard and often die young because they have little medical care and their diet is often deficient. They plant rice and hunt deer, wild boar, monkeys, squirrels, porcupine, and honey bears. Once they used poison arrows, but today they use guns and rattan traps.

After the day's work they sit in the longhouse exchanging gossip, making fishing traps, carving tobacco holders and intricately designed knife scabbards, and weaving palm baskets.

The Dyaks believe this world is possessed by good and evil spirits. Messages are received through omen birds and dreams, and from examining the livers of slaughtered pigs.

Hanging from longhouse doorways and the roof were small, flat, woven baskets with offerings of rice and fruit for the spirits.

The Sea Dyaks (also called Ibans) still worship the spirit of the famous pirate, Rentap, who came from the area and fought the White Raja.

He built a 300 metre fort of ironwood atop a hill near the river. It took the raja several attempts to capture him. He finally succeeded by sending a brass cannon and 100 Malay soldiers, and the fort was demolished.

In the evening we sampled Willy's delicious Chinese cooking, seated on the floor of the chief's quarters while he and his handsome wife watched us eat. The menu was chicken in soy sauce, prawns in batter, fried rice, fresh bamboo shoots, green beans with shrimps, hot pineapple sauce and tea. Later the chief's family ate what was over.

Chief Minggat, a fine-looking man of about forty, covered

in blue-black tattoos, chatted with us through Willy, who spoke
the Iban language.

'Sea Dyak men and women have equal rights,' the chief
said.

'The women also work the fields. There is free love before
marriage—the man just goes under the girl's mosquito net,
but he cannot court her for more than twenty-one days unless
he marries her.

'If he refuses to marry her, the chief fines him—perhaps
twenty pounds of rice, a sarong, money, a knife, a jar, or
a fighting cock.

'Marriage is a mutual decision. If the woman finds the man
unsatisfactory, she can easily divorce him.'

After dinner, woven mats were spread and chairs with backs
but no legs set out for the guests, and we enjoyed more
dancing by the light of kerosene lamps.

We clapped the show enthusiastically, then each dancer
in turn shook hands ceremoniously with each guest while
we murmured: 'Very good. Thank you.'

Then it was our turn. The gamelan orchestra of gongs
and drums, which has a central place in the longhouse, was
beating out a cha-cha-like rhythm. In no time, the young men
were up on the floor with me learning the cha-cha, while
chanting, 'One, two, cha-cha-cha.' This was followed by the
twist, and soon everyone was twisting precariously on the
round bamboo-slat floor.

The children, wrapped in long pieces of cloth sewn down
one side—sometimes used as a sarong and sometimes spread
out and sat in like a small boat, watched wide-eyed.

Then it was time for supper—broken cracker biscuits and
tea, triumphantly produced by Willy and received with great
acclaim by the Dyaks.

The other big success was the instant camera photos taken
by Marie, given as gifts and passed around with much giggling
and teasing, as the Dyaks recognized each other.

Having entertained us royally, it was time to get down
to trading. The Dyaks brought out their treasures for sale—
strings of glass beads (some over 100 years old), carvings
and woven mats.

The strings of beads were bought from Chinese traders
and used as money belts. Each bead was equal to a measure

of rice. The primitive carvings were of dragons, birds, toy dolls, warriors. The woven palm mats had beautiful designs of stars, moon, deer and flowers. I bought a tobacco pouch, a fierce carved 'man walking in the jungle', and some beads.

Sarawak has ten tribes—the Ibans or Sea Dyaks, the Land Dyak (also called Bidayuhs) the Melanaus, Muruts, Kayans, Kenyahs, Kedayans, the Kelabits, Punans, and the nomadic Bunans.

The head man of the longhouse is called the *Tuai Rumah* (elder of the house) and is elected by representatives of the longhouse families.

The Iban people practise healing rituals in which the witch doctor sits in a swing, sometimes with a white cloth on his head. He says prayers and sprinkles holy water. Primitive-looking healing statues are placed near the sick.

When I asked to photograph one fat cherub being breast fed, the mother said: 'Baby too tiny for photo' (at least that's how Willy translated it).

When Borneo became a British Crown Colony for eighteen years after the Second World War, the British proclaimed that anyone taking a skull on a headhunting expedition would be executed. But, during the war, the headhunters had a field day against the enemy. The pride of one longhouse was the skull of a former Japanese Minister of Education, his rimless glasses and gold teeth polished scrupulously every week.

Headhunting is now totally taboo but it's not so long since no self-respecting Dyak girl would marry until her fiancé brought home a head to prove his bravery.

It was time for bed. Travellers once slept in longhouses, sharing accommodation with grunting pigs, fighting dogs, chickens, crowing cocks, crying babies and late-arriving huntsmen. One traveller described a night there as 'a night in hell'. Nowadays visitors sleep in the more convenient and private bamboo and thatch guest house, away from the prying eyes of the Dyaks, who once squatted around their guests watching their every move throughout the night.

The guest house consisted of two bedrooms, one for men, one for women, separated by a corridor leading to the 'Western-style plumbing' bathroom and toilet. There were no beds. Our rubber mattresses were spread on two raised wooden platforms. Kerosene lamps threw eerie shadows on the thatched roof. In the toilet a huge spider occupied one wall. Marie, armed for all occasions, demolished him with a spray from her insect repellent can. A curious rat quickly disappeared.

Unfortunately, the Western-style handbasin let me down, collapsing in the middle of my wash, smashing the lamp and leaving me hanging on for grim death (to avoid a fractured toe), and hollering for help.

Marie and her mother made curious preparations for sleep. First Marie brought out their two floppy animal toy mascots— Flubby and Dubby, reassuring them that they would be safe even though in the Borneo jungle, and not to be afraid.

Their bedtime ritual continued with the pouring of a stiff gin and tonic each, followed by the swallowing of two sleeping tablets each.

'Nothing ever wakes us,' they choroused.

I lay in the dark, listening to the whirring, grating, chirping, rustling sounds of the jungle. There were strange noises as if a box of marbles were being rattled, and a noise like pods being rattled in a box. A bird made a whip-cracking sound, ending on a high note like a question mark.

The night was alive with the noises of crickets, birds, nocturnal animals, pigs grunting, and the voices of returning hunters.

There were noises of small animals rustling on the roof. Frogs croaked. But what really alarmed me was feeling something scamper across my leg, followed by a rustling at my head. I was sure a rat was on the prowl after my foolishly placed bunch of bananas. Then I felt the creature scurry across my leg.

'Marie!' I yelled.

A very sleepy voice said, 'What?'

'A rat just ran over my leg!'

'Oh, don't worry,' She replied. 'One just ran over my face!'

By 4 a.m. I could stand it no longer. I roused Marie and we tried to light a pressure lamp, succeeding only in spilling the kerosene on the floor. Even our hastily summoned guide, Willy, couldn't get it alight. I lit a candle (death by fire was the least of my worries) to keep the rats at bay and slept fitfully until dawn.

Breakfast was cooked by Willy on a Bunsen burner attached

to a gas cylinder. We ate fried eggs, bread, fried bananas, tinned jam made of egg and coconut, fresh bananas and tea. The longhouse kitchen was a bright place with tin trays painted with vivid red flowers, pink plastic dishes and highly coloured Western-style calendars.

We enjoyed the trip back down river through the rapids. We passed huge yellow and red flowers, red, purple and green parrots, butterflies with soft dusty blue spots, small huts in rice fields and thick jungle lianas.

Only an hour's flight separates Sarawak from Singapore but, in that time, the traveller spans a century or more, travelling backward in time to a simple, primitive way of life.

LIFE IN CALIFORNIA

TO the average Australian, the Californian way of life is zany to say the least.

Take Californian pets for instance. One pet owner cuddles her house-trained boa-constrictor, another loves to pat her pet shark.

American exotic pet shops do big business in California. It's just another way of doing your own thing—part of the mad but amusing lifestyle in the land of gurus, oranges and movie stars.

Roseanne, sales director of the Santa Monica Hotel where I stayed, kept her pet shark in an aquarium at home and told me it loved having its head stroked. She was heartbroken when she had to move and couldn't take her pet with her. But the couple who moved in were just as keen to adopt her unusual pet and give it a good home.

Friends of hers, a married couple, kept a boa-constrictor in the lounge room, and gave it lots of hugs to keep it happy (they could not afford a pet psychiatrist). It was allowed to roam the house, except when nervous visitors called.

And, shades of the British television comedy, 'Fawlty Towers' and waiter Manuel's pet rat, I actually met an American businessman whose children kept two pet rats. No, not hamsters, nor tiny, pink mice, but the big grey variety.

Apparently rats were used at the local school for lessons on the facts of life. Pupils were invited to buy a pet rat. His six-year-old son did not need much persuasion to acquire a rat of his very own, but was heartbroken when four-year-old sister sat on it and killed it.

Sympathetic teacher sent home another rat but, meantime, father had bought one from the pet shop. The two rats were given the run of the house which the family had recently moved into.

Enter friendly neighbourhood housewife with a fresh-baked cake to welcome them to their new suburb (a typical American gesture). She asked to use the bathroom and unsuspectingly entered only to emerge screaming that there were rats in there. Despite reassurances, she fled, never to return.

I got the story from the father who couldn't understand what the fuss was about.

'Mice are nice, but rats are better,' he claimed.

Llamas, crocodiles and snakes are just some of the other pets sold by exotic pet shops.

Other shops cash in on pet owners' fantasies. One, in Farmers' Market in Los Angeles, sells T-shirts for dogs with slogans such as 'Male Chauvinist Puppy', 'Fire Hydrant Inspector' and 'Super Stud', as well as jewelled collars, little porkpie hats, rubber ducks, toy mice and Muppets. White collars and black ties are available for doggy's formal occasions.

A fancy gift shop in Santa Monica displayed the *Dog and Cat Good Food Book*—an illustrated guide to dog and cat nutrition, with recipes such as egg-nogg, munchies and fish cakes for your cat; dog biscuits and meat loaf for your dog.

'Do people really cook special meals for their pets?' I asked a Californian friend.

'Sure thing,' she replied.

'One friend of mine was convinced her cat had developed cancer because of unwholesome eating. She now cooks it organic meals and freezes a week's supply ahead.'

Chocolate is another Californian passion. The state is a chocolate addict's paradise.

You can buy notepads with emergency messages such as, 'Bad day, send chocolate quick', and, 'Things getting worse, more chocolate'.

Chocolate speciality shops sell T-shirts, stickers and posters praising chocolate, recipe books for chocolate addicts—one recipe was for 'chocolate reefers'. You can even buy a car bumper sticker which warns: 'I brake for chocolate' (a play on 'coffee break' and 'car brake').

On a three-week visit to California I was constantly entertained, surprised, delighted, amazed, shocked at times. Americans were friendly, informal, generous and hospitable—and definitely into doing their own thing for enjoyment, kicks or 'just because'.

Australia was 'in'. They loved our 'darling' accent, our 'real neat' films, and above all, our television advertisements promoting Australia and starring comedian Paul Hogan.

'How ya goin', mate?', and, 'Put another shrimp on the barbie', had become catchphrases.

'How do kangaroos mate?' asked a Californian friend, Geri Jean Wilson, with utter seriousness.

'Do they do it in the pouch or how does the baby get there?'

I promised to ask the zoo when I got home and let her know (I did).

My first impressions of Los Angeles on an early evening arrival were of an eerily luminous sky, palm trees incongruous against glass skyscrapers, and Spanish-style haciendas. Later, exploration revealed Art Déco style architecture—not surprisingly, as Hollywood's heyday was in the 1930s.

Smog diffused the image to a smudgy Turneresque landscape. Only in Los Angeles you don't insult the Angelinos by calling it that—it's 'mist'. That slightly unsettling feeling that illusion and reality, magic and myth are inextricably mixed, is one of the attractions of a visit to California.

The hotel where I stayed in L.A., the Bonaventure, was a typical businessman's hotel downtown. Yet it was also the set for films such as *Star Wars* and *Buck Rogers*. Its futuristic lobby, with its towers, waterfalls and glass skylights, was an ideal setting for outer space.

From my bedroom window a neon-lit 'Jesus Saves' glittered from a nearby rooftop.

In San Francisco, my hotel, the Westin St Francis, received kings and heads of states and washed the coins used for guests' change every day. Why? Tradition.

'Baghdad on the Bay' they called San Francisco—at least that's what its famous columnist, Herb Caen, dubbed it. (I had dinner with Herb, his girlfriend, and Clint Eastwood in Carmel.)

I didn't find any Arabian sheiks in the city but I did find a 'living statue'—a man standing stock still on a dust bin holding a collection box; a seaman with a parrot on his shoulder; break dancers; and youths 'pop locking' (doing weird movements which 'pop' the joints).

Actors definitely did their own thing. The night I attended the Curren Theatre to see Al Pacino in the play, *American Buffalo* by David Mamet, the audience had to wait until opening time in a draughty foyer while Al and his cronies played poker on the stage (the curtain was up ready for the opening scene).

Right on eight there was a scramble for seats, mine being so high in the balcony that I could neither see the action nor hear the mumbled dialogue. The knowledgeable had quickly snapped up the hearing aids (hire two dollars) supplied for the deaf, plus binoculars. I left at interval.

In squeaky clean Beverly Hills, an exclusive L.A. residental district, I saw a council employee vacuuming the sidewalk. There were trees but no bird droppings.

'The birds fly upside down here,' I was told.

Dressing up in fancy gear and giving impromptu street performances was also part of the Californian style.

Outside Hollywood's Mann's Chinese Theatre (formerly the Sid Graumont Chinese Theatre) I met a Western gunslinger dressed in black with side guns who told me he was a professional 'mannekin'. I guess he meant a male model. His eyes were completely blank as he told me he had been a guest on the 'Mike Walsh Show'.

A gypsy, covered in bangles, beads and badges, gave me an unsolicited blessing, murmuring, 'No harm will come to you'—reassuring in a city with a horrendous crime rate.

Eccentrics flock to Venice beach in droves at weekends. They break dance—a spirited combination of twirling headstands, handsprings, robot-like movements, and foot-shuffling pantomine, roller skate or simply parade.

A Negro, dressed in a dinner suit, walked beside a woman wearing a snake entwined around her neck. An elderly woman skate-boarded past.

The crowd were simply carrying on the eccentric tradition of the rich American tourist who, returning from a trip to Venice, Italy, decided to recreate its canals in Los Angeles. The canals he built at Venice are now filled in, but the tradition of doing your own thing continues.

As one Angelino commented to me: 'When God made the world he shook it up and all the nuts and bolts fell out in L.A.'

Names were another way of showing individuality. Junk shops and cheap, trendy fashion boutiques on L.A.'s Melrose Street had names such as 'Retail Slut', 'I Love Juicy', 'Wacko', and 'Fantasies Come True'.

Personalized car number plates told the world their owner's preoccupations.

'Bad Love', read one; 'Can't Count', another (surely its owner was an accountant), 'Car Fun' (a Romeo, perhaps), was another. One bumper sticker implored, 'Kiss a Frog'—the owner obviously not a prince since the old saying is, 'You have to kiss many a frog before you find a prince.'

Californian limousines are the longest and sleekest in the world. One I noticed had a television set and cocktail bar inside. Another, an old-fashioned Excaliber, had a number plate, 'Suzie', plus four car horns decorating the bonnet, and searchlight-sized headlights.

Even marriage ceremonies are different in California.

'Couple to wed in burning house', headlined a San Francisco newspaper. The firefighter groom and his fianicée married in an abandoned house set ablaze.

'Fire fighting is a big part of my life,' the bridegroom explained.

'This wedding in the burning house is my way of incorporating my job with my wedding.'

The bride added: 'I'm not nervous. It's something different.'

The wedding party knelt close to the ground to breathe fresh air below the smoke. The bride wore a white fire helmet and a veil treated with flame retardant. She held a fire extinguisher as well as a bouquet.

The groom wore a red helmet and they lifted their respective fire helmets to kiss. The groom's buddies controlled the blaze and the pair left on a fire truck for the reception at the fire station.

Californians also come up with novel ways to solve community problems. When prostitutes plying their trade in the streets of West Berkeley in San Francisco made life intolerable, local residents set up community patrols.

Whenever they spotted a prostitute, they followed her until she left.

'We stood within three or four feet of the hooker, which seemed to make them nervous,' said one resident.

The patrol's tactics so disconcerted the prostitutes that they climbed fences to get away. Business dropped off. Problem solved.

At Long Beach, near L.A., oil rigs offshore were disguised as condominiums (home units) to keep a residential look to the area. But you could wake up one morning and find one of the 'condominiums' had moved to a new spot.

The old liner, *Queen Mary*, now a hotel and tourist attraction, is moored at Long Beach. It is reached through a mock Tudor village. A wedding reception was in progress the afternoon I visited the liner. That evening a plane flew overhead towing an illuminated sign, 'Congratulations George and Shirl from Mum, Dad, Grandma and Grandpa'.

As Paul Hogan says in his popular advertisement calling Americans to holiday in Australia, we have a lot in common with the Yanks, but we speak a different language.

In America you don't queue, you get in line. You don't ring a friend, you call her. You press for the elevator, not the lift. You ask for the check, not the bill. You pay with bills, not notes. You walk on the sidewalk, not the pavement. Praise is phrased, 'that's real neat', not, 'that's wonderful'.

The language can get impossibly complicated when ordering eggs for breakfast. The waitress mumbles rapidly: 'Over and easy, lightly, over medium, over hard, or over very hard.'

This duly sorted out, I opted for 'over and easy'—done both sides, medium gooey inside.

But as former Australian prime minister, Malcolm Fraser, said: 'Life wasn't meant to be easy.'

'Grits?' she asked.

'Pardon?' I replied.

Grits it seemed was a hot cereal made of Southern corn, powdered fine, and served on the same plate as your bacon and eggs. You could eat it with hot tabasco sauce, jelly (jam), marmalade, honey or brown sugar. Hot breakfast dishes came garnished with lots of fruit, including pineapple, melon, orange—even kiwi fruit—to make them look 'real pretty'. American breakfasts are always enormous. You start with a cup of coffee as soon as you sit down as an 'eye opener'. Or you can opt for a Bloody Mary (vodka and tomato juice). Every time you put down your cup, it is quickly refilled— they call it a 'bottomless' cup. You pay only for the first cup of coffee. You soon learn not to bother ordering tea, which is lukewarm water with a teabag sitting in the saucer waiting to be dunked.

If bacon and eggs are too conventional for you, you can try Belgian waffles with whipped butter, maple syrup and walnuts, a stack of pancakes with maple syrup and bacon, or fresh strawberries and whipped cream. You may opt for French toast—thick bread slices dipped in egg and milk, buttered, flavoured with sugar and vanilla, deep fried and served with whipped butter and sugar.

The language of ordering other meals can be just as confusing. Entrées are known as main courses, while what we call entrées are 'starters'. Salads are a separate course and big enough usually to feed a horse. Everything is wickedly fattening with dollops of whipped cream, whipped butter or mayonnaise.

The pies are especially fattening—Boston Pie (yellow sponge cake, custard, sweet chocolate topped with sliced almonds and icecream) or American Mud Pie (chocolate pie crust with icecream, caramel sauce, cream and nuts).

Even simple food comes with strange (to Australians) accompaniments. At the upmarket Fairmount Hotel on San Francisco's Nobb Hill, I was served delicious plump oysters with a choice of horseradish or red-hot tabasco sauce.

'Northerners like the horseradish, Southerners the tabasco,' the waiter explained.

Exotic alcoholic drinks are also popular in California. At the Pelican's Nest, a seafood restaurant in Santa Monica, I could have started my meal with a 'Magnificent Seven', a lethal mixture of vodka, rum, gin, triple sec, orange juice, pineapple juice and grenadine, or a 'Pelican Punch'—light rum with Myer's rum, apricot brandy and fruit juice.

With the main course (sorry, entrée) I could have had Long

Island iced tea spiked with vodka, gin, rum, triple sec, sweet and sour, a splash of Coke, and a lemon wedge.

Desserts included icecream dishes spiked with vast amount of liqueurs and, if I could still see the menu by then, I could have had Mexican coffee loaded with tequila and kahlua liqueur.

Tipping is an American custom which hits Australians right between the eyes—fifteen per cent is customary, more at classy joints. You pay porters, waiters and waitresses, room service, taxi drivers—anyone who provides a service. Wages are very low (three dollars an hour is not unusual for waiting staff) and employees rely on tips for a living.

Romance California-style can have a twist. One wealthy haberdasher passed a certain salesgirl on his staff every day for years, without as much as a word. Then, out of the blue, she got a written message from her boss asking her to meet him in his office after work.

She thought it meant dismissal, or at least a pass from the boss. Instead, the first words he ever spoke to her were, 'I've admired your work, will you marry me?'

She thought about it for a week, then said yes. They lived happily ever after in the penthouse above the business. Anyhow, that's how our guide told it as we passed the owner's building, the famous Olivetti Building in Los Angeles.

And if that's not the Californian way of life—zany with a happy ending—I don't know what is.

ON CLIMBING AYERS ROCK

THE Japanese say: 'He who never climbs Mt Fuji is a fool. He who climbs it twice is a greater fool.'

I feel the same way about climbing Ayers Rock. I'm unathletic, not as young as I used to be, and rather craven-hearted when it comes to scaling mountain peaks. But I'm proud to say that, unlike many who wear a T-shirt boasting of their climb, I did indeed reach the top.

What else could I do when George, seventy-two, offered to 'give me a hand up the difficult bits'. If I can do it, believe me, anyone (well, almost anyone) can.

If the thought of climbing the 300 metre scarred and pitted

monolith turns your knees to jelly, you can cheat and buy
a T-shirt inscribed, 'I really did climb Ayers Rock', but you'll
never experience that glow of achievement that comes with
actually doing the climb.

When our coach driver called for names of rock climbers
I dutifully put up my hand, and he duly noted my name for
the 9.15 a.m. victorious climbers' picnic breakfast at the base
of the Rock next morning.

That evening we met some of the survivors of that day's
climb. One girl limped in to dinner with a sprained ankle,
moaning that it took her fours hours to get down.

And two athletic-looking young men told us the climb was
'horrific' and 'worse than you could possibly imagine'.

The official (park ranger) estimate of the climbers' death
toll is twelve, four from falls and eight from heart attacks.
Our coach driver said thirty-five had died on the Rock since
1948. I hoped he was exaggerating.

It was just as well that I read the commemorative plaques
at the base of the Rock after, not before, my climb. One
told of a man in his sixties who died from a heart attack
on the summit. 'He achieved a lifetime ambition', it stated,
but whether his ambition was to climb the Rock, or die on
it, wasn't clear.

We climbers retired early. My room-mate, a fit bushwalker
in her twenties, woke me at 2 a.m. by calling out: 'We've
overslept!' She had dreamed we had missed the climb. No
such luck.

The whole coach party rose at 6.30 a.m. to stand in the
chilly dawn and watch the magnificent Rock come to life
in shades of glorious pink and red.

Fortified by a cup of tea, the brave, or foolhardy (depending
on whether you were a climber or not), set off for the Rock.

Noting my craven look, George reassured me he would
'carry your cameras and look after you'. It was all right for
him. He was fit, with the confidence that comes from walking
five kilometres a day, still worked as a plumber and planned
to go trekking in the Himalays. He was always in the lead
on our walks.

Alas, there was no turning back.

We were warned not to run down the Rock. Some chance!
Bare feet and thongs were also out. Slacks, or jeans, a shirt,

light pullover and stout rubber-soled shoes were the order of the day.

Our coach pulled up at the Rock where a chain ran up what looked like a perpendicular ascent to the horizon. Our driver cheerfully informed us that the end of the chain was not the summit. There were quite a few steep bits after that.

But first we had to traverse Chicken Rock, the chainless preliminary ascent which sorts out the lions from the lambs. This is where many would-be climbers chicken out. Hence the name.

'If you don't think you can make it to the chain, forget it,' advised our driver.

But I was concentrating on the statistics of the climb: that seventy-five per cent of visitors actually climb the Rock and that, even before the chain was erected, twenty per cent went up.

Trying to ignore the notice which warned that no responsibility would be taken for death or injury and that it was a difficult climb, I literally raced up Chicken Rock like a mountain goat, before I could change my mind. I passed a woman slipping and sliding in leather-soled shoes. She finally abandoned the attempt. A man was attempting the climb in bare feet, a dangerous practice.

The Rock looked implacable, a place of mystery, of strange Aboriginal myths. And here we were penetrating the once-forbidden heights of *Yulara*, the ancient Aboriginal name for the Rock, which means 'place of the howling dingo'.

George was right behind me with my two cameras securely attached. Ahead were a family from our coach. Dad, Andy, was battling up with a nine kilogram backpack, his video camera and seven-year old son, Ian, running behind attached by a rope around Dad's midriff. Mum and twelve-year-old son brought up the rear. I hung on to the chain and pulled myself up, hand over hand.

All you could hear was the climbers' heavy breathing, a few asthmatic wheezes and the cold wind's whistle.

Ahead of me, incredibly, an American tourist straddled the chain, clinging by hands and feet for dear life. If he had slipped, he would have ended up very saddle sore.

The wind took my breath away and it seemed I had to stop every five minutes or so to rest. The ascent seemed

interminable. Just when I thought we were reaching the summit, the mountain curved inwards and another ascent became
visible.

Andy's hat went flying off and he yelled to twelve-year-
old son not to try to retrieve it. Becoming a little more daring,
I turned and looked down. Far below, the coach looked like
a toy and people like ants stared up at the human chain
ascending the Rock. I was standing gazing down a curved
chute which slippery-dipped straight to the plain. I was tempted to sit down and hug the Rock, but luckily we were nearly
to the level section where the first length of chain ends.
Climbers rested here before attacking the second short stretch
of the chain.

My athletic room-mate was already over the next rise. Many
climbers give up after the first chain section. I was determined
to make it. Andy, just ahead, sped up the next bit so fast
that young Ian was left dangling and gave a piercing yell.
Royce, another climber, leaped forward and gave the kid a
push from behind which landed him on Dad's back, where
he clung until the worst of the climb was over

Once past the chained climb, the really hard bit starts. Steep
ascents with nothing to cling to. Loose slopes. Skidding rubber-
soled shoes. Walks across ridges with sheer drops below. Now,
instead of hand over hand, it was one foot after another,
feeling for a firm hold.

Then came the crevasses. We still had to traverse more
Rock to the summit. You had to slither, slide or run down
slopes with enough velocity to get up the other side.

But now there were the views. The magnificent round,
purple domes of the Olgas thirty-five kilometres away, the
vast desert plain and, closer up, the waves, curves, shining
pools of water, indentations of the monolith's summit, each
natural feature wreathed in myths from the Dreamtime.

Then the fantastic sense of achievement as we took each
other's photographs and signed the climbers' book. I felt like
Scott reaching the South Pole, Hillary on Everest.

Then the happiness of going down the chain watching the
tentative efforts of chain-clinging, apprehensive climbers on
the way up. And the fun of boasting that the climb 'wasn't
so bad'.

Trying not to let your legs run away with you, as you made

a gradual descent. In the distance I could see the American still straddling the chain on his way down.

Now I could boast that I had climbed Ayers Rock. But that's where I met my Waterloo. A woman friend of my age group topped my account with a quiet: 'But I climbed it before the chain was erected!'

CAMPING IN THE WILDS OF KAKADU NATIONAL PARK

SOME people are born campers, others achieve camping skills, and some have camping suddenly thrust upon them, as I did.

I had never camped before when I booked myself on a safari adventure through Kakadu National Park near Arnhem Land in the far north of the Northern Territory. I certainly did not know what I was letting myself in for. If I had read the fine print which advised a medical examination for the not so fit, I might have had the odd misgiving. I have never been the Girl-Guide type and my outdoor survival skills are nil, but I am always willing to try a new adventure.

We set off from Darwin in a four-wheel-drive, with eight travellers squeezed in, sitting facing each other on benches. They were all young, fit, former Girl-Guide types except for an elderly, fit, experienced camper, Bob, and new chum, me.

Our driver, Henk, was a larger-than-life colourful character, wearing a felt hat with sweeping feather, brief shorts and bush shirt. He was to prove a combination of Harry Butler 'In the Wild', Lawrence of Arabia adventuring in the desert, and bossy Rumpole of the Old Bailey. He also had a fund of scary, hairy stories of camping misadventures with which to frighten new chums. True, or untrue, Henk certainly knew how to send shivers up my spine.

First there was the story of the buffalo which got entangled in a camper's tent guy ropes in the middle of the night. The buffalo took fright and galloped off, dragging the tent with two terrified campers inside—well, that's how Henk told it.

'Good one!' he laughed, using a favourite expression.

Then there were the 'bird-eating spiders' which came out

at night, not to mention the feral cat which got into the tool box and scratched the driver all over when he tried to remove it. There was the motor-bike rider who had been killed by a buffalo who came from nowhere and ran into him. And the friend injured when a wild horse jumped on his car.

And what was I to make of the snake which Henk said came in through the window of the four-wheel-drive and fell under the driver's seat before getting into the back among the passengers who jumped out in record time?

'Only a harmless black snake,' reassured Henk.

When it came to camping near the wildlife paradise of Yellow Waters, I didn't have a clue about putting up my tent. All the Girl-Guide types and Bob had their tents up in a trice while I was still fumbling. I decided to throw myself on the mercy of the fittest-looking girl and it turned out a good choice.

'I was born in a tent', she said as she hammered in my tent pegs.

'Dad wanted a boy but made the best of me and took me camping since I was a tiny kid.'

In gratitude I pumped up her air mattress.

There were no showers available for our pre-dinner clean-up. Instead, we took it in turn to drag up a bucket full of dirty water from the creek and hid behind a tree soaping and sloshing ourselves clean.

Dinner in the wild was quite an achievement—steak, potatoes, tinned vegetables and tinned fruit salad and cream cooked by Henk on a camp cooker. A perfect sunset burnished the water. Wallabies watched us. A couple of buffalo wandered into camp after food scraps.

'Those who play up get scraps thrown outside their tent and will have to cope with the wild animals who forage,' warned Henk.

I hoped he was joking. The reason we were camped at Yellow Waters was that a crocodile had wandered up among campers at the usual camp at Jim Jim, after scraps, on the last trip.

There was more talk over dinner of enormous spiders, howling dingoes, rampaging water buffalo and hungry crocodiles.

Henk was a wild character who soon taught us his safari
jungle call: 'We are the wild life... whee-eee-eee!' He was
also the 'one who must be obeyed'. He had led an adventurous
life. A Dutchman, he had lived in South Africa, sailed a
barquentine with an international crew from Norway to Sydney, climbed mountains and endured a suppurating leg in
Nepal, suffered cholera in India, explored South America and
sailed with smugglers in the South China Sea. (He didn't
realize they were smugglers when he shipped aboard.)

'Those who can't keep up get left behind,' Henk warned.

When some of us had flagged in forty-degree temperatures
walking to the Norlangie Rock without the needed water
supply, to view the Aboriginal paintings, he had yelled at
us to keep up or else. The Rock is famous for its paintings
of the 'Dreamtime'.

That evening after dinner we drove into the nearest hotel,
the Cooinda, owned by the Kakadu tribe but with a white
manager. Henk surprised us by demonstrating his skill at
playing the didgeridoo. He had lived with a tribe in the
Western Desert in Central Australia—just one of his
adventures.

Ross, an Aborigine we met at the bar, kept repeating
proudly: 'I am Kakadu mob man.' The hotel's Aboriginal
owners have put a limit on how much any Aborigine can
drink. They are allowed four cans of beer to drink in the
hotel and six to take away. They are not allowed to stockpile
them.

Back at the camp I explored the area around my tent by
torchlight but found only a few tiny frogs and a huge spider.
The chef at the Cooinda Hotel had told of being bitten by
a huge huntsman spider and weeks later he still had the marks
to prove it. The sounds of the bush were not reassuring—
hums, stirrings, scraping. What were those dark shapes I could
see through the tent flaps?

Having done up the tent flaps securely, I fell asleep. About
two in the morning I woke and tried to pluck up courage
and head for the bush with my torch to answer a call of
nature. Which was better—a burst bladder, a charge from
a wild animal or a mauling by a rampaging crocodile? No
more tea at bedtime I decided. The bush loo won out, and
my only encounter was with some tiny insects and ants in

the dry leaves which left a legacy of horrid itchy little bites
on legs.

Morning came, which meant folding tents and squeezing
them into a minute tent bag. I thought I had done well, as
I placed my tent pegs in the box.

'What do you think you're doing?' yelled Henk.

'Those pegs have to fit in the tent bag. Start again.'

About six attempts later I finally got tent, pegs and guy
ropes into the bag. I was the last one for bacon and eggs.

That day we cruised the Yellow Waters Lagoon. Pythons
hung from trees, long-legged Jabirus strutted along the banks
and logs came alive as crocodiles slid quickly under the water.
There were fifty varieties of reptiles including five venomous
snakes and both freshwater and saltwater crocodiles. The
pythons were not venomous, we were told.

We spotted Magpie Geese, sharp-clawed Whistling Kites,
Little Pied Cormorants, black-faced Terns, graceful white
Egrets, Blue-winged Kingfishers, China Flycatchers and Nan-
keen Night Herons.

Kakadu National Park takes the visitor back into a mysterious primeval land where magnificent scenery and abundant
wildlife leave an indelible impression.

'No one who goes into Kakadu comes out the same person,'
a park ranger had told me.

In times long vanished Kakadu was part of a land bridge
between Australia and South East Asia. Across this bridge
people, plants and animals migrated between continents. Traditional links between Aboriginal owners and the land go
back some 50,000 years.

Only in recent times have visitors gained access to this
fascinating country. In November 1978, the traditional Aboriginal owners leased more than 6000 square kilometres of
their land to the National Parks and Wildlife Service to be
managed as a national park.

Kakadu lies about 220 kilometres east of Darwin, with the
sealed Arnhem Highway making access easy, but many of
the most spectacular sights such as Twin Falls and Jim Jim
Falls can only be reached by four-wheel-drive and on foot.

The park lies between the South and the East Alligator
rivers which empty into Van Diemen Gulf to the north. It
is home to myriad species of birds and animals, which include

the ferocious saltwater crocodiles, the milder freshwater ones, brumbies (wild horses), buffalo, kangaroos and wallabies.

The park is a paradise for our photographers, bird watchers, bushwalkers, fishermen and nature lovers. Its most spectacular feature is the Arnhem Land Plateau with a 500 kilometre-long sandstone escarpement featuring magnificent rock formations caves and waterfalls.

Visitors can opt to drive and either camp or stay at South Alligator Motor Inn, or Cooinda Motel near the Yellow Waters Lagoon. They can also take a coach tour with motel accommodation provided, or a wildlife camping trip by four-wheel-drive which goes to otherwise unreachable areas.

Safari tours may not always operate during the wet season, usually October to March, depending on road conditions. The 'wet' is, however, a great time to see wildlife.

Our tour left Darwin early one morning and headed for the park, with the first stop at the Ranger Park Headquarters where visual displays told of the park's history and attractions and information was available on routes and park conditions.

Bushwalkers were asked to clear proposed itineraries with the ranger before setting out, told not to swim in the holes without seeking advice from a ranger (because of crocodiles) and never to swim where there was a crocodile warning sign.

After our lagoon tour on the second day we took off for remote Jim Jim Falls along a horrific sixty-eight kilometres of rough track which took us about three and a half hours to travel. We lunched in a dry river bed among ghost gums and set out again only to get bogged down in soft black 'bull dust'. We got out and disconnected the trailer then pushed the four-wheel-drive through the dust which turned us to the shade of Negro minstrels. It was in our nose and throat and saturated our clothes.

Back aboard, Henk led our war cry: 'We are the wildlife... whee-eee!'

Before dinner at our camp we swam in a billabong, Henk having reassured us that the one crocodile we spotted behind a branch was a freshwater one, not a man-eating saltwater one. But, after our swim, Mike the ranger told us that a croc a short distance further away could be a saltwater type.

Our swimming-hole crocodile was small, 'only four foot long'.

We had very civilized pre-dinner wine with crackers and cheese and cabanossi sausage.

That night some in our party went looking for crocs by torchlight, Mike having told us you 'can see their red eyes in the dark'.

We rose at 6.30 a.m. next morning to hike to the head of Jim Jim Falls, on the way climbing 'boulders as big as apartments', as Henk put it. The one kilometre rock scramble would take about an hour he said. It took me two and a half hours getting in and out, including a swim at the foot of the falls, where water cascaded down a 150 metre cliff.

Remembering how I had lagged behind in the forty-degree temperature the preceding day, I wondered how I would manage to keep up with the Girl-Guide types. I need not have worried. If you did not keep up, you were left behind.

As I laboured up the boulders I could see the rest of the party ahead taking their rest break. By the time I reached them they were off again. I simply plodded on.

But the effort was worth it—swimming at the base of vividly coloured massive boulders and sheer cliff face.

After lunch we took off for Twin Falls, a twenty-kilometre drive then a short walk to a river canyon where we were expected to hop onto plastic air mattresses and paddled down the canyon to the falls. Between each gorge we had to traverse red-hot rocks carrying our air mattresses on to the next bit of water.

'What about crocodiles?' I nervously asked Mike.

'Don't worry, the last saltwater one was seen here over three years ago,' he reassured.

'The freshies are nothing to worry about.'

I was determined not be last. What if the croc had returned and was lurking about. We inflated our air mattresses, dived in on them and paddled up the gorges under the massive orange sandstone cliffs of the Arnhem Land Faultline Escarpment.

'Don't float over that way,' Henk warned our oldest camper, Bob.

'There's a freshwater croc there. They're not dangerous but it's the mating season and he may be a bit aggressive. They bite when they're annoyed.'

I asked Henk: 'What would you think if your wife was eaten by a croc?'

The 13-storey impressive white and vermillion fortress-palace of Tibet's god-kings, the Dalai Lamas, is reflected in a man-made lake in the centre of Lhasa. The Potala dominates both physically and spiritually the lives of the Tibetan people.

A typical ornately-decorated bus found in Afghanistan, Iran and Pakistan. Roofs carry more passengers, bikes and luggage. Unlucky last minute passengers cling precariously to doorways.

Jerusalem's stunning Dome of the Rock is sacred to Jews, Christians and Arabs alike. On the rock inside the temple Abraham prepared to sacrifice Isaac, Solomon built his temple, and a footprint commemorates Mohammed's leap to Heaven.

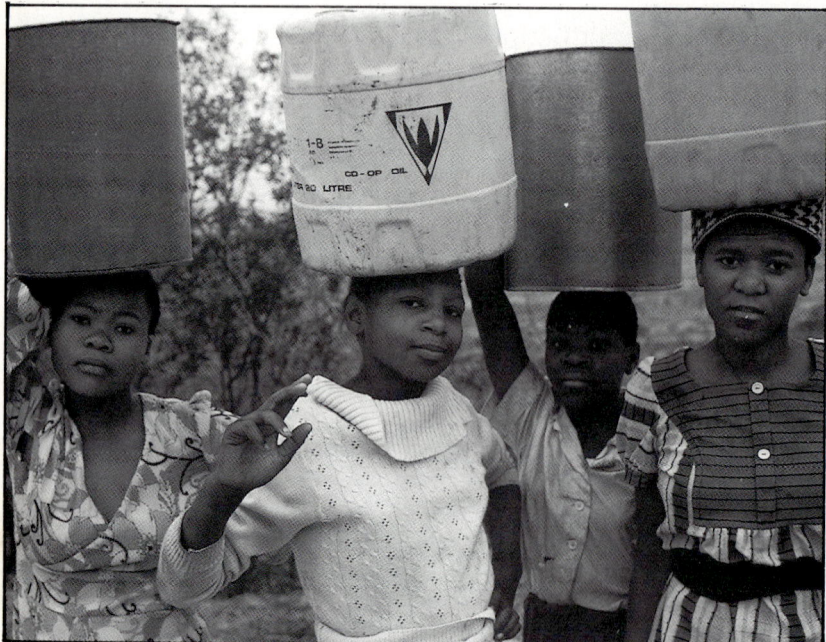

A familiar sight on South African roads — children, carrying cans of water home to their villages, clown for tourists.

'I'd think it must have been hungry,' he answered laconically.

We finally came to a beautiful white-sand beach in an amphitheatre of massive orange cliffs and water delicately coloured green and orange in the shallows, emerald green where it grew deep. We were in a rainforest with huge Carpentaria palms, kintai palms, milkwood, and herringbone fern. A perfect spot. The only other access is by helicopter.

I trailed the field again on my way back. What's more, my air mattress sprang a leak. One of the 'Girl Guides' transferred me to hers and nonchalantly swam the rest of the way.

That evening the sky was blood red with bushfires burning in the distance, a full moon, and jungle sounds as Henk blew on the didgeridoo to summon us to dinner. We had already used the 'summer trees' (as Henk explained, 'Summer for men and summer for women', and taken turns to draw up a bucket of dirty river water for our evening ablutions, soaping and sloshing water behind a tree.

'Plenty of ABCs [another bloody crocodile] around,' warned Henk.

But by now, our last night, we felt we could cope with anything the wilderness had to offer. We had become our rallying call—'We are the wildlife...'

A 300 kilometre journey the next day took us back to Darwin and civilization, but we were indeed changed.

'No one who goes into Kakadu comes out the same person.'

PLACES 1

ISTANBUL AND BEYOND—
TURKEY

ISTANBUL has been celebrated in many a mystery thriller
and spy movie as a colourful, intriguing, mysterious city, with
just a spice of danger.

Spies were murdered on the fabled Orient Express as it
raced towards Istanbul, priceless jewelled daggers were stolen
from Topkapi Palace-Museum, and the daring spy, Cicero,
escaped to South America by ship from its harbour.

East meets West in Istanbul, which is only fitting for a
city which bestrides two continents. The city, like Rome, is
built on seven hills and, like a city from *Tales of the Arabian
Nights*, it has 1001 minarets. Its exotic blend of basilicas,
aqueducts, mosques, palaces and fountains—relics of its
Roman, Byzantine and Ottoman past—make it unique.

It certainly captures the imagination. Here French writer
Pierre Loti spun his exotic tales, Byron swam the Hellespont,
Eartha Kitt sang of its sinuous rhythm in 'Üsküdar', and Peter
Ustinov stole its fabled jewelled dagger from Topkapi Palace
in the movie *Topkapi*.

Legend says it was founded by the Megarians who came
from Megara in Greece in 660 B.C., and originally called
Byzantium after their commander, Byzas, son of the demi-
god, Semestras.

The city later became Roman and, when the Emperor

Constantine moved the capital of the Roman Empire from Rome to Istanbul, the city become known as Constantinople after Constantine, who made it the capital of the Byzantine Empire. The name was changed back to Istanbul in 1930.

Constantine believed seven was a lucky number, so he built the city on seven hills. It was invaded many times during the fourteenth and fifteenth centuries by the Turkish Ottoman forces. Sultan Mehmet II captured the city after a long siege in 1453, bringing to an end the Byzantine Empire, and since then Istanbul has remained Turkish.

On my first morning in the city, I woke to a breathtaking view from the window of my room in an old inn in the Turkish quarter (as opposed to the international area with its big hotels and office blocks).

The Blue Mosque floated like a huge pale blue pearl in the morning mist, guarded by its sentinels—six slender minarets. My first close-up view was in the evening. A V-shaped flight of birds wheeled over a rose-coloured sky as I left my shoes at the door and shuffled in oversize felt slippers through a heavy baize curtain into a carpeted interior swimming in blue light, reflected from exquisite sea-blue tiles.

The Turks call it the Sultan Ahmet Camii. It was built by Mehmet Aga, on the orders of Sultan Ahmet I, in 1616. The sultan gave orders that the mosque was to have four minarets, as no mosque could surpass Mecca, which had five minarets. The sultan then went off to war.

When he returned, he was furious to find that his architect had built six minarets. In Mecca, another two minarets were hastily added to make seven. An incongruous note in the mosque is a grandfather clock, a present from Queen Victoria.

Facing the Blue Mosque across a small garden and pool is the Aya Sofya (St Sophia), the church where emperors were crowned during the Byzantine era.

It was built as a Christian basilica by the Emperor Constantine in 347 B.C. and rebuilt after a fire by Justinian in the sixth century A.D.

After Sultan Mehmet conquered the city, he converted the church into a mosque with four minarets, in the sixth century. Once it held porphyry columns from the fabled Temple of the Sun in Heliopolis and decorations from the temples of Rome, Athens and Delphi.

From the minarets of its mosque (and others), the muezzin's call to prayer rolls out over Istanbul, echoing across the Golden Horn to Üsküdar in Asia. The faithful pray, sitting on their heels, heads bowed: 'Allah is good, Muhammad is his helper', while the priest sits in a decorated niche in the mosque's interior, facing Mecca.

Today a museum, it is justly famous for its beautiful mosaics and the Muslim geometric patterns and calligraphy (one of the finest arts of the Muslim world).

But the loveliest mosaics in Istanbul are in the old Church of St Saviour in Chora (a suburb), which the Turks turned into a mosque with minaret. It is now a museum with exquisite mosaics and frescoes dating from the eleventh and twelfth centuries, including a superb head of Christ.

One of Istanbul's unusual sights, the Sunken Palace, or Yerebatan (sunken cistern), built by the Emperor Justinian, is situated near Sultan Ahmet Square, near St Sophia. Its 336 beautiful pillars are said to be reminiscent of a palace. With its arches and columns and dank underground water pool it is rather eerie.

My favourite mosque is the Eyub Mosque on the Golden Horn, a peaceful place of worship, its courtyard crowded with hundreds of fluttering pigeons, perfume sellers, stalls crammed with prayer beads, scrolls and copies of the Holy Koran.

It was built in honour of the Prophet Muhammad's standard bearer, Halid Bin Zeyd, who is buried nearby.

When Sultan Mehmet found the grave in 1453, he ordered a magnificent tomb and mosque built.

Pilgrims wash their feet and rinse their mouths, women chatter, a pilgrim kisses a tattered beggar, pigeons coo and flutter.

Inside there is perfect peace as pilgrims meditate in a pale cool greenish light under a golden chandelier.

Strolling through the nearby cemetery with its magnificent view of the Golden Horn, you come to the Pierre Loti restaurant which has the best view of Istanbul and provides water hubble-bubbles for patrons and delicious perfumed *loukoumi* (Turkish delight) and thick Turkish coffee.

Another favourite spot was near the Galata Bridge which spans the Bosporous, separating the Eastern from the European side of the city, with its shops, restaurants and theatres.

As dusk falls, the minarets, domes and towers seem to float in mist. The bridge is a string of lights, the golden ferries and ships glide like caterpillars across the water. Each side of the harbour glows with bright lights to rival the 'dressing' of pleasure ships and cruisers.

Businessmen sip tea in little *chai* shops and smoke water-cooled hookahs, mattress makers sit in shop windows sewing mattresses and quilts, the muezzin's call to prayer floats from the minarets. A roaring trade is done in rings of poppy-seed bread sold by street sellers. Shoeshine men stand in rows beside their shiny brass shoe stands.

Messenger boys scurry around with trays of tiny glasses of golden tea and sugar lumps, an essential lubricant to fluent social conversation and business deals. The bread men sit on camp stools on corners. The smell of rose-flavoured, almond studded, Turkish delight, wafts from a candy shop.

In open-air cafes, customers drink thick Turkish coffee and potent aniseed-flavoured *raki*, and consume sweet pastries such as *baklava* and *halva* in vast quantities.

Istanbul smells of spices, fresh bread, rose-perfumed *loukoumi*, dank buildings and salt spray.

The city seethes with people, muffled or in modern clothes. Crowded bazaars reek of pungent spices, street photographers hide under old-fashioned camera hoods and say the Turkish equivalent of 'smile at the dickey bird' while they pull the bulb.

Crossing the Bosporus by the Galata Bridge from the Asian side to the European side, you gaze up at the *Galata Kulesi* (tower) built by the Genoese as a watch tower within their ramparts in the Middle Ages (1216). Another version of its origin claims it was built by a Roman Emperor, Anastasius Dilosis, in 507 A.D. The towers of Istanbul are as prominent a part of the skyline as the minarets. Bayezit Tower, within the university grounds, was built in 1828 as a fire-watching tower and now houses a coffee house and has a fine view of the city.

Kiz Kulesi—the Maiden's Tower—was built as a signal tower in the time of Constantine. It got its name from a legend about the Emperor Constantine's daughter. A sorcerer said she would die from a snake bite. To save his daughter, the Emperor built the tower in the middle of the sea. She lived there safely until one day a basket of grapes was sent up to her. A snake crawled out and killed her.

You can catch a ferry from near the Galata Bridge which takes you down the Bosporus as far as the Black Sea. You pass the castle of Rumeli Hisari (the Thracian Castle) built in 1452 and boasting three towers. In summer concerts are given, and sometimes Shakespearean plays are staged here.

The shores of the Bosporus are dotted with castles such as the Genoese Castle and the Anatolian Castle built by the Turkish architect, Yildirim Beyazit in 1395, 24 years before the Turks conquered Istanbul. At the time the castle was built, the walled city of Istanbul was part of the Byzantine Empire but the Turks controlled the Bosporus area. Sariyer, then (15 years ago) a fishing village with quaint wooden houses (now a fashionable suburb of Istanbul), is a good place to break your journey. It has lots of good fish restaurants and a quaint mosque with water troughs where men wash to purify themselves before entering. From here you can catch a bus back to Istanbul.

Topkapi, now a museum, is a real palace. Its old *seraglio* (harem) is surrounded by high walls where once eunuchs guarded its beauties as they bathed in rose-perfumed sunken baths. Here in the palace sons of slave girls (potential rivals to the throne) were thrown over the palace wall into the Bosporus.

Nowadays the palace, built by Fatih Sultan Mehmet in the sixteenth century, gives a glimpse into the world of rich, cruel sultans. There are priceless jewels, Sung and Ming pottery. There are Turkish paintings, the throne room with its gold throne, the prophet's room where Allah's cloak is preserved in a casket, and the richly embroidered costumes of sultans including the blood-stained garments of the assassinated Osman II. The treasury has huge emeralds, and diamonds. One famous diamond called the 'Spoonmaker's' diamond occupies the whole of one display cabinet. It is a rare 84 carat diamond surrounded by 49 smaller diamonds. Jewellers from all over the country used to travel to Istanbul to admire it. There are gold thrones studded with precious jewels, a prince's jewel-encrusted cradle, and, of course, the fabulous dagger with its three huge emeralds and watch set in the handle, which was stolen in the plot of the movie *Topkapi*.

Visitors can see rose gardens, the sultans' reception rooms

and what must be the only loo in the world where an attendant pours rose-scented water over your hands.

Nearby the Archaeology Museum has the reputed tomb (sarcophagus) of Alexander the Great, works from the early Christian and Byzantine period and archaeological treasures from Sidon, Miletus, Ephesus and Troy.

The Dolmabahce Palace, a little further out of town, was built in 1854 and is a mixture of European and Turkish architecture. The plan resembles the old Turkish grand houses. Kemel Atatürk once lived here. Today it is a museum, but is still used for state receptions and guests have included King Faisal, the late Shah of Persia, and a former president of Italy.

The palace has 300 small rooms, twenty-six large ones, and a huge cathedral-like reception room with a chandelier weighing two and a half tonnes, a gift of Queen Victoria. The clocks are still stopped at the hour of Atatürk's death. One of the bathrooms boasts a bath made of precious jasper, known as the *Sultan's Bath*.

But Istanbul is not all history and ancient buildings. Its Grand Bazaar, also known as the Covered Bazaar, is almost a city in itself. It covers many kilometres and a shopper can easily get lost in its labyrinthine mazes. It has more entrances than a rabbit warren.

The bazaar was commenced in 1461, and rebuilt in the sixteenth century. Each street has one type of tradesman. It's a shopper's paradise with many treasure bargains—alabaster vases, antiques, carpets, leather suits and coats, exotic gold and silver jewellery, table linen, hookahs, carvings, precious stones.

Trays of refreshments are carried in from the tea shops to loosen tongues stiff with bargaining.

The harem rings are three to five rows of gold or silver, set with small colourful jewels, and said to be worn by ladies of the harem. The puzzle rings are gold or silver hoops whose strands are intricately woven together. Legend has it that the wives of sultans wore them. The sultan could always tell if his wives were unfaithful while he was away because if they took off their rings, they fell to pieces. It takes a lot of practice for the tourist to be able to put them together.

The Spice Bazaar (also known as the Egyptian Bazaar) sells

mainly spices—heaps of red, blue, green and brown powder.
It also dispenses delicious tea, fruit, honey, meats and pastries.
The famous restaurant, Pandelli, lies within its labyrinth.

A cheap and easy way to get around Istanbul is by *dolmush*,
a cross between a bus and a taxi which travels fixed routes.

I found Turkish food delicious—*doner kebab*, thin slices
of lamb from a revolving spit, seafood, rice *pilaf* with pine
nuts, spices and raisins, eggplant or tomatoes stuffed with
spiced, minced meat, *dolmades* (minced meat in cabbage or
vine leaves), *koftes*—herb-flavoured meat balls. The desserts—honeyed pastries such as *baklava*, milk desserts
sprinkled with rose water or simply yoghurt—were delicious.

I also enjoyed belly dancing (many nightclubs at hotels
provide this entertainment) and of course I had to sample
a Turkish bath.

I had my Turkish bath in a huge old Roman-like stone
establishment with high ceilings which was Istanbul's public
bath house. I took soap and shampoo, stripped and donned
wooden clogs. Water troughs in alcoves brimmed with steaming water from taps. Attendants threw hot water over me
and over the floor to raise steam. One attendant vigorously
washed my hair then, as I sat on a central circular stone
dais, scrubbed off my beautiful suntan. Finally she threw a
bucket of water over me and I emerged as clean as a new
pin.

In the old days matches were made in the bath houses.
Mothers would pick out a bride for their sons in the bath
house and the attendants acted as go-betweens.

But Istanbul is not all there is to see in Turkey, and it
was time to head for the countryside—wild mountains, horsemen herding sheep, olive trees shimmering in the sun.
Turkey was also gaily painted wooden carts, camel trains with
loads of cotton, women in purdah with enveloping head
scarves. It was the muezzin calling to prayer from slender
minarets, dazzling white salt pans, black goats in a dry river
bed.

Pergamum is famous for its ancient Greek and Roman ruins
which crown a steep hill. The terraced outdoor amphitheatre,
which cascades down the mountain side, glows golden in the
setting sun, its acoustics as perfect as when its third century
A.D. audience crowded its 30,000 seats.

Broken columns give silent testimony to once beautiful temples, theatres, libraries and centres of healing. In the seventh century A.D. the Arabs burned the city, which was reconstructed in the fourteenth century by the Seljuk Turks and later by the Ottomans.

The Aesculapium, the centre of healing, was devoted to the god of medicine, Aesculapius. According to inscriptions found, the mute spoke, the blind were given sight and many sick were cured by means of suggestion, dreams, sun and water baths, drugs made from plants, dramas and games.

In the underground passages of the centre, patients disturbed in mind were locked in with snakes to frighten them back into their wits. Those who could, slept, and in the morning the temple priests interpreted their dreams.

Ephesus is said to be the site of the final home of the Virgin Mary and the reputed burial place of St John the Apostle. St Paul wrote his epistles while visiting the city. It is also the Roman city of the time of Claudius (41 A.D.). The ruins reveal the beauty of its theatres, temples and baths. Along the wide, majestic Marble Street and the Arcadian Way, chariots once drove.

If it weren't for a fire bug who burned down the temple in its heyday, you could still visit one of the Seven Wonders of the Ancient World, the Temple of Diana. But the House of the Virgin Mary and the Church of the Virgin Mary (second century and reputedly the first basilica dedicated to the Virgin Mary) can be visited.

Izmir is a beautiful seaside resort where you can ride in a hooded carriage, with a fringe on top, or promenade the seafront watching the rows of hookah-smokers puffing at their water-cooled hubble-bubbles.

Or you can visit Hellenistic ruins, aqueducts, Roman baths, archaeological museums, mosques, caravanserais (inns where caravan traders stopped).

Gallipoli—a place of pilgrimage to Australians—preserves its memories of brave battles in pill-boxes, barbed wire and concrete blocks. But many young warriors sleep in peace under the rustling pines of a small cemetery at Anzac Cove.

It is not far from there to Canakkale. On the way you pass by a fortress with red-striped sentry boxes guarded by troops, soldiers dressed as colourfully as toy soldiers . . . orange fishing nets drying in the sun, and fish markets reeking of their catch. You can buy little handfuls of nuts, scooped from glassed boxes on wheels by itinerant vendors, or ride in gaily painted carriages.

Troy is redolent of history. It is not one city, but nine, each built on the ruins of its predecessors. Sitting under the rustling pine trees drinking potent Turkish wine, the ghost of Homer breathes through the ruins and Helen and her lover come alive. The sea, which once lapped the walls of Troy, has receded.

But once, from its ramparts, the sails of the boat which came to rescue Helen were sighted. The tombs of Hector and Priam are thought to lie under two mounds in the ruins. No one knows what became of the Trojan horse.

There are few more beautiful places than central Turkey. I remember my journey to Pamukkale. Our way lay through a green valley between purple hills. Trains of donkeys with workers from the fields, women loading cotton bales onto a truck, a peasant woman bowed under a load of firewood passed in a panorama as the bus sped through the evening.

The hills and valley glowed gold, then rose pink. The hills became blue silhouettes against the last gold glow of sunset. Green trees shimmered in pink light and a pale moon rose. Along a dry river bed a biblical-looking shepherd herded sheep. Night swallowed him up with the nearby green stream. The stars swam in a black sea and the lines of farm workers continued their journey home by starlight.

In Pamukkale we swam by starlight where ancient Romans had cavorted—in hot spring water, our feet touching ruined Roman columns lying on the floor of the hot baths. This was once a fashionable Roman spa called Hieropolis.

But even more spectacular than Hieropolis are Pamukkale's sheer, white calcified cliffs which cascade in scalloped lily ponds of blinding white, right down the cliff face to the grey-green plain below.

It looks as if a snow storm has transformed the mountain, but the white wonderland is caused by calcium deposits from an underground river, which is also the source of the hot springs. Rocks, cliffs, shrubs, stones, even ferns, have been iced with dazzling white.

The terraced rock pools—scalloped tier on tier of overhanging pools—hold bright blue water. You can swim in the lily-pond shaped pools, suspended between blue sky and green valley below.

Dinar is a pretty village with beautiful mosque and gaily costumed women, who wear baggy pants and gauzy face veils.

Ispartor makes attar of roses. Egridir has a heavenly blue mosque and a turquoise lake which reflects the purple, orange, pink and yellow of the surrounding mountain ranges.

Konya is the city of the Whirling Dervishes. The name means 'image' or 'icon' and it was named after Medusa. Legend says that Perseus slew Medusa here and hung her head on the city gate. All who looked at it were turned to stone.

The founder of the Whirling Dervish sect, Mevlana, the mystic and poet, is buried in a green-tiled mosque. In the nearby Dervish Museum, you can listen to the whirling music used in the trances of the sect and see the robes and conical hats they wore.

The most eerie landscape in the whole of Turkey is the Valley of Goreme. This is the land of the cave dwellers, the troglodytes. It is a strange, petrified valley with rocks twisted into grotesque shapes by centuries of wind and rain. The elements have also carved out caves in the rocks.

Modern cave dwellers, swathed in gossamer-like scarves and baggy pants, their eyes curiously surveying the strangers above their purdah masks, sit in cave-home doorways. Their hands are busy with spinning, quickly turning the wool on a long stick-like hand spindle. Biblical figures—little old bearded men in white skull caps—trot by on panniered donkeys.

At night an enormous moon floods the valley with light. It makes the twisted, contorted landscape even more eerie as it illuminates great gaping holes in rock faces, pinnacles and pyramids of torturous rock, which glow luminous white and yellow among the deep shadows of crevasses.

During the seventh century A.D. persecuted Christians fled to Cappadocia to escape death. Here in the Goreme Valley, they built their cave homes and churches, hidden deep in caverns where they could worship in safety.

The four main churches are known as the Church with Columns, the Church with Sandals (which takes its name from footprints caved on the rock floor, said to be a copy of Christ's), the Church of the Buckle and the Church of the Apple (after features of the frescoes, I surmised).

We looked in vain for an apple or a Garden of Eden among the complex painted frescoes, but could not find one. All the churches are richly decorated with Byzantine wall frescoes, many sadly defaced over the years by the Muslim Turks. The oldest frescoes date back to the beginning of Christianity.

Turkey has some beautiful Black Sea Coast resorts, like Trabzon (Trebizond)—I've always wanted to see it since reading Rose Macaulay's hilarious *The Towers of Trebizond*—and Samsun.

On the Aegean lies the town of Bodrum, site of another of the Seven wonders of the Ancient World—the mausoleum of King Mausolus. Not a trace remains, but there is a fine Castle of St Peter and pleasant swimming.

Unfortunately this time our itinerary did not allow for exploring the delights of the Black Sea Coast or the Aegean Coast. Instead, we continued on to Iran, Afghanistan, Pakistan and India. Turkey had proved an exotic beginning to our long journey.

COVENT GARDEN

'IT'S nice, dear, but it's not like it was. I could smell the flowers from streets away,' murmured the little old Cockney lady. She could have been a ghost from the past, an aged Eliza Doolittle, Bernard Shaw's famous flower girl who became a lady. We stood gazing at the trendy speciality shops, boutiques and smart restaurants of London's beautifully restored Covent Garden.

It was also a far cry from my own memories—queuing up at 5 a.m. on frosty, bitter black winter mornings outside the Royal Opera House at Convent Garden for tickets to opera and ballet seasons.

Steaming mugs of tea from a mobile stall in the market kept us going until an attendant arrived at 8 a.m. to hand out numbered tickets entitling us to queue once again at a designated hour, according to our place, once the box office was open. We loved the market's air of excitement, the noise, good-humoured chaffing, heavenly smell of roses, lilac, violets and hyacinths as we slipped on cabbage leaves and narrowly avoided barrow boys' barrows.

In 1974 Covent Garden fruit and vegetable sellers packed up and moved to Nine Elms, their new site near Vauxhall. Twentieth-century traffic had become too much for the historic market and more space was needed.

Today's Covent Garden may have gone upmarket and become a tourist mecca but it still has the excitement, colour and atmosphere which made it a favourite haunt of artists, writers and visitors when it first started as a fruit and vegetable market in the early 1800s.

The 1830s central market building, the focus of the market for over 300 years, has been beautifully restored, with colonnades, twenty great copper lanterns each topped with life-size pineapples hung under looping girders of light-blue cast-iron, which support vaulted glass roofs, and within, Victorian-style shop fronts.

The cellars, which once stored bananas, now sport shops with such names as Culpepper the Herbalist (herbs and spices), Whistles, Crocodile, and Knickers (fashion).

Elizabeth David, the famous cookery writer, has her shop, Covent Garden Kitchen Supplies, designed to look like a Victorian pantry.

Peelers, a licensed restaurant with traditional English dishes, was named after the famous police force set up by Sir Robert Peel. Bow Street Police Station is just around the corner from the market.

Henry Fielding, the novelist, and his blind brother, Sir John, were magistrates at Bow Street. Sir John founded the first detective force, the Bow Street Runners, later absorbed by Peel's Metropolitan Police in 1829.

The corner Body Shop sells natural cosmetics, the Doll's House antique dolls, hand-made dolls' houses and miniature furniture. The Dairy Centre sells English cheese and foods cooked with dairy produce.

Thornton's is an old-established family chocolate and toffee firm, while Feen's stocks venison, quail and guinea fowl, quail eggs and gull eggs in season.

Pollock's sells toy theatres and cut-outs, antique dolls and toys. Fern's sells tea and coffee. The Craft Work Gallery,

Strangeways, the Market Gift Shop and Casa Fina sell crafts, gifts and ceramics.

Wrought-iron flower stands salvaged from the old market are now used for open air stalls. Covent Garden is the only London shopping complex open six days a week, until 8 p.m.

But Covent Garden is more than shopping. The beautiful cobbled piazza echoes with light music ranging from reggae to classics. Buskers dressed in traditional striped pants and bowler hats twirl black umbrellas, and perform comedy routines, while music student trios and quartets play Mozart and Haydn near by.

Covent Garden with its ninety-four listed streets and alleyways is a wonderful place to explore on foot, but it helps to know a little of its wonderful 600-year history.

In the early thirteenth century Covent Garden was the convent garden to Westminster Abbey and the field and orchards were tended by the abbey's monks. During the reign of Henry VIII, all church lands were seized. So, in 1552, the convent garden and a field, Long Acre, were given to John Russell, first Earl of Bedford, for services to the crown.

In the 1630s, the fourth Earl of Bedford commissioned Inigo Jones, Surveyor to the King's Works, to design London's first residential square and, trying to save money, specified that he wanted a church 'not much better than a barn'.

Jones' response was to design 'the handsomest barn in England', St Paul's in Covent Garden. Fine houses for gentlemen with arcaded walks soon surrounded the square called The Piazzas. Both square and houses have since disappeared.

Inigo Jones was a man of the theatre who designed elaborate costumes and scenery for court masques written by Ben Jonson.

St Paul's in Covent Garden has long been known as 'the actors' church'—for over 300 years, in fact. David Garrick worshipped here, Ellen Terry's ashes rest here and commemorative services are still held on the death of famous theatre people.

In 1662 Charles II granted charters to two theatre companies, the Theatre Royal, Drury Lane, which opened in 1663, and Covent Garden Theatre (now the Royal Opera House), which opened in 1732.

In 1670 the Earl of Bedford received a charter to 'hold forever a market' for fruits, flowers and vegetables. For the next 300 years the market filled the square and surrounding streets and market traders rubbed shoulders with theatregoers.

But by 1828 overcrowding was a problem and the Bedford family obtained the right to rebuild the market. In 1830 Charles Fowler's Market Building opened (named after the designer), replacing the untidy stalls. This building is the centrepiece of Covent Garden today.

The Floral Hall was finished in 1860 and is now the London Transport Museum, which tells the fascinating story of nearly two centuries of London public transport.

The Jubilee Market was built in 1904.

In 1918 the market and surrounding properties passed to Covent Garden Estate and, in 1962, were acquired by the Covent Garden Market Authority. The Greater London Council bought most of the market buildings and land in 1974.

Today you can still see the Earl of Bedford's arms and motto, 'Che sera sera' (What Will Be Will Be) on the market buildings.

Covent Garden has a long cast of famous people. Pretty, witty Nell Gwyn started as an orange seller at the Theatre Royal, Drury Lane, and ended up as Charles II's mistress.

Other notables included David Garrick the actor, writers Pope, Sheridan, Dryden, Samuel Pepys and Fielding, painter and chronicler of low life, Hogarth, and actor/manager John Philip Kemble. Boswell and Johnson, that inseparable duo, were frequently seen.

Seventeenth- and eighteenth-century writers and artists lived in houses surrounding the Piazzas and met in coffee houses and taverns.

The Georgian-style coffee shop in Russell Street was once the home of Thomas Davies, actor friend and contemporary of Dr Johnson who first met Boswell there on 6 May 1763. Boswell, knowing Johnson's anti-Scottish reputation, stammered: 'I do indeed come from Scotland, but I cannot help it.' Johnson retorted: 'That, sir, I find is what a great many of your countrymen cannot help.' Nevertheless, the friendship flourished.

The Lamb and Flag, a pretty house in Rose Street, claims to have been the scene of the attempted murder of the poet Dryden. Its other claim to fame is that both Charles Dickens and Samuel Butler drank there.

Charles Lamb and his sister, Mary, lodged at 20 Russell Street (now the Covent Garden Gallery) from 1817 to 1823. Mary, who was ten years older than her brother, had fits of madness. In 1796 she had killed their mother.

Charles gave up his own chances of marriage to look after his sister. Together they wrote *Tales from Shakespeare* for children. While living in Covent Garden, Charles wrote the famous *Essays of Elia*.

Near St Paul's Church is a plaque which reads: 'Near this spot Punch's Puppet Show was performed and witnessed by Samuel Pepys 1662.' The Italian puppet show became popular in England and the character Pulcinella gradually became Punch and acquired a wife, Judy, and dog, Toby.

Nearby, Professor Higgins hid behind a portico of St Paul's to take down the 'horrible' English of flower girl, Eliza Doolittle.

Browsing along Floral Street you come to six bookshops, the ultra-modern Dance Centre of Covent Garden which gives lessons in dance, and next door, the expensive, exclusive Sanctuary, a fitness and beauty centre.

Performers and stage hands from nearby theatres still drink at the pubs, the White Horse and the Nag's Head, on opposite sides of James Street.

One of my favourite spots is Neal's Yard, a tiny flower-filled courtyard off Neal Street, with bakery and tea room, whole-food warehouse, flour mill and dairy (delicious icecream and yoghurt sold), and a dovecote with fluttering, billing and cooing doves.

Dr Johnson once said that when you tire of London, you tire of life. The same, I think, could be said of Covent Garden.

TRADITIONAL JAPAN—
LAND OF SHOGUNS AND
SAMURAI

ECHOES of a romantic medieval Japan with its powerful warlords and warrior clans linger in the ancient *samurai* towns on the island of Honshu.

Those were the days when feudal lords presided over magnificent banquet halls filled with graceful ladies of the court and brave *samurai* (warriors). Their imposing castles with their brilliant court life were surrounded by mansions of retainers and enclosed by deep moats for protection against the greed of powerful rival *shoguns* (lords).

Who could resist the charm of medieval towns such as Hagi and Tsuwano where moats are filled with rainbow-hued carp, brilliantly robed dancers perform in vermilion and golden shrines and kimono-clad ladies perform the tea ceremony in parks famed for cherry blossoms or tread the ancient measures of court dances.

Having thoroughly enjoyed the book, *Shogun*, by James Clavell, I was delighted to have the opportunity of visiting these old *samurai* towns near the westernmost tip of the island of Honshu. It's a Japan few western tourists see, but it's all there for the adventurous traveller prepared to venture off the beaten tourist track.

On my visit, I learned a lot about Japanese-style living. I learned to eat raw fish, cold rice and pickles for breakfast, to enjoy bathing Japanese style, soaping and rinsing outside the bath before soaking in steaming hot water. And I learned to bow—when meeting people, farewelling travellers, and in lifts as passengers got in. I even ceased to marvel when a whole line of people bowed in unison as their friends sped off in a departing train. No casual waves here!

I confess I never sorted out which slippers to wear in a Japanese house. I knew to discard my shoes before entering, but I usually got mixed up when it came to changing bedroom slippers for corridor slippers and these for bathroom slippers.

I saw scenes which have changed little in centuries. Japanese wooden houses with little figures of upturned carp on their tiled roofs as a charm against fires. Country peasants wearing *mompe* (trousers), *wappari* (jackets), boots and *tenugui* (head towel) looking like figures straight out of a Japanese woodcut print. Proud kimono-clad mothers carrying babies papoose-style on their backs, tucked neatly inside loose jackets. Misty mountain scenery reminiscent of old paintings. Kimono-clad ladies ceremoniously sipping tea; brilliantly robed temple dancers performing for the glory of Shinto gods in temple courtyards.

In contrast there were modern scenes. A family group—mother in colourful kimono and *obi* (sash) lunching with kimono-wearing father, and daughter in neat English-style school uniform. Crash-helmeted schoolboys in military-style uniforms and white sandshoes roared past on motor bikes.

My first hotel, a Western-style one in Fukuoka, had a 'morning set' of toothbrush and paste, a freshly ironed *yukata* (bath robe-cum-dressing gown) laid out on the bed and a thermos of hot water, canister of green tea, tiny tea cups and sweet bean-curd cakes neatly set out on the table.

I had begun my journey by flying from Hong Kong to the city of Fukuoka on Kyushu Island where I stayed overnight. Next morning I took the bullet train to Ogori and changed to a local train for Hagi, accompanied by a charming Japanese guide, Yoshimi, who spoke both English and French.

First we crossed the Kammon Straits by underground tunnel and bridge to the island of Honshu, and sped along the shore of the Japan Sea.

The crack Japanese bullet train provided a rapid, smooth journey. We glided past little fishing villages, 'sacred rocks' roped together to denote their 'marriage', terraced rice paddies and wheat fields, and wayside shrines.

The train journey was my first experience of the Japanese love of food, beautifully presented and decoratively wrapped. Fellow passengers tucked into gift-wrapped breakfast boxes featuring rice, pickles and other goodies, followed mid-morning by prettily wrapped bean-paste cakes, and finally lunch boxes.

These featured regional specialities such as kettle-cooked rice with steamed chicken and vegetables, *sushi* (raw fish with vinegar rice), or *norimaki* (raw fish or vegetables with cucumber in a steamed rice ball wrapped in seaweed). Other popular snacks were *sembei* (powdered rice with soy sauce and seaweed), bean-paste confections, and dried fish.

I conservatively opted for Western-style grilled chicken and rice followed by crème caramel, which cost me a mere six dollars.

Musical chimes and an announcement in Japanese warned of our approach to Hagi. This practical measure allowed us a few minutes to put on coats and have luggage ready.

I soon found that few people outside big cities speak English, that porters are a rarity and taxi drivers don't normally handle luggage. The idea is to travel light (only as much as you can handle yourself), take an English–Japanese phrase book and a guide book. We left the bulk of our luggage in the railway station cloakroom.

We stayed in Western-style rooms at the Grand Hagi Hotel which provided a *yukata* and a snack of bean-curd cakes and green tea in my room.

Hagi, an ancient feudal town of about 53,000 people, is famous for its seventeenth-century *samurai* houses, its beautiful Hagi-yaki pottery dating back 360 years and its role in providing statesmen and leaders for the Meiji Restoration of 1868 which marked the end of the *shogun* form of government and the return of imperial rule. It is also known for its oranges, fishing industry and boiled fish paste (definitely an acquired taste).

It is a charming little town with grey wooden houses with shingle roofs, traditionally trimmed pine trees, narrow streets which still follow the grid plan of the seventeenth century. Picturesque pottery shops and mysterious *samurai* houses embellished with wooden grills add to its character.

It's an ideal place to explore on foot or by hired bicycle. But, with little time to spare, we opted for a taxi and set out for Tokoji, the family temple of the once powerful Mori clan. No one spoke English, so I left the translating to Yoshimi.

The city, picturesquely situated at the foot of hills and near the sea, was founded in 1604 by Lord Terumoto Mori, feudal ruler of the Mori family clan, one of the powerful feuding *shoguns* (rulers) who schemed and battled for power. He was defeated in battle, and after being driven out of Hiroshima prefecture by the Tokugawa government in Tokyo (then called Edo) he fled to Hagi where he built his castle and turned the little fishing village into a prosperous town.

Lord Mori's powerful presence is felt most strongly in his family temple, the Tokoji Temple, founded in 1691. It is a Zen Buddhist temple built in the Chinese Ming style and with waiting rooms for visiting feudal lords.

Two huge gates lead to the wooden temple with its curved shingle roof and eaves decorated with carved devils. Bronze bells tinkle in the breeze.

Inside the temple sits a huge, calm, golden statue of Lord

Buddha meditating under elaborate gold chandelier-like ceiling decorations. The Zen Buddhist priests live in a simple wooden building nearby.

An impressive corridor of stone lanterns leads to the family cemetery where 500 more stone lanterns represent the lord's *samurai* and their servants. In earlier times they would have been buried alive with their masters, not merely represented in stone as they are here.

The Mori lords are represented by five imposing stone pillars on the right, their ladies by a similar number on the left. Mistresses, their children and servants are buried a little distance away.

Stone turtles support the columns. On their backs are Chinese characters which list the faults of each lord, making a personal history for Buddha. The turtle, traditionally a 'foolish animal' in China, carries the message that, although each lord had his faults, the Buddha should protect him in the hereafter.

Thus passes the glory of the world. The once-powerful Mori clan are turned to stone. Little too remains of their massive castle built in 1604—only a few walls and the moat at the entrance to beautiful Shizuki Park. The last ruler, wanting to show that *shoguns* no longer existed, once the Meiji rulers were restored, sold his castle in 1873 to an Osaka shopkeeper. It was destroyed the following year.

The park, which is alive with cherry blossoms in spring, has two nineteenth century tea houses where you can take part in the tea ceremony, after washing your hands in the little stone basin outside. The 'Hananoe-tai' tea house was once located within the grounds of Hagi castle and the feudal Lord Norichika-Mori used to see many of his patriotic friends and discuss affairs of state over the tea ceremony. Nowadays a tea ceremony is held on the seventeenth day of each month to commemorate his custom.

I visited one of Hagi's famous potteries nearby. Hagi pottery originated in the seventeenth century when two Korean potters came to Japan to teach the craft. There were once more than 400 kilns but today only about a dozen are working.

Students are attached to a kiln master and this particular kiln had ten students who will spend more than ten years learning the ancient technique.

I bought a beautiful apricot-coloured pot for about twelve dollars. One by a master craftsman could cost thousands of dollars. Besides, mine was fired in a gas-fired kiln, a less expensive and labour-involved way than in the huge old wood-fired kilns made of stone inside, mud outside, in which expensive art objects are fired.

The old kilns are used only once every four months for thirty hours continuously. I watched as clay was moulded into typically Japanese-style teapots. Red clay comes from a small island near Hagi and yellow clay from Bofu in Yamaguchi prefecture.

A piece of pottery made by a 'Living Treasure', an artist potter who has been designated a master craftsman by the government, is almost priceless. As well as items for sale, ancient bowls dating from the seventeenth century were on display.

Originally the pottery was made exclusively for the ruling Mori family. Today it bears a slight cut on the base because perfect was only for rulers, not commoners—the cut means it is not a 'perfect' piece.

A number of old *samurai* residences stand alongside warehouses in fascinating lanes not far from the castle. Their white mud walls display a lattice pattern and they are approached through wooden gates. Here too are the old residences of former famous statesmen and leaders.

The governor of the town, a descendant of the original owner, now lives in one. In the days when everything was sold by appointment to Lord Mori, the original owner did business with the feudal lord.

Lord Mori's doctor, and later, the sister of Prince Hirobumi Ito, first president of Japan, lived in Edoya Yokocho Street, which also has the famous traditional restaurant, the Nakamura.

Covered gateways with tiled roofs and old stone walls overhung with orange trees beckoned us to explore picturesque lanes. The orange trees were first grown in 1891 to provide a livelihood for the former 'soldier' class. In May and June the whole town is scented with fragrant orange blossom.

Hagi is also famous for its Shoin Shrine built to honour a patriotic schoolmaster, Shoin Yoshida, who was killed at twenty-nine after attempting to assasinate a high *samurai*.

He taught many famous students in his small academy between 1857 and 1860. Students included Prince Hirobumi Ito. Although almost all the students came from the lower class, many became leaders in the Meiji Restoration which put emperors back on the throne in place of *shogun* rulers. Students still come to have their photographs taken beside Shoin's schoolhouse. Even the present emperor came here 57 years ago when he was a prince.

Pilgrims to the shrine buy fortunes written on white scraps of paper. If they don't like their destiny, they simply tie the white paper to a tree and start again. One tree was covered with knots of white paper.

A stone washbasin with dipper stood at the right of the entrance and pilgrims scooped the water over face and hands to purify themselves. A shop sold little brocade-covered packages with bell attached containing charms for family household shrines.

Hagi is dotted with houses of former patriots and former clan schools. The Meirinkan, for instance, was a clan school built by the warlord Mori, where some of the *samurai* took lessons in the martial arts.

Two beautiful spots worth exploring are the Kasayama Hill, an extinct volcano, over 112 metres high, thought to be one of the smallest conical volcanoes in the world; and to the east, Myojin-ike, a natural saltwater pond formed by the explosion of the volcano, with swans and fish in its water.

We dined at a branch of the Nakamura restaurant on *tempura* (local fish, prawns and vegetables in batter), rice and local beer, sitting on woven straw *tatami*, divided from other diners by paper *shoji* (screens). *Ikebana* flower arrangements and huge black and white prints of Hagi's famous attractions decorated the restaurant.

Breakfast at our hotel next day was an incredible feast combining Japanese and Western dishes served 'viking' (buffet) style on plates with compartments which took toast, marmalade, fruit and hot dishes. Most Japanese happily mixed scrambled eggs and bacon with salad, dried salt fish, radish, boiled fish paste and rice with a raw egg broken into it.

The hotel had public bath houses for both men and women—huge rooms with vast square pools full of steaming water and alongside rows of taps and dippers. The idea was to sit on a stool, pour a dipper of water over yourself, soap and rinse, then hop into the bath for a relaxing soak. This experience cost one dollar.

Tsuwano, our next destination, was a couple of hours' journey away, with a change of trains at Masuda. The beautiful scenery included fast sparkling mountain streams, snow-capped mountains, green tea plantations, bare wheat fields and terraced vegetable gardens.

The pretty mountain resort of Tsuwano is known as Little Kyoto because of its rich cultural heritage. Its feudal rulers had been great lovers of learning and eagerly introduced the art and culture of the then capital of Japan, Kyoto. Tsuwano, population about 10,000, is, like Hagi, a medieval castle town. It is crammed with *samurai* houses, folk museums, shrines and temples. Set on a river, Tsuwano is surrounded by mountains and boasts many delightful small inns, tea houses, souvenir and antique shops.

We caught a taxi from the railway station to our hotel. I should not have been surprised that our taxi driver wore spotless white gloves with his chauffeur's peaked cap and neat uniform or that the taxi seats had lace doilies on the backrests. It is not unusual to see people in the streets wearing white surgical masks to protect others against catching their colds or flu.

Our Japanese family-style inn (*minshuku*) cost only twenty dollars a night each, including breakfast and dinner. We couldn't book in until 3 p.m.—a common check-in time in Japan—so we left our luggage and headed for the main street.

A huge peasant straw hat attached to the façade of a small restaurant attracted us to try the Mountain House's delicious 'mountain vegetables' lunch. This consisted of *sashimi*—with vegetables instead of the usual raw fish—white radish, vegetables cooked in various ways, thick mushroom soup called *nameko*, rice sprinkled with herbs, and bean curd (*tofu*) made of sesame grain. This magnificent repast cost $6.50 each and a large bottle of beer $2.

The meal was artistically presented with colours and textures complementing each other, on porcelain bowls and dishes set on a lacquered wooden tray, a feast for the eye as well as the stomach.

We finished our lunch with a dessert from the Mountain

Inn on the opposite side of the street—its trade mark on
the wall a giant straw slipper (*waraji*). It specialized in sweets,
and snacks including rice balls with salmon, salty plums,
noodles, Japanese fruit and frothy green powdered tea. We
sat around the *hibachi*—a charcoal fire in the centre of the
table—and Yoshimini tried the bean-curd soup with sago
(*shiruko*) while I sampled the sugared bean-paste cake. It
looked like fudge candy, was wrapped in pink and grey paper
and was a speciality of the Koinosato (carp) district.

In Japan sweets are not usually served with meals. If you
fancy a dessert or cake, you go to a coffee shop or an *amami
do koro* (place for sweet snacks).

Many Japanese restaurants feature a statue of a comic black
badger supposed to bring good luck. He has breasts like a
woman, a huge paunch, and clutches a bottle of Japanese wine
in a paw. With his hat pushed back on his head, he looks
as if he enjoys a good few drinks of *saki*, Japanese rice wine.

Tsuwano has about 15 medium-sized inns catering for visitors but they are often booked out by the Japanese in the
tourist season. There is also an inexpensive People's Lodge
and a youth hostel.

The small town is ideal for exploring by rented bicycle
or on foot. It teems with dwellings of old *samurai* warriors
and mansions of illustrious families, mainly located in central
Tonomachi Street. Most are of white-washed plaster decorated
with white lattice work, and wood—with ornamental tile roofs.

On a crisp winter day it was fun to explore on foot. The
roadside moats and water channels were crowded with jewel-
coloured ornamental carp—a symbol against fire, a real risk
in Japan where fires have decimated the wood and paper
houses. (Even modern tile roofs often feature carp on the
eaves.) Apple-cheeked children enjoyed tickling the plump
carp with long sticks.

Snow-clad mountains surround the picturesque town and
a small river runs through it. It is the scene for several colourful
festivals. Horsemen, dressed in brilliant medieval costumes,
take part in an annual archery contest in April. The 240 metre-
long track for the competition is laid out within the Washihara
Hachimangu Shrine which enshrines the guardian deity of
successive generations of feudal lords.

The White Heron Festival, with its brightly costumed procession and sacred dance of the White Heron, is held in July.

Antique shops are crowded with historic treasures. I noticed several beautiful pieces of the Edo period (1603–1867)—delicate blue and white dishes especially made for the emperor, and a brilliant orange plate.

Yorokan folk musueum is housed in what was once a clan school built by the eighth generation of the famous Kamei family to encourage clansmen in the pursuit of scientific studies and martial arts. It is surrounded by a moat filled with plump multi-coloured carp. In spring the window boxes are filled with purple irises. Opposite the museum is an impressive wooden covered gate, all that remains of the imposing family home of a once-powerful *samurai*, Mr Kuchiba.

Inside the museum we found old musical instruments, tea ceremony equipment, temple drums, ancient sedan carrying chairs on poles, household furnishings and utensils of country folk, dolls dressed in regional costumes, antique fanciful hats, old coins, lacquered mirrors.

Kyodokan, another folk art and craft museum near the Yorokan folk museum, is a two-storeyed structure of the Meiji style of architecture. Inside there's a large collection of historic materials relating to Tsuwano, masterpieces of fine art and the belongings of literary masters.

The Yomeiji Temple, a Zen Buddhist temple founded in 1420, has a study hall, lecture hall, belfry and hall for keeping *sutras* (sacred writings). The tomb of Ogai Mori—one of the great writers of the Meiji period—is to the left of the gate and the mausoleum of the once-powerful Kamei family nearby.

Tsuwano is also famous for its beautiful hand-made paper products. We visited the factory and saw how the wood is soaked, beaten, pressed to pulp, dried and steamed. On sale were men's jackets, purses, handbags, dolls, wall hangings—all made of paper—plus notepaper and wrapping paper.

Strolling along a street of stalls selling toys, china and food, we came to the imposing brilliant vermilion enclosed wooden walkway, its steps ascending the Shiroyama Hill to the richly decorated scarlet and gold Inari shrine. It was built in 1773 by a master of the Kamei clan to pray for peace and protection for his castle.

Inari shrines always feature a statue of the sacred fox, and this was no exception. Foxes apparently like bean curd and the shrine's statue of the sacred fox was being plied with offerings of its favourite food by pilgrims who lit candles in its honour.

We were lucky to see the shrine in festive mood on the Horse Day of the lunar calendar. In front of the gorgeous temple, worshippers bowed in prayer, while at booths to the right, attendants—men in white and blue robes, girls in red and white ones—sold holy charms.

The sweet sound of a flute and the rhythmic beat of a drum drew us to the side of the temple where brilliantly robed dancers performed on an outdoor stage. Inside the shrine Shinto priests in traditional white and gold robes, wearing elaborate tall black bonnets, officiated over sacred ceremonies in which beautiful girls danced before the altar waving golden decorations.

A three-minute ride by lift from near the shrine brings you to the site of Tsuwano Castle. All that remains is a series of old stone walls, but the trip is worth it for the magnificent view of town and country.

We ate that night at our inn in the family dining room. Bean curd and mushroom soup were served in covered lacquer bowls and we helped ourselves to rice from a huge electric rice cooker. Beautifully displayed dishes appeared—boiled fish paste coloured pink and white, turnip-like white lotus root, bean curd stuffed with vegetables, raw fish with soy sauce and grated green radish, and steamed chicken with orange slices.

The other guests, a young Japanese couple, bowed politely as we sat, then remained glued to the coloured television on the wall where a sports programme showed young men riding bikes under water along an obstacle course. Above the television set was a traditional touch—the family altar.

My bedroom was small and simply furnished with fine straw matting, paper screen windows, a television set, a cupboard for bedding, a stand for clothes, a small table covered with paraphernalia for making green tea and draped with a cloth which hid an electric *hibachi* (warmer). The bedding consisted of a pillow and several padded coverings (*futon*). I put one on the floor as a mattress and draped three over the table so that the *hitachi* would warm my feet. The wintry mountain weather was freezing but I slept soundly enough.

Next morning I managed somehow to get through a typical Japanese breakfast of cold rice with a raw egg mixed in, soup with bean curd, seaweed, cabbage, sliced grated radish, pickles, boiled fish paste and green tea. Plodding around in outsize *benjo* (toilet) slippers, I also managed to slip on a wet bathroom floor and dislocate a thumb.

Before leaving the delightful Tsuwano, I climbed the mountain to pay my respects at the Church of Maria on Otome Toge Pass (the Virgin's Mountain Pass). It marks the place where 153 Christian Japanese who had fled persecution in Nagasaki were imprisoned from 1868 to 1873. All were tortured and 36 were killed.

Tradition says the Blessed Virgin Mary appeared to one of the martyrs, but there is no connection with the name of the pass. Legend also tells how it got its name. Many years ago a young woman from Tsuwano was betrothed to a prince in Kyoto but was rejected by him. Disappointed and disconsolate, she wandered slowly up this mountain pass and disappeared forever, giving the place its name. It was an unexpected postcript to a visit back in time to the powerful world of *shoguns* and *samurai*.

PONDICHERRY—AN INDIAN CITY WITH A FRENCH FLAVOUR

AFTER the bright sunlight, the little bar is dim, but you can make out the rows of French liqueurs, aperitifs and Napoleon brandy lining the shelf behind the bar.

You select a Dubonnet and order a fine herb omelette, catching a savoury whiff as the kitchen door opens.

The Hotel Continental was one of many little French hotels scattered along streets bearing French names. The town could almost be a French seaport but the heat is tropical, the drink waiter wears a turban and the sweeping promenade on the sea front is graced by a statue of Gandhi.

The place is Pondicherry in Southern India. The French departed in 1948 but the Gallic flavour of the former French colony remains to intrigue the visitor.

Pondicherry has the air of an outpost of an empire—the kind of place to which respectable European families exiled the black sheep of the family to a career in the army or trade. These empire-builders bore the white man's burden, often succumbing to tropical fevers. Many were buried in small Christian graveyards like the one a few kilometres out of Pondicherry.

Pondicherry, like ex-Portuguese colony Macau, has a slightly decadent, faded and plushy atmosphere preserved in the faded pastel pink, yellow and blue plaster houses, the baroque splendour of cathedral-like churches and the solid, square, fort-like public buildings—court house, hospital and college.

It was all part of an impossible dream of empire which brought not only French, but Dutch, Portuguese and English to India, and managed to swallow and digest most invading cultures. But Pondicherry still seems an exotic hybrid grafted onto the local variety of Indian cities and never assimilated into the mainstream of Indian life. Perhaps that is its fascination.

The city is set on a sweeping bay, absolutely flat to the horizon. A solitary steamer lies far out, casually giving off the odd puff of smoke. The heat is overwhelming and palm trees, rice paddies and lagoons all shimmer in the heat haze.

The little Indian street vendor, oblivious of the fierce sun, trundles his barrow piled high with rough wooden fiddles. He selects one and plays a piercingly sweet Indian air. But the dark-eyed beauty of eleven with the yellow hibiscus tucked in her long glossy black plaits, sings not a Hindi chant, but the French song 'Alouette'. Yet her graceful schoolgirl friend in the long cotton skirt and blouse is India personified. She stands motionless listening, holding a pink rose under her nose like a figure from a Rajput painting.

The charm of the sprightly tune is impossible to resist and I chose a violin from the pile of rough wooden string fiddles, ten cents' worth of the plaintive air of India. I never managed to coax a tune from it.

The bazaar is crowded with coconuts, mangoes, curry powders and spices. French croissants are piled among the sugary Indian cakes. I wonder who eats them for breakfast now.

Pink and white bougainvillea cling to white walls and gateways, yellow trumpet flowers, bright red hibiscus and sweet-scented yellow and white frangipani make a riot of colour and scent. In the square the pink and cream church rings the 'Angelus'.

Trishaws carry black and yellow family-planning posters but, judging from the crowds, nobody reads them. The market is piled with green and black grapes and mounds of pink, plastic shoes. Peasants carry golden pots coolie-style on poles, and rickshaws and pony carts deftly carry their loads of beautiful women in rainbow-coloured saris, like old-fashioned bouquets of mixed flowers. Country women squat on the pavement husking purplish-brown onions, throwing them into the air from palm-woven platters.

Pondicherry is a popular excursion from Madras, about 290 kilometres north. Indians come down for a day or two to have a few drinks in a non-prohibition city. Madras is 'dry'. Alcohol in Pondicherry is expensive and the local brew of beer costs seventy cents a bottle and is flat and tasteless.

But Pondicherry's main attraction for foreign visitors and Indians alike is the Sri Aurobindo Ashram founded by Indian patriot, yogi and sage, Sri Aurobindo. It is one of India's largest *ashrams* and pilgrims come from all over the world to search for truth here. They can live on very little at the *ashram* which holds over 2000 residents.

The *ashram* buildings are scattered throughout the town, so it's common to see bearded young men in sandals and European and American girls in shorts and shirts cycling everywhere.

The *ashram*'s main office is a colonial-style building with cool, colonnaded verandas, and high-ceilinged rooms with whirling fans. Peacock feathers, potted palms and a vase of flowers added an indefinable touch to the portrait of 'Mother' and her guru, the white-bearded Sri Aurobindo.

'Mother' was a Frenchwoman who joined the *ashram* in 1920, became its president and, when I visited the *ashram*, still made rare appearances mainly on her birthday, although she was 94. (She has since died.) Her slogan, under her portrait, read: 'No words; acts.'

The *ashram*'s secretary, Mr Navajata, a former successful Indian businessman, now working full time at the *ashram*, made me welcome. Having driven from Madras by taxi just for the day, I had to choose between seeing either the *ashram* or 'Auroville'—'City of Light'—the world's first universal city.

From small beginnings Auroville was to become a laboratory seeking living answers to the world's problems and creating ideal circumstances for people's greatest potential growth and contribution to humanity, according to Mr Navajata.

It was to be a garden city covering nearly 390 square kilometres and with a final population of 100,000. Workers from all over the world were giving their labour freely and architects and engineers had volunteered their services, including the chief architect, Frenchman Roger Anger, who had planned some revolutionary buildings.

The city was to be self-supporting with its own industries and agriculture. Already it had a printing press, kindergarten, school, community hall and health centre, orchards, grain fields and vegetable gardens. It had roads, wells and electricity. There was to be an international university dedicated to seeking peace, with no entrance qualifications or exams.

In this 'utopia' there would be no personal property or private income. Needs would be provided for from community income. The then Prime Minister, Indira Gandhi, had called Auroville 'an exciting project for bringing about harmony using different cultures, and for understanding the environmental needs for man's spiritual growth'.

On the sunbaked plain where Auroville was evolving there were no signposts but my taxi driver persevered and we finally came to the city centre, a marble mosaic lotus-shaped foundation stone. It was laid in February 1968, when young people of 120 nations came together for the ceremony, bringing soil from their native land to fill the core of the foundation, symbolizing human unity.

There were nine settlements, most in an early stage. I visited 'Aspiration', which housed 70 in thatched cottages, surrounded by well-kept gardens, but would eventually accommodate 2000.

There was a neat community hall and a kindergarten. The community's entertainment was provided by the colony's musicians and artists, supplemented with recorded music and visits to Hindi movies in Pondicherry.

Plans were going ahead for cultural pavilions to preserve each country's culture. The first was to be the Tibetan pavilion.

A model fishermen's village, film studio, artists' colony and world trade and information centres were planned. Auroville's founders hoped that, with its unusual way of life, it would become a world-famous tourist attraction and they were planning regular conferences, seminars and youth camps.

The surrounding Indian villages also benefited from the new city whose citizens, believing they were responsible for their neighbours' welfare, had arranged free medical care, built a school, put in electricity and provided clean drinking water and free milk for mothers and children. It seemed a brave venture in a troubled world.

In the cool of early evening I journeyed back to Madras. The sun was a huge yellow ball, its light diffused through the mist. Cattle and goats were being driven home, villagers squatted beside the road cooking in pots over small fires of sticks. Women gathered water at wells. The gray shiny rice paddies shimmered gold as they caught the setting sun.

We passed a country shrine with a god painted in garish colours and two huge plaster horses, and further on, a French church as big as a cathedral. Its spires jutted above a straw-matting village instead of the neat French farmhouses the church led you to expect.

The sun poised for an instant on the edge of the world, then quietly slipped over.

Perhaps the French slipped away in the same quiet fashion, leaving a faint Gallic flavour drifting among the spices, the curry and incense of Pondicherry.

SOUTH AFRICA

WHERE else in the world would you find old Cape Dutch farmhouses, tribal witch doctors dispensing strange concoctions in African medicine shops, oriental bazaars, curio shops, elephants crossing the road in game parks, carpets of exotic wildflowers and primitive tribal dancing.

It is hard to decide what to see in a short holiday in South Africa. Perhaps an adventurous trip to the Kruger Game Park to see wild animals at close range. Durban with its sweeping beaches and colourful Indian market. Cape Town with its stunning coastal scenery, vineyards and picturesque architecture. Then there is the superb scenery of the coastal Garden Route, or the soaring Drakensberg Mountains with their Bushman paintings—or the goldmines of Johannesburg.

But, with all its excitingly different attractions, South African lifestyle has many similar aspects to the Australian way of life. Barbecues—called *braiis*, surfing, lots of sport and outdoor living, a sunny climate, gum trees, excellent beer and wine.

There is a good network of transport by plane, train, bus or hire car. English is widely spoken. Accommodation and meals are very reasonable.

In just over two weeks I travelled by regular plane, light aircraft, train coach and car from one end of South Africa to the other—from Kruger National Park, a game reserve in the north to Cape Province in the south. I visited Cape Town, Port Elizabeth, Plettenberg Bay, part of the famous Garden Route, and an ostrich farm in Oudtshoorn in the Little Karoo Desert.

Like me, most overseas visitors arrive in Johannesburg, a bustling city nicknamed the 'City of Gold'. Gold was discovered in 1886 on the widow Oosthuizen's farm at nearby Langlaagte by her lodger, George Hamilton, an Australian prospector. The news spread, diggers arrived from Kimberley and a tent town sprang up. Rich prospectors called 'Rand Lords' built palatial homes, many still standing.

I took a trip to Heia Safari Ranch to watch the famed Mzumba African Dancers re-enact ancient legends to throbbing drums, while the women chanted. Zebra, springbok, impala, ostrich and blesbok roamed free in 110 hectares of parkland. Other attractions included a barbecue, swimming and horseriding. Overnight accommodation was provided in thatched *rondavels* (round native-style huts), but you could (as I did) take a day trip, booking ahead for meal and performance.

Gold mine visits are organized by the Chamber of Mines. The Simmer and Jack Gold Mine is a nineteenth century mine restored to the atmosphere of early gold-rush days, and there is tribal mine dancing on Sundays (except the third Sunday of the month) at one of the mines. Admission is free but you have to book ahead or take a tour.

Johannesburg has many museums and art galleries including

A pretty Borneo Dyak dancer dressed in hand-woven finery and silver ornaments welcomes visitors with a wide grin.

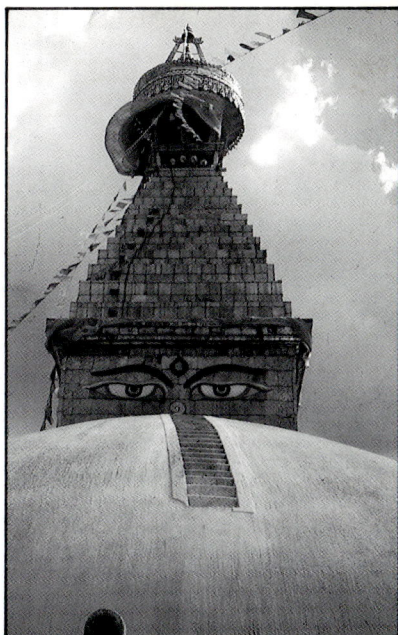

The mystic eyes of Buddha decorate the four sides of the temple at Bodnath guarding the Katmandu Valley below.

Chief Minggat shakes hands with me after his group's colourful dancing display. Later that evening I had to reciprocate by teaching the Dyaks Western dances.

On a country road, a young Tibetan boy carries a light coracle boat of cured yak hide on his back. These boats are easy to launch in the fast flowing streams and Tibetans are skilled in sailing them.

Huge fallen statues of horse heads once decked the soaring capitals of the fabled city of Persepolis. Sited on a high platform of rock, its ruins still evoke the splendour of this ancient Persian city.

the Africana Museum with thousands of treasures recording South African history, the Jewish Museum, Museum of Military History, South African Railway Museum, the Adler Museum, which includes an African medicine shop, and the Johannesburg Art Gallery.

The city's zoological gardens has over 5000 hectares of beautiful grounds with 'open cages' for larger animals.

You can also visit a diamond and a gem-cutting works.

Historical landmarks include the Old Fort (now a prison), St Mary's Church in Jeppe Street, the Rissik Street Post Office, the Rand Club, where mining magnates dined, and the Great Synagogue with its blue dome, a replica of the Byzantine mosque of St Sophia in Istanbul, built by Emperor Justinian in A.D. 537.

You can shop for beautiful Masana handwoven pure wool tribal rugs, gemstones such as malachite and tiger's eye, shells, semi-precious stones, ivory jewellery and carvings, snake skin handbags, African handicrafts. Basuto tribal paintings, tapestries, Swazi mats, wooden bowls and baskets from Botswana, African masks, diamonds and gold jewellery make interesting buys.

Durban, on the Indian Ocean, is South Africa's most famous seaside resort. The city was founded in 1823 as a tiny trading settlement, named in honour of the governor of the Cape, Sir Benjamin D'Urban. It has a mixed population of Europeans, Coloureds, Indians and Bantu people (black South Africans). Restaurants serve wonderful seafood and Indian food. Entertainment is centred on the broad, sweeping Golden Mile promenade, bordered by gardens, amusement centres and luxury skyscraper hotels. At night the promenade glows with strings of coloured lights.

There is lots to see. You can stroll along Marine Parade, visit the dolphinarium where daily shows by dolphins and Cape fur seals are held. You can ride a rickshaw pulled by a Zulu driver in elaborate costume and towering feather and bead headdress. Nearby you can buy colourful bead dolls, bead jewellery and other beaded objects ranging from bottle covers to table doilies from Zulu women.

The Indian market is a stone's throw from Durban's commercial centre. Bargaining for curious and exotic jewellery is great fun.

The Hindu temple, Saptah Mandir, is decked with exotic images of Hindu deities. The Juma Mohammedan Muslim Mosque in the Indian quarter has gold-domed minarets which tower over the built-in arcades below. It is open daily, but you must make an appointment with the Islamic Propagation Centre for a free, guided tour.

The da Gama Clock, in its graceful cast-iron monument, in the Victorian Embankment gardens, was given by the Portuguese Government in 1897 to commemorate Vasco da Gama's discovery of Port Natal in 1497.

The green palm-shaded Francis Farewell Square was named after Lieutenant Francis Farewell who founded the city as a permanent trading post in 1824. Public buildings include City Hall which houses the Public Library and the Durban Museum and Art Gallery, and is almost an exact replica of the Belfast City Hall in Ireland; the Cenotaph and statues and plaques immortalize famous people and events in South African history.

The Old Fort and Warriors' Gate once housed a British garrison entrenched against the attacking Boers in 1842. The magazine, which once held the garrison's arms and gunpowder, is now a small interdenominational chapel flanked by quaint cottages which house pensioners. The Warriors' Gate is a museum with battlefield trophies from around the world.

Further afield, the Natal Anti-Shark Measure Board at Umhlanga Rocks gives a fascinating glimpse into its work of making Natal beaches safe. There is a free conducted tour, lecture and shark film on Wednesday afternoons at 2.30 p.m. You catch a bus to Umhlanga, the seaside resort, then a mini-bus to the Board. If you go early, you can fit in a swim at the beach and lunch at the grand Cabana Beach Hotel, a luxurious Spanish-style hacienda. The hotel puts on evening concerts of tribal dancing.

Other tribal dancing displays are held on Sundays at the railway recreation grounds in Wellington Road, or at Kwa Mashu, an African township to the north of Durban, where competing teams of gyrating Durban Africans perform for the crowds.

Further afield, the Valley of a Thousand Hills is a Zulu reserve area. You can visit a traditional *kraal*, Phezulu Kraal, which is a living museum village offering a magnificent view of the valley. Bare-breasted women in sarongs and beads, and warriors with shield and spears, dance, leap and stamp. There are demonstrations of spear-making and pot-making and, inside the *kraal*, tapes are played to give visitors an idea of the proud Zulu culture.

From Durban it is a five- or six-hour drive via historic Pietermaritzburg to the magnificent Drakensberg Mountains (Mountains of the Dragon). The Giant's Castle Game Reserve below the sheer face of Drakensberg is a photographer's paradise and a naturalist's delight—eland, reedbuck, wildebeest, jackal, baboons, leopards, klipspringer and birds such as giant kingfishers, black eagles and black storks abound.

You can climb, walk, fish for brown trout, go horse riding. No visitor should miss the ancient cave paintings of the Bushmen; you can get recorded tapes on their culture and history from the camp office. Accommodation is in attractive camp huts set in beautiful gardens overlooking the Bushman's River valley. Or you can stay, as I did, at Champagne Castle Hotel, among towering mountain peaks.

Cape Town, on the Cape Province coast, is known for its craggy Table Mountain. It has spectacular sea and mountain scenery, great seafood, shops, restaurants, theatres, superb wine-growing areas, and quaint Cape Dutch houses. Sir Francis Drake rounded the Cape of Good Hope four centuries ago in the *Golden Hind* and called it 'the fairest cape we saw in the whole circumference of the earth'. Tourists driving along the spectacular peninsula road would have to agree.

For the best view of Cape Town, take a seven-minute ride on the Table Mountain aerial cableway to the summit, 1067 metres above sea level, for a stunning panorama of city, coast and mountains. It is open from 9 a.m. to 6 p.m. and in summer the cable car runs at night. Table Mountain is floodlit at weekends and nightly in summer.

The Castle, the oldest standing building in South Africa, was completed in 1679. It is in the shape of a five-pointed star, with each bastion bearing one of the titles of Prince William of Orange. The beautiful Van der Stel Gateway leads to the main courtyards. The castle houses the William Fehr collection of antique glassware, paintings and furniture, the state banqueting room, the military and maritime museums, and the dungeon.

Bokaap Museum in the Malay area recreates traditional Cape Islamic life and culture. Koopmans de Wet House belonged to a wealthy citizen in the eighteenth century. The Cultural History Museum was once a slave lodge.

Choose a fine day to take the spectacular scenic tour of the Cape peninsula. You can do a circular drive along the superb Atlantic coast marine drive, past Hout Bay and Chapman's Peak to the Cape of Good Hope and Capet Point, returning via False Bay resort. Resort towns include Sea Point, with its flower-decked rockeries and mini-railway, pretty Camps Bay with its wide stretch of white sand beach, the small cove of Llandudno, and Hout Bay with its fascinating fishing harbour.

You can take a launch trip beneath the cliffs of Chapman's Peak and Sentinel Rock and across the Duiker Island with its colony of seals and sea birds.

The Cape of Good Hope nature reserve is a 7680 hectare reserve on the southern tip of the peninsula. Here are springbok, bontebok, ostrich, zebra, baboon, eland, many species of birds and—in spring—carpets of wildflowers. A little bus, the 'Flying Dutchman', takes tourists to a rocky ledge above Cape Point where you look out over the Cape of Good Hope with its sharp rocks and pounding waves, one of the most perilous spots in the world for ships.

On the way back to Cape Town, it's worth a stop at Simonstown, an old-world village and one of the oldest seaports in South Africa, with army buildings built in 1814.

Stellenbosch, a 300-year-old town in a beautiful tree-filled valley, is another interesting trip. Named after a Dutch governor, it is the heart of a wine area and is also renowned for its lovely Cape Dutch and Cape Georgian houses. Cape Dutch houses are white and gabled, with thatched roof and wooden shutters. Cape Georgian have no gables, a square look, mullion windows and rounded doors.

Interesting buildings to explore are the Cape Dutch houses in Dorp Street—for instance, La Gratitude built in 1798, and the Burgher House built almost 200 years ago and displaying antique Cape furniture, silver, glass and copper. Don't miss the Rembrandt van Rijn Art Museum in a Cape Dutch House and the Brandy Museum which illustrates the history of brandy in the Cape with displays of wonderful old copper stills and pictures of old implements (brandy was first distilled here in 1672).

The town square is bordered by beautiful buildings, such as the arsenal where ammunition was once kept for emergency attacks by Hottentots. The bell would be rung to raise the farmers who ran for guns and ammunition.

The lovely Rhenish and Anglican churches are also worth visiting.

A wine-route map and printed guide are available from the public relations officer, Stellenbosch Wine Route Co-op Ltd, 208 Mill Square, Stelenbosch 7600 (P. O. Box 204). Stellenbosch Wine Route has eleven estate wine cellars and four co-operative wineries within twelve kilometres of the town. Most offer cellar tours, you can taste more than 100 wines, and enjoy beautiful scenery and old homesteads. You can buy wines, cheese, Old Cape preserves and relishes, enjoy a barbecue or try a wine house, often set in restored Cape Dutch houses. Other area wine routes include the Breede River Valley, Paarl Wineway and Tulbagh.

Wine houses date back to colonial times when locals gathered for a glass of wine, a bite to eat and a good gossip. Today they provide typical regional wines and Cape cooking such as *water blommetjie bredie* (stew prepared with water hyacinth flowers), venison pie with saffron rice and sweet potatoes, or a 'slave' dish of mutton casserole.

Try to plan for lunch at the Lanzerac, a beautiful three-star hotel, which dates back to 1692 and was granted to three freed slaves. Later an adventurous sergeant in the Dutch East India Company bought the farm. He also prospected for copper and hunted escaped slaves.

The present house, built in 1830, was bought by a Mrs English in 1922. She made extensive alterations and started producing wine under the name of Lanzerac. The hotel has a famous restaurant featuring a lavish smorgasbord lunch. You can try farmhouse soup, Cape Malay pickled fish, home-made fish cakes, cold fish buffet, *bobotie* (a Cape Malay dish), rare roast beef with pickled walnuts, roast leg of pork with apple sauce, roast Karoo lamb with mint sauce, and a grill. After that there's a dessert buffet and cheese board. Staff wear colonial costumes.

You can fly either from Cape Town or Durban to Port

Elizabeth, then follow the glorious Garden Route north by car or coach to Cape Town. If time is short, fly from Port Elizabeth to Plettenberg Bay, do part of the route on a day trip to the Tsitsikama National Park and Storm River and the next day continue on the Garden Route to the town of George, then turn inland to Oudtshoorn to visit an ostrich farm.

Port Elizabeth attractions include museums, a snake park and tropical house and an oceanarium. Worth seeing is the historic museum at Castle Hill, which is the oldest surviving private house in Port Elizabeth. It was built in 1827 by the first colonial chaplain. Donkin Street has a row of quaint Victorian terrace houses and Cora Terrace (off Bird Street) has Regency-style houses, once used as officers' residences in the mid nineteenth century.

The Port Elizabeth Publicity Association operates half-day and two-day trips to tourist attractions.

Be sure and take the 'Apple Express', a diminutive steam train which, since 1906, has chuffed along a sixty-one-centimetre-wide line. It is painted apple green with a red apple insignia. Every Saturday, from June to the end of January, South African Railways runs a one-day return 'Apple Express' excursion seventy kilometres up the line through beautiful country to Loerie in the apple-growing Langkloof Valley. You must book at the South African Railways main line ticket office in the Feather Market Hall, on the western side of City Hall. You can also book and buy a box lunch from the Port Elizabeth Publicity Association in Market Square.

Plettenberg Bay is a good base for touring the Garden Route, which includes mountains, coast, rivers, lakes and forested national parks.

I stayed at the splendid Beacon Island Hotel, perched spectacularly on a peninsula, where the staff wear sailor costumes. My favourite restaurant there was the Captain's Cabin, built under sea level. Floodlit breakers dash against casement windows, while candles gleam on scarlet linen, and staff in period costume serve delicious seafood.

Leaving the Garden Route at George, you go through the Outeniqua Pass into the Little Karoo Desert, to Oudtshoorn, where you find an ostrich farm, sample ostrich omelette and *biltong* (dried stips of meat) and see an ostrich race. The

Cango Caves and a crocodile farm are other attractions in the area.

From Oudtshoorn you can go by road, or fly to Cape Town. That's where the luxurious five-million-dollar Blue Train starts for Pretoria via Johannesburg. You can also travel in the opposite direction. You have to book well ahead, as the train is very popular.

From Johannesburg you can do a five-hour drive, or take a forty-five-minute flight to Nelspruit, gateway to Kruger National Park. From Nelspruit you drive fifty kilometres to the Numbi gate entrance. You can also fly by light aircraft from Johannesburg to Skukuza (in the southern part of the park) or Phalaborwa (in the centre). I stayed at Skukuza, the largest camp, in a small *rondavel* (round hut) with screened veranda.

The best time for viewing animals is in the early morning or late afternoon when they come to the waterholes. You may sight elephants, antelopes, cheetahs, zebra, giraffes and many other animals. The road from Skukuza to Lower Sabie, called 'Road of Lions', is also good for viewing. I saw giraffe, warthog, elephants, hippo, buffalo, baboons, zebra and a lion resting under a distant tree.

With such a wealth of sights and experiences, visitors are guaranteed not to forget South Africa in a hurry.

GREECE'S DODECANESE ISLANDS

THERE is an Oriental indolence and charm to the Dodecanese Islands, a chain of twelve Greek islands afloat in the shimmering blue of Mediterranean sun and sea, off the coast of Asia Minor.

Hundreds of years of Turkish occupation have left their mark in the minarets of mosques which still dot the islands, the habits of old men drinking sweet, thick Turkish coffee under the plane trees and swinging their *komboli* (worry beads), and the wild, sinous Greek-Oriental music which hangs heavy in the hot, still air.

Kos, green and fragrant with sweet-scented wild herbs, was the birth place of the father of medicine, Hippocrates, who taught and practised the healing art here.

Patmos, with its white cubist houses and peaceful harbour, its clear air and strong, cleansing winds, is the Island of Saints. St John the Evangelist saw visions, dreamed dreams and wrote the *Apocalypse* from a cave here. And St Christodoulos founded the massive monastery which crowns the island.

Kalimnos, rocky and barren, but alive with coloured houses tumbling down its slopes and jaunty fishing caiques crowding its harbour, is the home of the brave sponge divers who risk their lives diving off the coast of North Africa.

Rhodes is the island of the medieval Knights of St John of Jerusalem, the Crusader whose splendid palaces, castles and battlements still enchant the visitor.

Kos has a curved, tree-lined harbour front, busy with crowded open-air cafés and crowded with shipping—masts of yachts and fishing caiques, excursion ferries, boats and cruisers. It is overlooked by the old battlement walls of the Knights of St John's fortress.

Time passes as in a dream in Kos. In the main square, under the shadow of a minaret, the clock stands forever at 6 p.m.—teatime. The fierce heat has abated and the cafes pile their chairs into the square. Soon waiters are busy bringing thick sweet coffee, icecream, crème caramel, rice pudding and rich, sticky pastries. In the post-siesta daze, visions of green melons, white-washed houses with purple bougainvillea and white jasmine and sweet-smelling lemons tantalize the visitor.

In the evening the action moves to the seafront where the harbour craft are dressed with coloured lights, families promenade and diners watch the passing parade while consuming vast quantities of fresh fish, kebabs, stuffed tomatoes, moussaka, pastries, all washed down with the vitriolic *retsina* wine, the tamer white and red island wines and the flattish beer.

The lottery seller waves aloft his banner of lottery tickets and the peanut man, basket over arm, bends obsequiously and proffers pistachio, salted sunflower seeds, round nuts and peanuts. The air is mild, the pavements hosed down of their heat, bikes whizz around like fluttering sparrows. The cicadas' noise quietens to a soft drumming. Cats miaou and prowl under tables waiting for fish, manna from above.

Further out in the countryside an open-air taverna resounds with the mesmerizing beat of bouzouki music as locals and foreigners join in Greek dances.

From the seafront you can catch a bus which takes you on a tour of the island. Masticara village is memorable for women hand-spinning wool and old men of the sea mending yellow fishing nets. Flocks of goats are driven through narrow streets, tiny white-washed chapels sport domed roofs.

Kefalos is a long, curved pebble beach with crystal clear water for bathing. You can enjoy a meal of fresh fish, wine and melon for a few dollars and eat to the insistent wail of recorded bouzouki music. Kardamania is the loveliest village on the island. Its caiques are laden with fruit and vegetables for other islands. Its sparkling champagne sea tingles on the bather's skin.

On the seafront many tourist agencies provide excursions to other islands, local tours, and visits to the Turkish coast at Bodrum, the site of the ancient city of Halicarnassus, which boasted one of the Seven Wonders of the Ancient World, the lavish tomb of Mausolus, from whose name 'mausoleum' derives.

One of the most enjoyable island pastimes is bicycle riding. Kos is the Greek bicycle island and thousands of tourists soar and sweep like moths across the luminous landscape en route to explorations of ancient ruins. Or they prop their little bikes at secluded pebbly beaches where they lie and listen to the cicadas' shrilling or the crepitations of wind among the sun-burnt thistle-strewn grass.

Early one morning before the sun rose, I cycled through the cypress-pine avenues, past the shining olive groves, the ripening figs and sharp-smelling pine trees to the Aescul-apium, the old Greek centre of medicine where Hippocrates cured patients and taught using scientific medicine based on observation, experiment and experience.

Before the time of the great physician, Hippocrates, who was born in Kos in 460 B.C., priests worshipped the god, Aesculapius, and cured patients with sacrifices, baths, the sleep cure, divination by dreams and by fasting.

The fourth century B.C. Aesculapium is now in ruins—sunbaked stones, broken columns, pieces of statues across which lizards scurry. The air is full of sound—donkeys braying, frogs croaking, cicadas and crickets drumming. The view from the plateau on which the Healing Centre is situated is stunning, across the yellow and green plain to the purple-blue sea and the grey stony islands.

Kos abounds in ancient ruins—Greek theatres and stadium, Roman houses, the medieval castle of the Crusaders. Near the Lotzia Mosque Spring is the 2400-year-old plane tree under which, legend says, Hippocrates taught medicine, and St Paul the Apostle preached.

From Kos to Patmos by boat usually takes about four hours. The day I braved the perils of the sea, it was very rough and I arrived in the saintly isle pea-green with seasickness, after a five and a half hour purgatorial journey.

The island's only two taxis were otherwise engaged, but I was given a lift by a jolly American woman in a panel van who drove me up to the fortress-like Monastery of St John the Divine, which was built in A.D. 1088 by St Christodoulos.

As we wound up into the clear blue air, the high winds sweeping through the white-washed village of Chora, it was like being on top of the world—exhilarating and a little frightening.

Looking across the beautiful island with its indented bays, the American said: 'Living on this island is the nearest thing to the "Greek Experience".'

We whizzed past priests in long black robes and stovepipe black hats and only just got into the fortress-monastery before closing time, midday. The treasury is full of wonderful old chalices, vestments and paintings. The library has old documents including a fourth century gospel of St John, thousands of historical documents and manuscripts dating from the sixth to the nineteenth centuries. It also has exquisite miniatures of the ninth to fifteenth centuries.

The origins of the island date back at least to the fourth century B.C. The goddess, Artemis, and the god, Apollo, were worshipped here. In A.D. 95, St John the Divine, apostle and evangelist, was exiled to Patmos from Ephesus—where he had preached Christianity—on the orders of the Roman Emperor, Domitian.

In the monastery library are details of the apostle's life and acts including a duel in miracle-making between St John and the local priest of Apollo, Kynops. Popular legend has it that St John defeated Kynops and turned him into a stone where he still lies in the depths of Skala harbour.

Two middle-aged Swiss ladies (used to mountaineering) accompanied me straight down a donkey track on the mountain side. I slithered and slid like a mountain goat, while an astonished old man riding a panniered donkey gazed in disbelief.

Our destination was the cave of St John, half-way between the monastery and the port. The white-washed entrance house boasted a bird singing in a cage, pink oleanders in pots, bearded priests and a black-clad housekeeper.

Candles lit the chapel of the cave. Our guide pointed to the rock ledge where St John rested his arm while he read and wrote. She said the rock had been split in two when St John saw his vision and heard the words: 'I am the Alpha and Omega' (the Beginning and the End).

Later, I took a local bus which wound down through the tranquil fields and trees which stretched to the rollicking purple sea with its splinters of brown islands. I only just caught the boat.

Kalimnos is quite a different experience. A two-hour journey from Kos, it is a mass of multi-coloured houses tumbling down slopes to the harbour where fishing smacks huddle. You can almost hear the mermaids singing.

The tangle of ropes, sponges, dried seahorses and shells on the seafront, the blue sea glittering and the huddle of butterfly-coloured sailing boats seem the perfect setting for mermaids.

But the strangest story told by the islanders is not of mermaids but of a giant fish which swallowed a sponge diver.

Sponges are the island's livelihood and each spring the sponge-fishing boats set off for the north coast of Africa to harvest the sponge beds off the coasts of Egypt and Libya.

The diving season begins in May, ends in November and is preceded by a big festival. The people sing, dance and make merry or, as an island barber put it: 'The men eat, drink and enjoy themselves because they may die tomorrow'. They brave sharks, cramp, blocked air pipes. The products of their labour, sponges of all shapes and sizes, adorn the shops on the waterfront.

On the day of sailing the priest blesses the boats and the men who sail in them and the islanders who are left behind wave their handkerchiefs and cry, for who knows how many will return. And the sailing men cling to the masts and lean over the sides waving back. It will be six months before they see the island again.

As he sat clipping sponges on the seafront in between customers, the island barber told me of the fish which swallowed the diver.

Four years ago, he said, a naked diver in the ocean depths came on a huge fish. It opened its mouth and swallowed him whole. The fish got more than it bargained for and vomited the struggling man back. Shades of the biblical Jonah and the Whale.

'I swear it is true,' said the barber.

'The man came out covered with scratches from the fish's teeth.'

The barber also told of the two Australian writers who once lived a couple of doors from the barber shop. George Johnston and Charmian Clift lived in a blue and white house with a green door and a shoemaker's sign above it and had one of the best views of the harbourfront from their balcony. While living on the island, Charmian wrote a novel about the drama of the sponge divers' lives.

In a small factory, tucked away in a side street, I watched barefoot, brown-skinned boys treading the sponges to expel the air, then packing them in hessian bags for export.

When the divers gather the sponges, these are black, covered with a brown 'milk'. The divers throw them into a woollen blanket on board and barefoot workers tread the sponges to squeeze out the 'milk' until the sponge is dead. Later, sponges are washed in a special liquid to bleach them and bring out the yellow tinge.

In winter, when the diving season ends, men play cards, relax, dance, sing, get drunk, gossip. Who knows what the next season will bring?

Sponges are the best tourist buy. The highest quality are called *fina* (fine), the lesser grades are *kapadika* and *tsimouhes*.

But Kalimnos is far more than sponge diving. Tourists pouring off the steamer from Piraeus (the port for Athens) or from the island of Kos (two hours away by boat and with an airport linking it with Athens) usually make for the seafront cafés to sit and dream over the scene—multi-coloured fishing smacks in harbour, cats foraging under tables, warm liquid sunshine, black-robed, bearded priests with stovepipe hats, their hair in a neat bun at their necks.

The men at side cafés twirl their worry beads and drink thimbles of black coffee followed by iced water. The salty lemon sea smell pervades the narrow twisting streets.

The town is spread like an amphitheatre of coloured toy houses in orange, green, ochre, pale yellow and white round the harbour stage with its backdrop of sailing caiques and old fishermen mending orange nets. Silver-domed churches dot the panorama and a couple of brown windmills crown the hill.

The best beaches, Botsaliakia, Kantouni, Mirtes and Misouri, are reached by taxi, shared with up to eleven people and quite cheap. A closer beach, Vathi, is reached by buses which leave from the waterfront.

My taxi to Misouri held a Greek-Canadian girl, three children, and six locals. We rattled across the hot, sunbaked island through dry stony country alive with pink oleander, punctuated by stone fences and dotted with silver-domed Greek churches with minarets (a relic of the Turkish occupation).

At Misouri black-clad women with white head scarves bathed in their dresses. Under a group of green trees young tourist campers chatted among their haversacks.

After a quick iced-lemonade dip in the purple-blue sea, I climbed to the restaurant and lunched on fresh lobster and fish, washed down with cold white Lindos wine from Rhodes. The label bore the legend: 'When the Gods of Olympus were distributing the treasures of the world, they gave Rhodes as a bridge to the Sun God. From this everlasting bond between the Sun and Rhodes, we see the fruits of this union in this wine that delights everyone's heart'. Tomato and cucumber salad, crisp bread and bright pink watermelon rounded off the meal.

You could get a hotel room at Misouri dirt cheap or stay in a private home for even less.

Kalimnos has a past which goes back into the mists of myth. Homer mentioned that Kalimnos, then called Kalydnae, took part in the Trojan War, providing 30 ships.

Today, with its colourful feasts, its dances and folk lore, its enchanting seascapes, Kalimnos lures the tourist without any help from mermaids.

Rhodes, another Dodecanese island, is a different scene.
Entering the harbour, you automatically look for the Colossus,
one of the Seven Wonders of the Ancient World, which
'bestrode' the harbour before the giant statue was destroyed
in an earthquake.

It stood thirty-four metres high, a bronze statue of Helios,
the Sun God and patron of the city of Rhodes, which did
not actually bestride the harbour as usually depicted but stood
on the shore, its torch held aloft, a shining beacon to ships.

It was built in 227 B.C. by Chares of Lindos, in thanksgiving
for deliverance of the city from an unsuccessful siege by a
Macedonian prince, Demetrios Polyorketes. Mythology says
that Zeus gave the island to his son, Apollo, the Sun God,
who named it 'Rhodes', the island of roses, after his sister,
Aphrodite, whose symbol was a rose. Some people say the
rhododendrons which flourish on the island are its 'roses'.

The island was colonized from Crete about 1500 B.C. and
became a Minoan trading post. It took part in the Trojan War.
In 338 B.C. it was conquered by Alexander the Great. History
records that it came under Roman rule and was visited by St
Paul who came ashore to shelter from a storm at Lindos.
Later, it came under Byzantine, Persian, Venetian and Genoese
rule. Then, in 1309, the Knights of St John of Jerusalem
made Rhodes the crossroads of the Crusades as crusaders
stopped there on their way to the Holy Land. It was captured
by the Turks in 1521 and the conqueror, Sultan Suleiman
the Magnificent, expelled the Greeks from the city to make
way for Turkish immigrants.

It was occupied by Italy during the Italian-Turkish War,
then by the Germans during the Second World War. Finally,
it was united with Greece in 1948.

The old walled Turkish city has a bustling oriental air with
its little shops, markets and square with open-air restaurants,
arcades and the latticed balconies of Turkish houses. A double-
balconied minaret dominates the scene.

Most tourists love this old Turkish area where they can
bargain and shop to their heart's content and watch cop-
persmiths, cobblers and embroiderers at work.

Along busy Socrates Street, you come to the entrance to
the Street of the Knights with its beautiful 'inns' or houses
of the nationalities which comprised the order. The knights'

city with its cobblestone pavements, building façades decorated
with gargoyles and oriel windows is a beautiful example of
a medieval knights' community.

The Street of the Knights leads to the solid grandeur of
the Palace of the Grand Master, reconstructed by the Italians.

In summer a Sound and Light performance each evening
recreates the last siege by the Turks which ended the rule
of the knights.

Mandraki Harbour is a favourite place for a stroll. Its
entrance is guarded by graceful columns topped by statues
of golden deer. The harbour has a fortress on one side, the
beautiful Church of St John on the other. Graceful white-
sailed windmills are floodlit at night. The name Mandraki
comes from *mandria* meaning a 'flock of sheep' because for
centuries small sailing boats from Asia Minor brought sheep
to market here.

In summer there are excursions to the Valley of the Butterflies. Thousands of colourful butterflies arrive each year
at the end of May, leaving with the September rains. At rest,
their veined yellow wings are camouflaged as they hang from
under leaves. But, when the trees are shaken, they rise in
a bright vermilion cloud, revealing the brilliant red underside.

The ruins of the second-century city of Kamiros make
another interesting excursion. You can wander among the
remains of market place, temple, houses and acropolis of the
abandoned city, which was once a Minoan trading post.

On Mount Filerimos there are ruins of a temple of Athena,
and a beautiful Byzantine church whose tenth century chapel
has frescoes carved by the knights.

Lindos, founded in the twelfth century B.C., has the most
beautiful natural harbour, dominated by the dazzling white
of the acropolis, with its Temple of Athena Lindia. Through
its Doric columns you can see the dazzling sea far below
and the cove where St Paul landed in A.D. 51.

On the mighty cliff slopes white-washed houses rise in
terraces to the foot of the acropolis, which is entered through
the medieval fortifications of the Knights of St John, who
built a castle here.

You can ride up to the acropolis by donkey, a wise move
in the heat of summer. Coming down by stairs is easier and
gives glimpses of doorways decorated with ceramic plates and

courtyards with black and white pebble mosaics. In cobblestone alleys Greek handicrafts and souvenirs proliferate in dim, cosy shops. Ornamental windows and doorways proclaim houses once belonging to the knights. Byzantine chapels gleam with silver-haloed dark-eyed saints and are perfumed with incense.

The harbour is picturesque, alive with yachts. It is bliss in the heat of summer to drink cold wine, then lie buoyant in the lemon salt sea gazing up at the castle fortifications and sun-burnished dazzling white acropolis.

Rhodes by night has plenty of entertainment including Sound and Light performances in the Garden of the Grand Master, open-air folk dancing in the old town, classical theatre, Greek dancing in tavernas in the Old Town and the Wine Festival in the Rhodini Gardens where you could drink as much wine as you liked for a few dollars.

Between the airport and the city lies the Coney Island-like modern area crammed with high-rise hotels, beaches dotted with umbrellas and thatched beach shelters. Most tourists stay in this area, which is just like any other ritzy beach resort.

The Dodecanese Islands reward the traveller with the 'Greek Experience'. What is this experience? To borrow a phrase: 'To those who have experienced it, no explanation is necessary, to those who have not, no explanation is possible.'

TIBET

HOLY men chant Buddhist texts, small boys sing for alms, monks in maroon robes finger *mala* (prayer beads), picturesquely costumed women knit beside stalls crammed with jewellery, brass Buddhas and silver-embossed boxes.

The scene is the Barkor, the market place of the holy city of Lhasa, capital of Tibet.

Over all looms the massive palace-fortress of the Dalai Lamas, the Potala.

Exploring Lhasa is like stepping back into medieval times. Until recently, it was the Hidden Kingdom, a remote and mysterious land ruled by god-kings, the Dalai Lamas. Foreigners, particularly westerners, were not welcome. Only now is Tibet slowly joining the twentieth century.

The country of esoteric religious practices, myth and magic, has been called the Forbidden Land and the Land of Snows. It is the model of Shangri-La in James Hilton's romantic novel, *Lost Horizons*.

Nowadays tourists are being admitted—approximately 1000 in 1984 and a total of only 4000 in the four years after Tibet opened its doors to formal group tours in 1980. A few independent travellers get there, but a packaged tour is more convenient, since there are no coaches for transport to tourist sites and little accommodation.

A 1000-bed hotel, the Lhasa Hotel, had just been built when I visited a year ago (1985) and the small hostel where we stayed took about thirty people. There were also a few cheap little inns in the old quarter.

Apart from a small town near the border with Nepal, only three cities or towns are open to tourists—Lhasa, Shigatse, where the Panchen Lama, a 'living Buddha' and the second most important religious leader (the Dalai Lama is first) lives, a day's journey away, and Shan Nan, a half-day journey from Lhasa.

The Tibetans are of Mongolian stock and practise a Tibetan form of Buddhism, known as Lamaism (after the lamas, or teachers). It borders Kashmir, Nepal, Sikkim, Bhutan and Burma. The Chinese marched into Tibet in 1950, and in 1965 declared Tibet an autonomous region of the People's Republic of China. The landscape encompasses fertile valleys, rugged, forbidding mountains, glaciers, marshes. Its widest river, the Yarlung Tsampo, becomes the mighty Brahmaputra as it flows into India.

American travel writer, Richard Halliburton, one of the heroes of my youth, took the hazardous journey to Tibet in the 1930s, returning with tales of the fabulous Potala and the child god-king. I found it hard to believe I was actually visiting this remote land of snows, guarded by the world's highest mountains, the Himalayas.

Our two-hour flight from Chengdu in Southern China took us over the roof of the world. Beneath us, majestic snowclad moutains stretched to infinity. At other times they became slate-grey with deep shadowed valleys like a moon landscape. In one cleft, perhaps a dry river bed, two small villages appeared.

Early travellers, traders, Buddhist missionaries, explorers and armies had traversed this inhospitable landscape by pack train, travelling on donkeys, horses or camels. They risked their lives in treacherous weather conditions, landslides and rough tracks. We tourists, a small party on a Jetset tour, breakfasted in comfort high in the sky on sweet buns, cake, orange cream wafers, sweets and jasmine tea—a normal-style Chinese breakfast. Most passengers were Chinese.

We landed in a wide valley and began our two and a half hour journey by bus to Lhasa, our road running beside the mighty Yarlung Tsampo River.

The air was crystal clear, the sun warm, the limpid river reflected the clouds and the landscape seemed to sparkle in the clear light, Shangri-La indeed.

Our guide warned us to take things very slowly to avoid altitude sickness, common at this height of 4300 metres. Everywhere we went, a green canvas bag of oxygen went with us. We came to be glad of a few whiffs to revive us when the thin air made us breathless.

The passing parade fascinated. Tibetan women, clad in *tchuba* (woollen tunic), woven striped apron and jacket, carried babies or had water carriers slung on backs. Some wore floral headscarves, others had long braids wound around their heads, entwined with ribbon.

The road was narrow and winding. A bad accident, in which a Tibetan tractor driver was killed colliding with a car, had held up all traffic for an hour.

Donkeys trotted by laden with sacks and straw matting. Vast horizons of water, sky and mountains unfolded. The mud-walled, white-washed villages spouted multi-coloured prayer flags from their flat roofs. Some were gaily decorated with reds, blues and greens, with vermilion or pink under the eaves. Some doorways bore mysterious signs—a sun, a wavy line to represent clouds, a moon.

A small, round coracle boat, made of cured yak hide, was being launched into the river. These light boats are carried on men's heads and backs like a giant mushroom hat. We passed fields of yellow mustard and purple lavender. Conical wheat stacks (wheat was first brought in by the Chinese) dotted fields. Into this age-old landscape, the Chinese had introduced electricity poles in certain areas.

As we neared Lhasa, we passed a 700-year-old red and yellow painted Buddha, seated in the lotus position, on a wall of rock, a mirror image in the small lake beneath. Flowers were set in front. On a nearby hill prayer flags fluttered, carrying prayers on the wind to Buddha. Throughout Tibet, similar images are carved or painted on hilltops or rocky walls. The country is still deeply religious.

We entered the Lhasa Valley and gasped at our first sight of the fabulous Potala. The white and vermilion palace-fortress of Tibet's god-kings stood thirteen storeys high, crowning a peak called Red Hill. Its golden roof shimmered in the sun. Soaring distant mountains lent a dramatic backdrop. The Potala dominated the country as far as the eye could see. Lhasa lay at its foot.

The countryside was wooded with birches, willows and walnut trees. We stayed at the Lhasa Hostel, a few kilometres from town. It consisted of stone cottages set in a garden. We slept three or four to a room. It was simple but quite comfortable apart from the grubby bathroom with its primitive temperamental geyser which rarely produced hot water.

After lunch we rested to acclimatize. I developed one of the symptoms of altitude sickness—severe headache. Others had vomiting or nausea. But, after a good night's rest, we were ready to explore next day.

The Jokhang Temple (Temple of the Precious One) in the heart of the city was our first stop. It is the most spiritual centre of Buddhism in Tibet. Built by a Tibetan king, Songtsen Gampo, in the seventh century, it enshrines the statue of the sacred Sakyamuni Buddha, said to have been brought to Tibet by the King's Chinese wife, the Princess Wen Cheng. She and his other foreign wife, a Nepalese princess, brought Buddhism to Tibet. In front of the temple stands a somewhat wilting willow tree planted by Princess Wen Cheng in A.D. 652.

Tibetan ladies in national costumes sat in the square outside the temple, twirling prayer wheels or fingering prayer beads and gossiping.

In front of the curtained entrance to the three-storey building, pilgrims prostrated themselves continuously in adoration, others twirled prayer wheels, murmuring mantras such as 'Om Mani Padme Hum' (Hail to the Jewel in the Lotus).

Inside, the air was thick with the smoke of burning yak-butter lamps, the walls slippery with grease, the atmosphere musty and the steep stairs narrow. The walls were richly ornamented and huge gilded Buddhas, including the benevolent Sakyamuni, sat encrusted with turquoise, coral and pearls, decked in rich silks and brocades. We followed crowds of pilgrims through scores of tiny chapels crowded with rich images on ornate gold thrones. Devoutly they refilled the lamps with yak butter melted over candles or left white or yellow prayer scarves.

The golden roof of the Jokhang was decorated with fabulous gilded dragons, bronze effigies of gods, bells, symbols of Buddhism, waterspouts in the shape of exquisite animal heads. From here you got a magnificent view of the Potala.

Outside the temple, the bustling market, the Barkor, was crowded with Tibetans in national robes, Chinese in blue Mao suits with green caps with red stars. Nomads from the country wore sheepskin jackets nonchalantly draped over one shoulder, leaving the other bare. Tibetan men kept their belongings in bulky cummerbunds wound around waists. The women wore magnificent jewellery of coral, turquoise, and other semi-precious stones.

One man carried on his back a long bamboo tube decorated with copper strips. This is used to churn yak-butter tea. The hard blocks of pressed tea imported from China are mixed with yak butter, soda and salt. The Tibetan's staple food is *tsampa*—roasted barley mixed with yak-butter tea to form a paste.

Stalls sold colourful yak-wool carpets, clothing, incense, cloth, knives, prayer wheels—a bewildering variety. Tibetan ladies clustered around the tourists producing little treasures such as jewellery or brass Buddhas from pockets. One even offered her own big hooped turquoise earrings.

Our next stop was the Norbulingka (Jewel Park), the Summer Palace and pleasure gardens of the Dalai Lamas. The original was built by the eighth Dalai Lama in 1783 but rebuilt in 1959 after damage due to shelling by the Chinese, which led the present (fourteenth) Dalai Lama who was in residence, to flee to India.

We entered through massive red doors with ornate brass decorations and tassels (Tibetan doors are fascinating), leaving

our shoes outside before treading on hallowed floors. Inside
there were paintings of Tibetan life and of Buddhist saints,
richly decorated walls and ceilings. The Dalai Lama's bedroom
had a finely curved gilded bed, vermilion and gold furniture,
brocade hangings and *thankas* (religious scroll hangings). The
god-king had sat on a lacquered throne in the reception room
to receive guests.

The Norbulingka sits in extensive beautiful gardens, now
popular with picnickers.

The next item on our fixed itinerary was a visit to a Tibetan
family—a farmer, his wife and five children (the sixth was
married). We were offered yak-butter tea (which tasted like
fermented milk), fried barley and nuts, and a potent local
brew called *chang*, made from barley.

The neat little white-washed cottage had a multi-coloured
painted ceiling, green and gold decoratively patterned cupboard, ornately carved altar. *Thankas* of Buddha hung on walls
surrounded by prayer scarves.

That evening we were entertained by a group of amateur
Tibetan singers, dancers and musicians in traditional costume,
with elaborate face makeup. As five musicians played variously
drum, cymbals, tambourine, lute, a horn instrument, a Tibetan
banjo, harmonica and xylophone, dancers leaped, twirled and
stamped, to great applause.

Next morning was devoted to the fabulous Potala, the winter
palace of the Dalai Lamas and former seat of government.

Our bus drove through the massive ornamental vermilion
gate half-way up the peak on which the Potala stood. We
then walked the 125 steps cut in the hill and entered through
the Door of Happiness. 'Potala' means 'high heavenly realm',
an apt name for this thirteen storey-high wood and stone
building which towers over the small medieval city below.

It was built on top of an ancient fortress on the rocky
peak, and contains two palaces, the spiritual centre known
as the White Palace (on top are the apartments of the Dalai
Lama) and the Red Palace, the former centre of secular
authority.

It was built in the seventh century by King Songtsen for
his two foreign wives (Chinese and Nepalese) who converted
him from the animist Bon religion to Buddhism.

The fifth Dalai Lama declared this king to be the first

reincarnation of the Buddha of Compassion and statues show a small figure representing this Buddha, wearing the king's turban as a symbol of incarnation.

This Dalai Lama (known as the Great Fifth because of his wisdom and political acumen) rebuilt and extended the Potala in 1645 after centuries of damage by war, fire and lightning. From that time on it became the religious and secular centre of rule (Tibet was a theocracy) until 1959 when the present Dalai Lama fled Tibet.

Inside, monks in maroon robes tended yak-butter lamps while pilgrims—some country folk in sheepskins—chanted *sutras* (holy scriptures) or prostrated themselves.

The gorgeous vermilion rooms had highly decorated ceilings and walls and were crammed with bejewelled, gilded Buddhas, many robed in silk or brocade. Tibetan faces glowed like burnished mahogany in candle light. As very small babies Tibetans are rubbed with yak butter and exposed to the sun to weather their skin.

There are over 10,000 chapels crammed with over 200,000 various deities. In a morning we could see only a few of the Potala's 1000 rooms. Steep ladders linking floors and dim light meant careful footwork was needed. Flickering lamps cast strange shadows in the gloom, recalling magical rites and secret ceremonials.

A constant chant of 'Dalai Lama, Dalai Lama' went up, sometimes whispered in our ears. Later we found out that the pilgrims were asking if we had any photographs of the exiled Dalai Lama.

Seven god-kings are buried in the massive *chortas* (tombs) within the Potala. That of the thirteenth who died in 1933 stands twenty-one metres high and consists of gold over a silver base. *Chortas* are gold and silver plated and studded with lapis lazuli, amethyst, rubies, jade, pink and red coral, huge diamonds. White or yellow prayer scarves left by pilgrims deck all images.

The Dalai Lama's private apartments included bedroom, prayer halls, reception rooms rich with gilded Buddhas, vermilion and gold furniture, splendid brocades, murals of paradise.

The roof was lavishly decorated with gilded umbrellas, wheels, lotus, conch shells, and strange mythical animals with protruding tongues jutting from roof corners. In golden days lamas stood here and blew their three and a half metre brass horns calling the faithful to prayer.

The Dalai Lama is chosen by monks who search carefully for a child with certain signs, such as a large head and generous ears, indicating wisdom. The child must recognize belongings of the previous Dalai Lama such as his prayer beads, silver pen, drum, eating bowl, and spectacles, despite being presented with skilful imitations. Sometimes, a dying Dalai Lama gives some clues—the district, for instance—where his successor will be found. An oracle may have a vision which helps the search. When the chosen child is old enough (two to six) he is taken to the palace and trained by the Regent.

The present Dalai Lama, like many predecessors, came from a humble peasant family. He was born in the village of Takster. Parents are given noble status when they move to Lhasa. This Dalai Lama as a tiny child is said to have claimed the former Dalai Lama's belongings as his own and addressed the monks, who found him, in the Lhasa dialect which he had no way of knowing.

Our final visit in Lhasa was to the Drepung monastery, built in 1416 and one of the great Tibetan monastery buildings. It used to house 8000 monks but now only 400 live there. Many monks have now been scattered and earn their living in secular occupations. Built into the side of a mountain, the monastery got its name which means 'heap of rice' from the honeycomb appearance of its many cells, numerous courtyards, fourteen dormitory buildings, schools, colleges and chapels.

Outside the monastery pilgrims had left *mani* stones, piles of stones, sometimes white-washed, inscribed with mantras (short prayers) and left in holy places all over Tibet.

The most spectacular room was the Prayer Hall with its magnificent multi-coloured brocade hangings, golden Buddha statues, ornately decorated walls, pillars and ceilings. Neat rows of maroon monks' robes lay in piles on the floor ready for the next service. Most of the monks seemed elderly but a few young boys are now being trained.

The climb up the rough cobblestone paths is steep and the thin air left me breathless. We passed typical Tibetan white-washed buildings with pleated cloth curtains at doors and windows.

The roofs of the monastery are embellished with gilded symbols of Buddhism—deer, wheels, huge gold-covered cylinders. The kitchen gleamed with burnished copper bowls and copper-bound wooden yak-butter tea churns.

We spent several days in the Tibetan countryside—but that's another story. Tibet was slowly modernizing but traditional life still went on. A final scene—my last memory of Tibet— drove this home. Our airport bus travelled to the tarmac over a road where barley lay, being winnowed by women who stepped aside to let us pass. A few hours later our jet plane, like a magic carpet, transported us back to the twentieth century.

UTRECHT, HOLLAND

LIKE Amsterdam, Utrecht is a city of canals. One of the most historic cities in Holland, it was founded by the Romans in A.D. 48. They named it *Trajectum Ad Rhenum* (place to cross the River Rhine) and put up a fortress to control the area.

In medieval times, Utrecht was a walled city, but only a few remnants of the walls remain.

During the Middle Ages the first canal, the Oude Gracht (Old Canal) was built to give access to the Rhine River. When that part of the old Rhine silted up, Utrecht lost its powerful position as a trade centre.

By then powerful bishops and counts possessed most of the Netherlands including Utrecht. In 1579 the Union of Utrecht was signed in the former chapterhouse of the cathedral.

The Netherlands provinces had tired of the eighty-year fight against the Spanish in the Eighty Year War (the Dutch War of Independence), and decided to unite and force the issue. The Peace of Utrecht in 1648 saw the end of Spanish domination. The Union of Utrecht later became the basis for the Netherlands State.

Utrecht was also the cradle of Christianity in the Netherlands, so it's not surprising to find many fascinating medieval churches, full of art treasures, and ruins of others.

All this I learned from my guide, as we sat eating bacon

and apple pancakes in the old 'Mint Cellar' (*Muntkelder*)
beside the Old Canal. The cellar was once the cloister of the
St Cecilia Convent. It was confiscated during the Reformation,
and subsequently used as a provincial mint, hence the name
'Mint Cellar'.

The canal is lined with former warehouses, now boutiques
or ethnic restaurants—French, Dutch, Italian, Spanish, Greek
and Mexican. You can sit out at a table overlooking the canal,
sip a drink and watch the passing boats. In the evening a
small orchestra sometimes plays on a floating platform in
the canal. You can also hire a canoe, row boat or motor boat
and head for a picnic in the Kromme Rhine (woods). Regular
tourist boats ply the canal.

Originally it was lined with houses but, after a weir was
built outside the city, the water level sank. People could not
get their goods off-loaded because the canal was below house
level. They solved the problem by building cellars beneath
their houses and ships unloaded into them direct from the
quays.

There are some interesting old bridges and markets in the
medieval quarter. A broom market once stood near the Bezem-
brug (Broom Bridge). The medieval-style lanterns were made
by a nineteenth-century sculptor. Quaint sculptures on the
bases include a broom seller and a witch on a broomstick,
the latter recalling old legends.

The Zoutmarkt (Salt Market) where salt for fish was sold,
is close by the Vismarkt (Fish Market) beside St Maarten
Bridge. Fish were laid out on a big stone slab and salted.
A statue of a fishwife, with several unlikely chickens tucked
under her arm, commemorates the market. In nearby Lichte
Gaard Street, interesting old gabled houses include one with
a clock in the façade. Ancient maps, antiques and old books
are sold in the area.

The nearby Buurkerkhof is Utrecht's oldest parish church.
There was a small church here as early as the tenth century.
The tower is from the second Gothic church. A three-aisle
hall church was built in the fifteenth century and enlarged
the following century. This is the church you see today.

In 1515, a nun, Sister Bertha, had herself immured in a
cell which was walled up against the church choir. She lived
there from the age of thirty until her death at fifty-seven.

She did this to expiate her shame at having been born the
illegitimate daughter of Jacob van Lictenberg, priest and dea-
con of the cathedral.

Sister Bertha was famous for her spiritual writings and
poetry and, when she died, the cathedral bells tolled twice,
not the usual once. There is a carving on the base of a lamp
post in the Salt Market which shows a little man bringing
her food.

Christenings, weddings and funerals took place in the Buurkerkhof and the various guilds held their meetings there and
had their own altars and crypts.

Bishop Bernold in the eleventh century had five churches
built in various city locations to form a cross known as 'the
cross of churches'. The first, the Romanesque St Peter's Church,
contains the tomb of Bernold, and has beautiful sandstone carved
reliefs of angels and the bishop. It was done in 1170.

The churches of St Maarten and St Salvator have disappeared and only the beautiful Romanesque cloister of St Marie's is left, and a few remnants of the monastic St Paul's.
St John's (or St Jan's) is a colonnaded basilica. Its present
front dates from 1682. It was rebuilt after a hurricane destroyed
much of the church. The thirteenth-century wooden roof has
now been beautifully restored.

The centre of the cross was the medieval cathedral which
once stood in the Dom square, but was almost totally destroyed
by a tornado in 1674. The lovely old cloisters remain. On
one wall there is a plaque to the memory of Willibrord, an
Anglo-Saxon monk who sailed from England to convert the
Low Countries to Christianity. The plaque features a sailing
ship, a church and the monk's name.

The cloisters also feature sculputures of scenes from the
life of St Martin, Bishop of Tours (France) in the fourth
century. The most famous scene shows him as a mounted
warrior cutting his red cloak in two and giving one half to
a beggar in rags. St Martin is Utrecht's patron saint and the
city takes its colours—red for his cloak and white for his
undergarment—from this incident.

Nearby is a rune stone of King Harold, whose mother
and father played a big part in the Danes becoming Christians.
The stone was a gift from the Danes in 1936, to mark Utrecht
as the site of the first Christian church in the Low Countries

and Scandinavia. It symbolizes the conversion of the Danes to Christianity by Willibrord.

The 112-metre-high Dom Tower (which stood apart from the former church) was being renovated when I visited. It is the highest church tower in Holland and its bells chime every fifteen minutes. Inside are two fourteenth-century chapels—St Michael's used as a private chapel by the bishop, and the Egmond Chapel, which houses an exhibition on the tower.

In the Dom square stands a statue of Count Jan van Nassau, one of the signatories to the Treaty of Utrecht in 1579.

For a complete change of pace we visited a museum of musical clocks, musical boxes and barrel organs, called the Speilklok Totpierement Museum.

The first barrel organ was introduced into Holland in the sixteenth century and soon mechanical musical devices were being built into furniture and clocks. They were so expensive that only the rich could afford them. They were often given as exclusive presents to kings and bishops.

After musical clocks came musical boxes. One played a tune while birds flew, another had a boat rocking under a waterfall. They became the rage and were installed in every conceivable object—under children's chair seats, in hand-made dolls which played lullabies, in manicure seats. Some early musical boxes had ten choices of music. Watches, and even snuff boxes, had small musical movements.

Street organs date from the eighteenth century. Small ones were called 'belly organs' and were worn around the neck, resting on the belly. The organ grinder played to attract customers to street theatre. There was usually a monkey and dog to entice child patrons and their parents. Money was collected in a copper box, the same kind still used today by street organ players. By the end of the nineteenth century large organs, with a perforated cardboard system inside, came into vogue.

Street organs were popular until the first part of the twentieth century and you can still see them on the street in Dutch cities. The big ones were ornately decorated with flowers, scenes and figures and pushed by men, or pulled by horses.

We discovered an orchestrion, a mechanical musical machine which featured a 1910 orchestra.

The museum gives regular musical recitals for visitors. We

listened as an enormous organ painted with roses, bathing beauties, swans, country scenes and windmills, ground out 'La Tarantella'. We also heard a 1926 piano roll of 'Swannee'.

The museum was shortly to be moved to the fourteenth-century Church of the Burgers and plans were afoot to hold dances to barrel-organ music, and build a coffee shop for visitors.

Utrecht has many interesting museums including one in St Catherine's, a fifteenth-century convent of the Knights of St John, which illustrates the history of Christianity in the Netherlands and includes displays of textiles, manuscripts, sculptures and paintings. A large collection of medieval art and paintings by Rembrandt, Franz Hals and other seventeenth-century artists is another attraction.

The vast underground shopping centre, Hoog Catharijne, (High Catherine), is also named after the saint. Heated and airconditioned, this subterranean city stretches five kilometres and has 200 shops, restaurants, an underground railway station, parking for 4000 cars, a music centre, concert hall and sports centre.

Utrecht's food specialities include *proffertjes*—little puffed griddle cakes, buttered and dusted with icing sugar, *boter sprits* (shortbread cookies) and *domtoretjes*—chocolate pastries shaped like the Dom Tower, filled with whipped cream and mocca and topped with Dutch chocolate.

I stayed at Les Pays Bas Hotel opposite a flower market overlooking Janskerhof Square and the Church of St Jan (or John). The hotel was originally owned by a duchess, who later converted it into a hotel. Visiting royalty stayed here both when it was a private home and later a hotel. It still has a gracious atmosphere with magnificent chandeliers and lovely old marble fireplaces.

We dined by candlelight at the elegant Le Restaurant Lorre overlooking the floodlit medieval Old Canal, ending the day as it had begun, in a typical old Utrecht cellar.

GUILIN, CHINA

WE could have stepped into a Chinese traditional scroll painting. The silken river was the colour of jade, the misty jagged blue hills rose in serried ranks to the horizon, the lush fields were emerald green.

Through this enchanting landscape ran rivers and lakes. Beneath were vast caves and mysterious subterranean rivers.

This is Guilin, a countryside renowned in poetry and painting. Famous ninth-century poet, Han Yu, wrote of the idyllic scenery along the River Li: 'The river forms a green silk belt, the mountains are like blue jade hairpins'.

It is not surprising that tourists flock to Guilin. I was there on a typical tour with Jetabout, the package tour division of Qantas.

Guilin's superb scenery strikes you as you get off the plane and gasp at the magnificent, but bizarre, formations thrusting up from the lush green plains. These *karst* formations erupted from the limestone seabed hundreds of millions of years ago when the land was covered by sea. Wind and rain have eroded them into mysterious shapes which change colour and form as light and weather change.

On the bus from the airport, the scenic landscape unfolded— spring-green rice paddies mirroring the clouds, oleander trees, tree-lined riverside walks, duck ponds, bamboo groves, waterways covered with lotus flowers, symbol of purity, and of the Buddha. Bearded old men in baggy black pants and tops fished from bamboo rafts. Elderly black-clad women in head scarves carried babies slung from their backs. Young peasant women in wide-brimmed straw hats trotted by with baskets of farm produce hanging from shoulder poles.

Our first stop was the poetically named Reed Flute Cave, the most famous of a number of local caves. Reeds which once disguised its entrance were fashioned by locals into flutes, giving it its name. Children clustered around the entrance, selling postcards or demanding 'bon bons'.

The cave dates from the Tang Dynasty (618–907) and the local people used it as a refuge from bandits and invading armies. A wet, slippery path descends 500 metres past stalactite and stalagmite formations bathed in coloured spotlights. Guides point out resemblances to wild animals, old trees and humans.

Guilin itself is a pretty little town with tree-lined streets. Street sellers hawk fruit and vegetables and clothes. Signs display bikes for hire. Floating restaurants on the Li River

bear such names as '18 Immortals Wine Boat' and 'Panda
Café'. The eighteen immortals, it seems, were powerful local
families with magical powers who conquered demons, according to popular mythology. The backdrop of undulating misty
blue hills adds a dramatic note to the town.

Guilin is a classical beauty spot, about 360 kilometres north-
west of Guangzhou (Canton), in the valley of the Li River.
It was settled in 214 B.C. when the Qin Dynasty rulers decided
to build the Lin Canal to link the Yangtse and Pearl rivers
via the Li River, and to transport provisions for the Emperor's
conquering armies.

The first Europeans to see Guilin were Portuguese sailors
made prisoners of war in 1550. Guilin in the seventeenth
century became the Ming dynasty capital, as the retreating
emperors fled from the Manchu conquerors. It was the national
capital again briefly in 1936. Many refugees fled here during
the war with Japan, and the town was a stronghold of
resistance.

We stayed at the Rong Cheng Hotel, at Banyan, on the
outskirts of Guilin, a huge new complex with a stone garden
mimicking the hills, the inevitable souvenir and antique shops,
as well as massage, acupuncture and bike hire services.

The highlight of any stay is the trip on the River Li which
winds among the scenic limestone peaks. It took a bus trip
of about two hours to reach a suitable stretch of the river,
which was at low level.

It was a beautiful drive, through thatched mud brick villages,
paddy fields richly green, lush fields of arrowroot, taro and
jute. We passed ragged peasants ploughing with water buffalo,
children in ragged blue Mao suits, fields of tall corn, women
with shiny long black pigtails, groves of orange trees.

Then suddenly we were right among the misty blue mountains which, close up, turned out to be green monoliths of
mottled dark and light shades, covered with moss.

As we reached our final stop, Yangdi village, tourists filed
past, protected from rain by oiled paper umbrellas and struggling to keep up with guides, despite the distractions of
hawkers. Lines of stalls sold ancient tobacco pipes of quaint
flowered enamel design, bamboo flutes, Chinese Mao caps,
postcards, old coins, one-string fiddles, 'antique' china, and
peanuts.

About thirty little ferries were lined up on the river. On board ours we were served jasmine tea, with scented flowers floating on top, accompanied by sugared squid strips and peanuts. Each bend of the river revealed a fresh panorama, as we made off in convoy on a grey overcast day—Chinese, Japanese, Europeans, Americans and Australians on board.

Peaks rose on either side, some needle-sharp, others rounded. With a good imagination, you could detect fighting cocks, flying fish, elephant trunks, a man in profile, horses— at least according to our guide. We passed mist-shrouded crags, lush valleys, bamboo groves, fishermen with their cormorants, sampans, bamboo rafts and shale beaches.

Our trip ended at Yangshuo, another small village which greeted the tourists ecstatically. Tourism and the free-market philosophy had meant unexpected riches and, according to those on their second trip, standards of living had improved dramatically.

Narrow lanes were lined with stalls selling bronze statues, clothes, paintings, teapots, jewellery, embroidered table cloths and 'antiques'.

Back at Guilin, we climbed Piled Silk Hill (poetic names abound) for a stunning view of town, hills, river and fields.

Guilin has other attractions: Fubo Hill with its temple dedicated to a local Han general, and the Pearl Returning Cave, where legend has it that a fisherman returned a stolen pearl to the dragon within. Seven Star Park has a small zoo and six caves, one of which contains hundreds of stelae and carved inscriptions, some dating from the Tang and Ming periods. Zengpiyan Cave is the former site of a stone-age village; Venerate the Country Temple contains a small museum displaying memorabilia of Dr Sun Yat Sen, the country's first president.

Our last dinner was aboard a riverboat, the Water Moon Restaurant, from where we watched a pale yellow sickle moon with a reddish halo rise, while a peasant woman on the next-door barge breastfed her toddler while cooking dinner.

Our dinner was typically Cantonese. Had we decided to sample local specialities, we would have dined at the Tonglai Guan Restaurant in Zhongshan Zhong Road where dishes include bamboo rats, scaly anteater, masked civet (wild cat), lynx, and tortoise stew with duck eggs.

Next day we left behind the world of Chinese scroll paintings and took off on our Russian-made plane (an Ilyushinn) for Guangzhou (Canton), a bustling business metropolis.

NORTH FROM ROME

MEDIEVAL cities, delicately painted frescoes on Etruscan tombs, Roman ruins and some of the best provincial cooking in Europe all lie within a few hours north of Rome, in the province of Lazio.

The medieval city of Viterbo, Tarquinia, one of the great cities of Etruscan civilization, Norcia, with its imposing Etruscan rock tombs, and Vulci, with its eleventh-century castle, and Etruscan and Roman ruins, are just some of the attractions of Lazio.

Viterbo, the 'City of the Popes', had its golden age during the mid thirteenth century when the papal court was established in the splendid papal palace. After Pope Clement IV's death in 1266, it took the cardinals two years and nine months to decide on a successor, the longest period the papacy had ever been vacant.

Their decision was forced on them because they feared a local riot. The citizens were already so exasperated that they had taken the roof off the papal palace hoping wind and rain would convince the cardinals to make a decision and move out.

Today the city is a treasury of palaces, churches, fountains and old piazzas. The picturesque medieval San Pellegrino Quarter has hardly changed since the thirteenth century. Its small square, houses, towers, alleyways, arches and outside staircases are a photographer's paradise.

Viterbo is an ideal city for walking and the tourist centres puts out walking-tour brochures which cover the main attractions.

We went at night when the buildings are floodlit and light and shadow add an extra mysterious dimension to medieval splendours, crammed with art treasures, and redolent of history.

The Piazza del Plebiscito (People's Square) is the historic centre of the city. Here you find the Palace of the Priori, the eleventh-century Church of Sant'Angelo, the old prison building, and the city's administrative offices which feature a beautiful clock tower built in 1487.

The papal palace was built between 1255 and 1267 and has mullion windows and a crenellated façade approached by a wide staircase. Opposite is the cathedral, which started out Romanesque style and had Gothic touches added later. Inside is the funeral monument to Pope John XXI, the only Portuguese pope. He died tragically in Viterbo in 1277 and is mentioned by Dante in the 'Paradiso'.

A crisp autumn evening gave us an appetite and we dined after our walk at Richiastro Restaurant (the name means 'courtyard'). Gastronomic delights for which the region is famous included *acqua cotta* (boiled water) which dates from the Middle Ages. The idea was that the poor farmers and shepherds boiled water with whatever they could find—vegetables, herbs, edible plants, even grasses.

Today the tasty soup contains vegetables, herbs, spices, fish stock, eggs and bread.

Another speciality is *pasta e fagioli*—tender yellow broad beans cooked with pasta. Of couse we had *bruschetta*, toasted bread rubbed with olive oil, garlic and salt.

Other famous dishes included wild boar, pheasant, hare hunter style and *tozzetti*, a hard sweet biscuit with nuts and chocolate bits that you dunked in dessert wine.

Worth visiting, and within easy reach of Viterbo, are the elegant Villa Lante with its Italianate garden, the Palazzo Farnese, and Parco dei Mostri (a park with sculptures of monsters).

The next day we headed for Tarquinia, about seventy kilometres away, through peaceful countryside—orchards, silver olive groves, wheat fields, grape vines, and red-tiled ochre and pink houses clinging to hills.

Tarquinia was a centre of Etruscan civilization which flourished six centuries before Christ. We started our tour in central Cavour Square with a visit to the National Tarquinese Museum, which is lodged in the beautiful fifteenth-century Vitelleschi Palace, once a cardinal's palace. It had a magnificent display of Etruscan sarcophagi, pottery, funeral urns, warrior helmets, tomb paintings and sculptures. Its crowning glory is the magnificent sculptured Winged Horses which once decorated the fourth century B.C. altar of the Queen Temple.

Opposite the museum is the Archaeology Travel Service which provides tours and guides.

The famous Etruscan painted tombs are a few kilometres from town. To get there you can take one of the taxis which leave regularly from outside the museum, and cost only a few dollars. Admission tickets to the tombs are obtained from the museum.

The Etruscans were a joyous, artistic people who loved life and believed that the good things would continue in the next life. The frescoes show a people who enjoyed the outdoors, sport, dancing and dining.

There are about forty tombs and we looked at two. On the walls of the Hunting and Fishing tomb (520 B.C.) vivid scenes spring to vigorous life. Dolphins spring from waves. Fishermen in a rowboat lower lines. A diver from the cliff is caught in mid flight. Hunters throw stones at swarms of soaring blue birds. The painting of the diver is the oldest surviving picture of a diver of ancient times.

It's a wonderful feeling to know you are looking at what the Etruscans six centuries before Christ painted and to experience vicariously the lifestyle of a remarkable people.

Death was not a sad event to the Etruscans. They held a big feast outside the tomb then, about a year or so later, the family came to stay in the tomb and enjoyed feasting, music and dancing. Some of the paintings are linked with these feasts, although the symbolism is not known. The Etruscan language has not yet been deciphered so they remain a mysterious race to the present day.

One wall showed girls with funerary crowns, dressed in delicate diaphanous fabrics, and dancers full of joyous energy listening to a double flute player.

On another wall a man carries a pottery container of wine. Children carry a rabbit, and a dog runs beside them, then horsemen and a man with two dogs appear. In another scene, girls make funerary crowns and servants bring wine.

The second tomb we visited was the Tomb of the Juggler. On one wall there is a juggler, a girl with candelabra, a young boy throwing a disc, and the oft recurring double flute player. Servants bring wine and food, entertainers sing and dance, a man sits watching their performance.

In a touch of humour a naked man passes a bowel movement, a rude gesture—the Etruscan answer to the bad fate represented by the blackbirds in the painting. His defence is to turn his back on the birds and defecate. In the inner chamber, there is a magnificent red lion and a blue panther.

After seeing the lapis lazuli blue, the earth red and sea green colours of the frescoes, I agree with D. H. Lawrence who wrote in his essay, 'Etruscan Places': 'If you want mass, go to the Romans. But, if you love the odd spontaneous forms that are never standardized, go to the Etruscans', the people who found the secret of joyful living and gave banquets to thank the gods for the pleasure of life.

Our next stop was Norchia, with its massive cube tombs cut in the cliff face. The most significant are the Tomb of the Three Heads (three divinities carved in the architrave of the door), the Lattazzi Tomb, and the two temple-like or Doric tombs which imitate sacred buildings with a gable-shaped space above the doorway, decorated with friezes. Only sixty of the estimated 100,000 tombs of the necropolis have been opened.

On to Vulci, through countryside dominated by a huge stone aqueduct—after stopping for a quick lunch (most Italian lunches are leisurely affairs of several hours) of prosciutto, sausage, bruschetta and the famous *cacciotta* which like *pecorino* cheese is made from goat's milk, accompanied by fragrant local wine. Cacciotta, a softer cheese than pecorino, has a reputation as an aphrodisiac and the Emperor Charlemagne was said to carry a supply in his saddle bag when he went abroad.

Vulci, with its ruins of Etruscan and Roman Cities, is a romantic spot. It was once one of the twelve powerful Etruscan city states, later an important Roman town. It has an eleventh-century castle and picturesque stone bridge over the gorge of the river. We explored the castle which now contains a small Etruscan museum and the Roman ruins where a villa, temple to Mithras, and bath house have been excavated.

As the blood-red sun touched the horizon, we made for the Casale dell' Osteria, which has been a farmhouse inn for over a century. Its old name was Farmhouse of the Old Papal Coin because grave robbers paid for dinner with coins they found near by.

We filled up on *acqua cotta*, a marvellous antipasto of ham and sausage meat made from wild boar, beans with onion and celery, olives stuffed with orange peel, chilli pepper and garlic, vegetables with onion, breadcrumbs and pepper, and cacciotta. Not to mention the bruschetta, the pasta with sausage, the grilled veal shank, the wild boar, potatoes, and dessert of tozzetti, the hard biscuits with almonds which we dipped in our *vino santo* (holy wine), a sweet red. Then we danced and sang before heading back to Rome under a full moon.

SOUTH FROM ROME

'WELCOME to those who come, health to those who leave. I give you the time through ancient science and art.'

I wondered if the picturesque town clock's message greeted the great artist, Michelangelo Buonarroti, on his arrival in the Italian spa resort of Fiuggi. Michelangelo, troubled by gallstones, had come to take the water.

So did his patron, Pope Boniface VIII, who was born in the district, employed Michelangelo in the Vatican and frequented the spa after a cure.

The entrance to one of the town's two spas bears the legend: 'L'Acqua di Bonifacio VIII', in honour of its distinguished former guest.

Fiuggi, in the province of Lazio, is only a few hours' drive from Rome and also has a rail link. It is one of the fascinating places south of the capital.

The resort makes a good centre for exploring nearby historic towns such as Anagni, 'the City of Popes', with its cathedral and palace of Bonifacio VIII, Alatri with its acropolis and cyclopean walls, Subiaco with its monasteries of saints Benedict and Scholastica, and Cassino with its famous Monte Cassino Abbey.

The medieval quarter of Fiuggi, with its narrow lanes, pastel-coloured houses with wooden shutters, geranium pots and washing festooning the alleyways, is a complete contrast to the smart spa quarter with its modern hotels and restaurants.

Regional food specialities included macaroni and noodles, lentils and pork crackling, lamb with tasty vegetable sauce, mountain ham and a variety of cheeses, sausages, pork chops and delicious macaroons, doughnuts with syrup and ring-shaped cakes.

The spas are set in parkland where the trees were turning autumn red, gold and brown and people promenaded, glass or mug of water in hand, chatting or listening to the pop band clad in what looked like waiters' uniforms.

The spa buildings are used for drama, opera, variety concerts, fashion shows, sporting events and conventions.

Three ski reserves are within twenty-five minutes' journey.

Our next destination was the town of Cassino, with the impressive Monte Cassino Abbey on the mountain summit, dominating the plain below. We wound up to it along a tortuous, hairpin bend road for about eight kilometres, enjoying stunning views.

The abbey was almost totally destroyed by bombing during the Second World War, but the monks, with international help, and aid from the Italian government, rebuilt it.

The abbey, the mother house, and most famous of all Benedictine abbeys, was built by St Benedict in 529, and has been destroyed and rebuilt many times.

The Benedictines kept up to their motto, 'Work and Prayer', and the monastery became a repository of European arts and culture through the ages. Some of its treasures were removed to the Vatican during the Second World War for safe keeping.

Today's building is a copy of the fifteenth century abbey. The museum is a treasure trove of illuminated manuscripts, embroidered vestments, Roman antiquities and precious jewelled artefacts.

The Hotel Pavone, where we lunched, had paintings of the bombing of the abbey, old war helmets, field telephones, guns and shells.

The next part of our journey was a complete contrast— to the seashore of the wine purple Tyrrhenian Sea, a land of Roman ruins, Mediterranean-style cream, pink and ochre houses, lemon trees and balconies with pots of red geraniums, scenic drives, stone walls and grape vines.

Formia was an old fishing village and is now a modern resort, on the rail junction for the Rome–Naples express.

A traditionally costumed folk dancing group, Le Tradizione, the girls in red and black with stiff lace headdresses, performed harvest, courting and fishing dances at our hotel, the Grande Albergo Miramare.

Formia is continuous with Gaeta—part of a band of beaches, bays, golden sand and shingles backed by rugged mountains. At Gaeta's Montagna Spaccata is a great cleft rock face with a sheer drop to the sea below, and nearby is a Turkish grotto.

Turks, pirates, and Saracens ravaged this coast for centuries and are still very much in the local legends, folklore, dances and place names.

The legend of Montagna Spaccata has it that a Turkish pirate, leaning on the rock, told the Christian ruler that he did not believe in Christ. Suddenly the solid rock was split in two and the Turk's hand was seared into the rock where you can still see the imprint of the five fingers today.

The beach at Sperlonga is the best in the Roman region, say locals. Sperlonga is a charming medieval town with steep, narrow, winding streets, workshops, rustic white-washed houses, little nooks and crannies. It looks somewhat like a village on a Greek island.

In the Porta Piccola Chiesa courtyard there is a delightful quaint painting, only fourteen years old, of the coming of the bloody Saracens, with swords and shields, in their warrior boats. The women in medieval gowns go to meet them bearing flowers. The accompanying story is in medieval language.

The Emperor Tiberius had a villa in the area and excavations have revealed many interesting relics now housed in a nearby museum. On the shore, the ramparts of a small fortress overlook the sea. It's well worth a climb to the belvedere for stunning views.

In the village, women carry baskets of washing on their heads to the public laundry, at the spring's source, and pound washing on the rocks.

A little further along the coast is Terracina, which once marked the borders between the Kingdom of the Two Sicilies and the Papal States.

Its Roman ruins include the Emilian Forum, buildings, a wall on the ancient Appian Way and the first century B.C. Temple of Jove Anxur perched on Mount St Angelo. The temple was once decorated with paintings and covered in gold which glittered in the sun. Ships from afar saw the glittering temple which acted as a beacon.

There is also a medieval village to explore, a twelfth-century cathedral, the eighteenth-century Braschi Palace and the nineteenth-century Church of the Holy Redeemer.

Another great attraction is the splendid Grappolo Duva restaurant which provided the best seafood meal I have ever sampled. The antipasto was a vast display—fetta with olives, white pizza bread with oil and rosemary, prosciutto and melon, seafood salad, calamari, mussels and prawns, fried sardines, fried zucchi in batter, pasta with seafood, rice croquettes, scallops in breadcrumbs, mussels on the shell, pink salmon, prawns with mushrooms.

After the first course (a buffet spread) came grilled prawns, fish and scampi, and then dessert—crème caramel, strawberry tart, a pretty mousse, or fruit—all washed down with jugs of fresh local wine. Coffee, liqueurs (Grappa La Lupe and Amaro Lucano), and chilled spumanti ended this ambrosian feast, which the manager told me could be had for under thirty dollars a head.

The location overlooking the sea, with gulls, fishing boats and an upturned rowboat, and a silver tide-streaked beach, was a perfect setting—and a fitting end to a journey into the Roman countryside.

BAVARIA

EVEN a short visit to Bavaria yields a marvellous variety of sights, sounds and experiences. Magnificent churches, palaces and castles, medieval cities, quaint villages, oom-pa-pa bands, beer festivals and superb scenery are just some of the attractions which lure visitors.

In just over ten days, I sampled the delights of Munich, Regensburg, Passau, Nuremberg and Frankfurt, with a side trip from Nuremberg into the Upper Franconian countryside.

Munich is many cities rolled into one. There is Royal Munich with its palaces, ceremonial roads, ornate fountains, castles; Religious Munich with its glorious old churches, processions and festivals such as Fasching (the pre-Lenten festival). And there is fun-loving Uproarious Munich with its world-famous Oktoberfest, when beer flows like water, its jolly pubs, cosy kellers and beer gardens.

Schwabing, described as 'not so much a village as a state of mind', is Bohemian Munich. Here in the student quarter, near the university, you'll find wine taverns, restaurants, pavement artists, little progressive theatres and jazz clubs.

Last, but not least, there is Olympic Munich, the area where the Games were held. Its many attractions include Olympic Hall which holds 12,000 and is used for pop concerts, the Olympic television tower with its panoramic view and restaurant. Another attraction is the BMW Museum adjacent to the BMW car factory (the initials stand for Bavarian Motor Works).

Munich is built on the spot where Benedictine monks had a monastery. Its German name, Munchen, means 'the monks'. In 1158 the Emperor Barbarossa gave Munich marketing and coinage rights and by 1255, the Royal Wittelsbachers had moved into the city and were closely linked with it until 1918.

The monks also gave Munich its famous beer. They held the brewing monopoly until the sixteenth century, when William V decided to start his own court brewery, the Hofbrau.

Visitors can sample the wonderful brew in beer gardens and kellers, but at least one visit should be made to the cheery Hofbrauhaus, with its ceiling gaily painted with food and wine designs. Built in 1890, its traditions go back to the court brewery. Commoners were not allowed to drink the beer until the end of the last century.

Regular customers sit at their own table and keep their own beer steins locked in a special cupboard to which they have a key. Only when one dies does his place become available.

Locals call the beer 'liquid bread' and a Norwegian writer, Knut Hamsun, described a quart of Munich beer as 'a regular meal'.

When the national theatre burned down last century, beer was used to fight the flames, since the water was frozen in the pipes. Later, beer drinkers had to pay a 'beer penny' tax to finance rebuilding.

In the nineteenth century, King Ludwig I made Munich one of Germany's most beautiful cities, leaving his mark on many buildings in the Old City.

Despite widespread destruction during the Second World War, rebuilt Munich is as beautiful as ever.

A tour of Imperial Munich should include the Residenz (Palace) with its magnificently decorated state rooms, fabulous Treasury with its court jewels and crowns, courtyards and fountains, antiquarium built to display antiques, and the splendid scarlet, gold and white rococo theatre built by a dwarf court jester with a gift for architecture. His name was François de Cuvilliés and he was jester to Elector Max Emanuel. Mozart's opera *Indomeneo* had its premiere here in 1781 and Mozart concerts are still held here.

Nymphenburg Castle, summer residence of the Royal Wittelsbach family, has a famous Gallery of Beauties, thirty-six paintings of lovely ladies chosen by King Ludwig I to be immortalized. They include his mistress, the notorious Lola Montez (who danced on the Ballarat goldfields and horse whipped a local newspaper editor who had criticized her performance).

The heart of Munich is the Marienplatz (Our Lady's Square) where tourists gather to watch the antics of tiny jousting knights when the *glockenspiel* (mechanical clock) strikes the hour.

Munich has 200 churches, but the pick of them are the late Gothic-style Church of Our Lady, the Renaissance style St Michael's, and the magnificent St Peter's Cathedral with its baroque and Renaissance altars.

Its many museums include the Alte Pinakothek with its masterpieces by Durer, Reubens and Altdorfer, and the nearby Neue Pinakothek with its French Impressionists and masters of the eighteenth and nineteenth centuries. The scientifically minded will also enjoy a visit to the Deutsches Museum of Science and Technology.

Munich's most popular festivity, Oktoberfest, started in 1810 to celebrate a royal wedding. It takes place over two weeks, ending the first weekend in October. Ten vast decorated beer tents hold 5000 people each. There are brass bands, folk-costumed processions, a fun fair, parades of colourful horse-drawn brewers' carts, a lot of downing of huge steins of beer and munching of tasty sausages and sauerkraut.

Munich makes a good centre for excursions to King Ludwig II's extravagant castles, Neuschwanstein and Linderhof, and to Berchtesgaden and Salzburg.

Regensburg, on the Danube, is one of the few cities in

Germany which still has an unspoilt Middle Ages character. About sixty per cent of the buildings are more than 300 years old and it has 1400 historical buildings and monuments.

In medieval times trade routes to Eastern Europe, Italy and Northern Europe passed through the city which also traded with Asia, Russia and the Orient. In earlier times, this was a Roman settlement and parts of the Old Roman Wall of A.D. 179 remain. Today's visitors march through the Porta Praetoria, as the Praetorian guard once did.

Bavarian dukes ruled the city in the sixth century until 788 when the Holy Roman Emperor Charlemagne made Bavaria part of his empire. It became an imperial city, subservient only to the emperor in the twelfth century, and part of Bavaria in 1810.

It has long been a favourite city of people with artistic taste. Goethe stayed at the White Lamb Inn on his journey to Italy in 1786 and may have patronized the historic sausage kitchen (Historische Wurstkuche) opposite, which dates back to the twelfth century.

Mozart visited Regensburg in 1790 and praised its hospitality, its food and wine and delightful music.

The sausage kitchen provides outdoor seating beside the River Danube. There's nothing more pleasant on a fine day than to lunch there on potato soup, its own special sausages and sauerkraut and a stein of beer, all this for a few dollars.

One wall of the kitchen is part of the Old Roman Wall. It was built in the twelfth century to serve the construction workers of the nearby Stone Bridge, the oldest bridge in Germany and the city's symbol. A statue of the builder, called the 'Bruckenmannchen', stands on the superbly designed bridge looking towards the cathedral.

St Peter's Cathedral was begun in 1250 but various parts were added up until the last century. It is a treasure house of art. It also boasts the longest established boys choir (founded 1000 years ago) called the 'Sparrows of Regensburg', who sing at Sunday Mass.

Other interesting churches include the white and gold rococo basilica of Our Dear Lady, and St Emmeram, a ninth-century church where the Prince of Thurn and Taxis and his wife, local royalty whose palace is next door, worship.

The cloisters and coach-house museum are open to the

public and, when the family are not in residence, the palace itself is open, apart from private rooms.

A wander around the Old Town reveals some marvellous ancient buildings, including the fourteenth-century Italian-style 'Patrician Towers' built for noble families by builders who had worked in Italy. Only twenty remain of the original sixty.

The rooms of the electoral princes, the Chamber of Diets and the torture chamber in the Old Town Hall (Altes Rathaus) are open to the public. The Old Town Hall's Gothic portal dates from 1408 and the baroque eastern wing from the seventeenth and eighteenth centuries.

After hearing the guide explain the horrors which went on in the torture chamber, it is a pleasant relief to sample some fragrant coffee and deliciously rich cake in the Prinzessin Coffee Shop opposite. It was the first coffee shop built in Germany. Another historic touch is 'Barbara's Kisses'. These are delicious liqueur-filled chocolates named in honour of Barbara Blomfield, who had an affair with Emperor Charles V and gave birth to an illegitimate son, Don Johann of Austria, famed for his victory over the Turks in the Battle of Lepanto. A traditional custom at the opening of Parliament was the presentation of chocolates to members by pretty girls, in memory of Barbara. These became known as 'Barbara's Kisses'.

Before moving on to our next city, we took a boat trip on the Danube to Walhalla, about 10 kilometres from the city. Built by King Ludwig I of Bavaria in 1842, it celebrates famous German musicians, writers and philosophers whose busts decorate the interior of the Parthenon-style building which stands high above the river.

Passau is one of the prettiest cities in Germany. It is sometimes called the Venice of Bavaria because it sits on an island where three rivers meet—the Danube (called the Donau), the Inn and the Ilz.

With its pastel-coloured buildings with red-tiled roofs, it has a Mediterranean atmosphere, largely due to its Italian builders.

The narrow streets are studded with arts and crafts studios, quaint shop signs, pretty buildings with flower boxes.

Open-air cafés line the riverside with its pleasure boats. Wooded hills and a castle on the opposite bank add to the scenic charm of the Bavarian city.

The 2000-year-old city was ruled by bishop princes from the thirteenth century to 1803, when Passau joined Bavaria. Until 1468 the bishop was also the patron of St Stephen's Cathedral in Vienna.

At night the city takes on a magical air with floodlighting colouring the ornate clock tower, onion domes of St Stephen's Cathedral and pastel-coloured buildings, for all the world like a vast stage set.

The glass museum (Passauer Glasmuseum) displays beautiful and historic glassware. It is housed in the Wilden Mann, an historic building which also contains an excellent restaurant where visitors can sample gourmet food such as venison, and wild mushrooms (*chanterelles*). There is also an inn with inexpensive accommodation.

In the museum a suite of rooms with quaint furniture is kept for visiting VIPs, who have included Neil Armstrong, the first man on the moon.

The cathedral, rebuilt after a fire in 1662, in Italian baroque style by artists from Lake Como, houses the world's biggest organ. We attended a magnificent classical organ recital, held every day at noon.

The Museum of Oberhaus Castle, formerly a Roman fortress, the New Residenz of the Prince-Bishops, and various chapels and galleries are well worth visiting.

Operas and drama performances are held in the Passau City Theatre, the former opera house of the Prince-Bishops, where Mozart performances were first held in 1783.

We took a coach excursion into nearby Austria, with a pleasant cruise back on the Danube on a Donau-Schiffahrts Linie boat. You can also cruise to Linz and Vienna or to Budapest.

Nuremberg's golden age was the fifteenth and sixteenth centuries, when it became an important trade centre. Its most famous painter, Albrecht Dürer, lived and worked here from 1471 to 1528. You can visit the Dürer House, below the castle, and now a museum. Hans Sachs, immortalized in Wagner's opera, *The Meistersingers*, also lived in Nuremberg.

The beautiful city (Nürnberg is the German name) was founded by Henry III in 1050. Its name means 'to the rocky hill'—a massive castle still crowns this hill. Friedrich, Emperor

Barbarossa, occupied the city in the twelfth century.

For centuries it was an imperial city until annexed to the Kingdom of Bavaria in 1806. Like Regensburg, it is wonderful city to explore on foot.

Its three most famous churches are the Gothic St Sebaldus, the Church of St Lawrence, both filled with art treasures, and the fourteenth century Church of Our Lady in the Market Place. The last has a quaint *glockenspiel* or ornamental clock and daily, at noon, the figures of seven Prince Electors rotate around the Emperor. People still gather water from the Beautiful Fountain (Schoner Brunnen) with its gilded figures and 'lucky ring', a turn of which ensures happiness. The present fountain is a nineteenth-century copy of the original built in 1318, and famous in song and story.

The annual Christkindlesmarkt (Christmas Fair) is held in the market, from the beginning of Advent until Christmas Eve. The traditional fair, which began over 400 years ago, is opened by the 'Christ Child', a seventeen-year-old blonde, curly-haired girl dressed as an angel in gold and silver, who reads a poem from the balcony of the Church of Our Lady. She is the city's symbol during the fair.

Part of the charm of Nuremberg is its child-like character. It makes beautiful wooden toys to delight any boy or girl, and its gingerbread could have come straight from a fairytale. The Toy Museum has a wonderful collection of toys from many centuries and countries. An International Toy Fair is held each year.

All over the city, pastry shops sell the delicious-smelling gingerbread in all varieties—spiced, with nuts, chocolate coated. The original recipe is over 600 years old. When *lebkuchen* (its German name) was first mentioned in local history, it was then a simple pastry baked in convent cloisters.

During the Middle Ages the recipe underwent a spicy transformation. Ships from Asia brought aromatic spices and the trade route between Nuremberg and Venice became known as the 'Spice Street'. Bakers now use cinnamon, nutmeg, cardamon, pepper, ginger and other spices in the gingerbread. By official decree, gingerbread baking became a separate trade from general baking.

You can buy one type of gingerbread called the *Kaiserlein* (Little Emperor) in remembrance of an occasion when Kaiser

Friedrich III, in 1487, invited all the city's children to receive a special gingerbread baked with his portrait.

The Imperial Castle, which dates back to 1040, is the city's most famous and interesting historical building, with a wealth of nooks and crannies to explore. It is surrounded by a moat, now dry. A popular story tells how a robber baron jumped his horse from the castle wall over the moat to escape capture and, incredibly, survived.

The handicraft market (the Artisan's Courtyard) near the entrance to the Old Town (now a pedestrian plaza) is the place to see local craftsmen at work making dolls, carving, painting on glass, weaving baskets. I bought some beautiful hand-made Christmas decorations there.

The Fembo House Municipal Museum is housed in a grand mansion dating from Renaissance and baroque times. Its exhibits show earlier local lifestyles. The Germanic National Museum has displays of German art and culture. Under the Old Town Hall, a torture chamber and medieval dungeons are open to the public.

Nuremberg, with its quaint buildings, perfectly recreated after the destruction of the Second World War, its pretty waterways of the River Pegnitz, romantic bridges and arches, and old alms-houses is the perfect city to explore on foot. When you get hungry, there are some marvellous places to eat, including the Nassauer Keller, a restaurant housed in a thirteenth-century noble's home, the oldest in Nuremberg. Cosy kellers, including one I tried in the Artisans' Courtyard, sell the wonderful spicy Nürnberg sausages with sauerkraut and potato salad and tall steins of cold beer.

Nuremberg's pride in lovingly restoring its historic buildings, and its traditional customs, makes it a rewarding city to visit.

We left Bavaria, and returned to Frankfurt for our flight home, after a day's sightseeing.

Frankfurt has had a major financial role since the Middle Ages. Nowadays it has more than 350 national and international banks and its airport handles some twenty-eight million passengers annually, making it the second busiest airport in Europe.

Its big international fairs—the book fair, automobile fair, textile fair and fur fair, make it a mecca for business travellers.

Frankfurt is the gateway to Germany for international air travellers and a good centre for exploring, with day excursions possible by train to such attractions as Heidelberg (fifty-three minutes), Rudesheim, a beautiful village on the Rhine (sixty minutes) and Wiesbaden, the State capital of Hessen (sixty minutes).

It is an elegant city with a green belt of five kilometres of parks and gardens replacing the city's old fortifications. Most of the main tourist attractions are within walking distance of each other, and of the attractive pedestrian area of smart boutiques and department stores.

It is wise to take a city coach tour to get your bearings. It lasts about three hours and is inexpensive.

The Goethe House is a 'must' on any tourist itinerary. Rebuilt after bombing during the Second World War, the house where the poet was born and grew up has authentic period furniture and an attached museum giving the city's history.

The heart of the city is the Romer, Frankfurt's city hall since 1405. In the stately Kaisersaal, banquets were held to celebrate the crowning of Holy Roman Emperors in the nearby cathedral.

In front is the picturesque Fountain of Justice, flanked by rows of medieval-style restored half-timbered houses. Nearby, St Nicholas' Church (1290), the magnificent Dom (cathedral), and St Paul's Church (never used as a church, but the seat of the first German Parliament) are well worth visiting.

The city has twenty-two museums, including an architecture and a film museum.

No visit would be complete without spending an evening in Sachsenhausen, the entertainment area across the Rhine, with its cider pubs and gardens, jazz cellars and bars. The atmosphere is cosy, the food tasty and the apple wine guaranteed to make you lightheaded.

Ten minutes by train brings you to Hoechst, a charming medieval town, with castles, ancient walls and one of Germany's oldest churches, St Justinian's.

Bavaria, with its romantic history, rich traditions and fun-loving people, provides a memorable holiday.

HOLLAND—THE RIVER VECHT COUNTRY AND CASTLE DE HAAR

THERE are few landscapes as tranquil as those of Holland, and the River Vecht countryside is one of the most peaceful.

Only thirty kilometres' drive from Amsterdam, the river meanders through green meadows, past browsing brown and white cattle, nineteenth century windmills, which regulate water levels or grind corn, and old farmhouses.

The tree-lined road, in the soft misty Dutch light, looks as it must have done centuries ago. We pass houseboats moored alongside colourful gardens, a cheese farm and the pretty village of Vreeland. Opposite a picturesque weighbridge and poplars reflected in the river, stands a charming restaurant, Der Nederlanden.

Driving along a narrow road we come to Loenen, with its graceful old church and stately *dorp*—village meeting hall.

The river can be explored at leisure on hired motor boats. Water travel has a long history. In the seventeenth century wealthy Amsterdam merchants, who made their wealth from trade with the East Indies, built lavish country mansions along the Vecht, travelling there by boat, drawn by horses on either bank. They came at first just for a day's outing, later for weekends.

Nowadays you can also rent a horse-drawn carriage in the delightful village of Breukellen and clip-clop along the riverside road, as we saw one couple doing, stopping at picturesque Castle Gunterstein for a photograph or two.

Further along, past the village of Klaar, we came to spectacular Nyenrode Castle with its red and white shutters and drawbridge. It is now a university for commerce students.

But it's the riverside mansions which are the main attraction. Centuries ago, noblemen and bishops from the nearby city of Utrecht built strongholds and castles in the area to defend themselves against enemies.

Most of the Vecht area was destroyed by the French in the seventeenth century. But, soon after, rich Amsterdam merchants who had made fortunes from trading with the East Indies, built their country villas and had magnificent landscaped gardens laid out. Quaint garden teahouses overlooking the river were popular and a few remain. Each bend in the road reveals yet another magnificent mansion.

We were on our way to de Haar Castle, a neo-Gothic edifice in a vast park—perhaps Holland's most magnificent castle. It belongs to a nobleman with the imposing title, Baron von Zuylen van Nyeveld de Haar.

First we drove through Haarzuilens Village, which he owns. The red, green and white colours of its buildings were the family colours. The De Vier Balken restaurant looked interesting and apparently provides excellent food for travellers.

We walked through the deer park and rose gardens to where the splendid moated castle rose, as in a fairytale, complete with turrets, balconies, casement windows and red and white patterned wooden shutters.

It was originally built in the twelfth century, first occupied about 1350, and destroyed in 1481, later rebuilt and enlarged. In 1672 French troops partly destroyed it and, neglected, it fell into ruin.

Enter a nineteenth-century fairy godmother, the Baroness Helena de Rothschild, who married the Baron de Haar, the present owner's grandfather. Together they set about restoring the castle with Rothschild money. Two hundred workmen laboured for twenty years, under the direction of architect Petrus Cuypers, to complete it. A whole village was torn down to create the vast park.

They travelled the world for three years collecting beautiful antiques and fine period furniture, fourteenth- and fifteenth-century Gobelin tapestries (the castle has three, said to be worth one million dollars each), ancient Chinese blue and white porcelain, and valuable paintings, many from other castles. Treasures include a small carriage in which the 'Sun King', Louis XIV, rode as a child. Every piece has a history.

The entire castle—200 rooms including about twenty bathrooms—is centrally heated. The dining-room table seats thirty-five. At the last charity ball held in the castle, 1200 people danced in the magnificent ballroom and two orchestras (including a Hungarian one) played.

The castle and formal French and English gardens are open to the public at certain times of the year. From August to October, and at Christmas, it is closed. As soon as it closes, staff get busy turning it from a tourist attraction into a first-class hotel, in readiness for the arrival of the Baron from Paris and his guests.

Ten servants are hired from the village and the Baron brings another twenty with him, as well as his own cook, Paul Amory, said to be one of the best ten cooks in Paris. Six servants work in the kitchen under a supervisor. A liveried servant stands behind every third or fourth guest at dinner, attentive to their slightest wish.

Amory has been known to produce a sugared model of the castle for dessert to mark its eightieth birthday in 1978, and another dessert shaped like a horse to celebrate the win of a racehorse bred by the Baroness.

The family also spend Christmas at the castle, this time without guests.

At other times, a staff of six—manager, two guides, caretaker and two gardeners—maintain the castle and grounds and keep an eye on the 70,000 visitors who come each year, to wonder at the extraordinary splendour in which the enormously rich live.

WOOLNORTH—HISTORIC SHEEP AND CATTLE STATION, AUSTRALIA

I felt like the heroine of the novel *Rebecca*, driving up the impressive entrance to 'Mandalay', as I passed through the gateway of one of Australia's oldest and most romantic cattle and sheep stations.

It takes a good twenty five minutes to drive from the gateway of 'Woolnorth', a vast 22,100 hectare property on the northernmost tip of western Tasmania, to the homestead.

The property has the same colour and romance that made 'Mandalay' memorable. Its mystery was maintained by closing it off to the public until recent years.

The original property took in an area from Bass Strait to the Indian Ocean. The company which founded it, the Van Diemen's Land Company, had so much power, that the first agent in Tasmania, Edward Curr, locked horns with Governor Arthur.

Such was 'Woolnorth's' status that its boundaries were

included in early maps of Tasmania. Even today it takes in sixteen kilometres of north coast and eighteen kilometres of west coast.

Started in 1825 by the Van Diemen's Land Company under direct charter from England's George IV, its history is bound up with that of early Tasmania. The first surveying of the north-west was done by the company, which also built the first road from Launceston to Burnie and was responsible for the first railway to the west coast from Burnie. You'll find some of the history of the company in the colonial museum at Burnie, now a fair-sized town, but originally part of the 'Woolnorth' estate.

Powerful Edward Curr took over management in August 1826, when he was only twenty six and just out from England. He was paid 800 pounds, which was a fortune in those days. He set up a home, Highfield House, which still stands at Stanley, a coastal village, once part of 'Woolnorth'.

George IV granted land on condition that the company settled nowhere else, and developed it. The company brought out people from England to work for them and, after seven years, gave them their own land to work as tenant farmers.

'Woolnorth' was like a vast feudal estate, with convicts and ticket-of-leave men working alongside free settlers. The company even had its own public holidays. One was the day on which tenants came to pay yearly rent and free whisky and other drinks were laid on.

Curr's falling out with Governor Arthur forced him to leave 'Woolnorth' in the 1840s when the governor made it difficult for the company to acquire the land they wanted, and to continue to impose their own controls. He settled in Victoria and was one of the main instigators behind Victoria's secession from New South Wales. 'Woolnorth', incidentally, is older than Melbourne.

The estate has its own ghosts, colourful characters and famous incidents. It is where the last of the legendary Tasmanian tigers (thylacine) were captured. Four tigers were taken alive by employees on the property near Cape Grim and sent to Hobart Zoo in 1908. The last known wild one was captured in 1933 and died in 1936. They are now believed to be extinct, although there have been unconfirmed sightings in the more remote areas of Tasmania. The tiger, a nocturnal marsupial, is orange-brown in colour, and lives by preying on wallabies, kangaroos, and small animals.

Sue, the charming wife of 'Woolnorth's' manager, Graham Gillon, is convinced that Tasmanian tigers still exist and that she herself made the last sighting in 1968.

'We had been to a party—and yes, I was sober—and, as we drove across Welcome Bridge on the way home, I saw a Tasmanian tiger run across the road. I have no doubt at all. It had stripes and ran pacing two legs together at a time.'

As for ghosts, Sue recalled that the ghost of a former employee, Bill Mason, was called up at a seance she attended.

'He had come to work at 'Woolnorth' from Scotland when he was seventeen after an unhappy love affair. He never left the place until he died. During his annual three week's leave he would work his way through a case of gin. He wanted to be buried at 'Woolnorth', but after he died, he was buried at Stanley.'

Another ghost is that of a charging black bull which many people report seeing near the lagoon.

'Workers used to shoot the wild bulls,' explained Sue, 'but the fearless black bull would charge them. When they finally shot him, they put his skull on a tree. It's gone now, but the ghost stories persist.'

It's surprising there are not Aboriginal ghosts considering that 'Woolnorth' was the scene of one of the worst Aboriginal massacres in Australian history.

It came about because of a fight between Aborigines and four Irish ex-convict shepherds, according to Sue. The site is called Slaughter Hill and the sea below, Suicide Bay.

'Sealers and shepherds were abducting Aboriginal women,' Sue told me.

'Curr had said that the Aborigines were not to be harmed but the fight escalated. A white man was speared, an Aboriginal chief killed.

'The Aborigines took revenge by chasing 113 Spanish Merino sheep over Slaughter Hill cliff. The shepherds were furious at losing these prime sheep which the company had outbid the King of Spain to acquire, and knew they would be in trouble with Curr. They waited their chance and ambushed the Aborigines, opening fire on them as they climbed the cliff.

'Many jumped into the sea. Those who survived were clubbed on the head and thrown into the sea. After the massacre, the white men chased the black women, who suicided by jumping over into Suicide Bay, with their children, rather than be captured.'

Not surprisingly, the company kept quiet about the massacre and it wasn't until some years later when George Augustus Robinson, who had the 'friendly mission' of rounding up the Aborigines to isolate them on Bruny Island, visited 'Woolnorth' that the story came out.

I made a private visit to 'Woolnorth' but tours were available several days a week and included a barbecue lunch of prime Scotch fillet steak, hamburger, sausages and salad, followed by fruit salad, plus a Devonshire tea in the afternoon.

Stock manager Ken Else and his American wife, Linda, give demonstrations of sheep shearing, a workout by sheep dogs and a cattle roundup. Ken grew up on his father's sheep station in Victoria, while Linda was from California and her father managed a ranch in Nevada. They both appeared in rodeos and agricultural shows with their beautiful stallions.

Our first stop on the tour of inspection was Suicide Bay. From the cliff you can see the Doughboys, two rounded green rocky islets which jut out into a turbulent sea. They were named by explorers Bass and Flinders.

Trefoil Island used to belong to the company and is a favourite spot for mutton birds which riddle the island with nesting holes. The federal government took it over and mutton birds and sheep provide a living for remnants of the original Tasmanian Aborigines (there are no full-blood people left).

Hunter Island is leased by a local family as a cattle property. Part of it is a national park.

Three Hummock Island was settled by a British navy commander and his wife and family after the Second World War. Eleanor Allison, the wife, wrote a book on the island where they lived and raised their family for thirty years. It too is now a national park.

To the left of Suicide Bay is Cape Grim where the federal government has established an air-monitoring station. 'Woolnorth', with the wind—mainly untainted westerlies—blowing for about ten months of the year, is said to have the freshest air in Australia and the monitoring station provides a baseline for air pollution. It is one of a network of stations around the world.

The coastline, apart from Cape Grim, is a wildlife heritage area and 'Woolnorth' has most of Tasmania's native animals—wallabies, wombats, echidnas, bandicoots, platypus, sugar gliders, tiger cats and Tasmanian devils. There are over 100 species of birds including hawks, native hens, black jays, and the long-beaked golden valley ibis. The company brought in Cape Barren geese to breed when these were in danger of dying out.

Tourists are taken to see the coastal location for the original settlement at 'Woolnorth', but only a well remains. Here too is the skeleton of the wreck of the *Colliboi* which beached here in August 1932, after springing a leak. Opposite the beach is Goat Island, included in the original company agreement. 'Woolnorth' has its own oyster beds, and good fishing for flounder, salmon, trumpeter, perch, parrot fish and abalone.

The tour continues with a twenty-minute walk to 'Woolnorth' Point and a hayride back.

It's all a far cry from the first visitors in the 1950s who were brought in by the manager to shoot wildlife in return for a bottle of whisky.

The original buildings were pointed out—the oldest are the mason's and the cookhouse cottages and the gaol (now a radio–telephone exchange), built from 1830 to 1840.

Most tourists take advantage of the chance to acquire a souvenir or two at the craft shop.

During my visit I lunched with Sue, Linda and Ken in the dining room of the attractive homestead which was built by a bachelor manager. Sue has restored the beautiful George III furniture which was bought second hand during the reign of George IV when the company was set up. She intends to house some of the archives in the restored Georgian bookcase. The gun on the wall which originally hung in the office came from Queen Victoria's armoury in the Tower of London.

An astonishing five tonnes of archival material on 'Woolnorth' are housed in the Archives in Hobart. Only one book has ever been written on 'Woolnorth' and that only covers the period from 1825 to 1840.

But 'Woolnorth' today is not just an historical treasure.

It's a working cattle and sheep station, the oldest Hereford stud in Australia. The property runs 3500 Hereford cattle and 14,000 Cormo (Corriedale–Merino cross) sheep. The estate's population of twenty-five consists of eleven permanent employees, six women, and eight children who go to school in their own school bus subsidized by the Government.

Sue says: 'We're only a shadow of the powerful company which originally asked for a million acres and ended up with 300,000 acres. The company should be one of the richest, but they sold land blocks over the years and we have to make do with what's left. Beef prices have fallen and the high upkeep of the property means a struggle.'

Despite this, 'Woolnorth' is a public company listed on the London Stock Exchange and nowadays has a number of European shareholders including an Italian count.

So, if you should visit 'Woolnorth' and the chef turning the barbecue steak turns out to be a charming man with an Italian accent, don't be surprised. The count apparently likes nothing better on his visits than doing a spot of cooking for tourists.

CAIRNS—
QUEENSLAND'S FAR NORTH

WHERE else but Cairns would you find the remains of a 'Noah's Ark' built by a Canadian in expectation of the end of the world?

Or a springtime Orange Blossom Ball held among the orange blossoms of an orchard? Or a paddlewheel steamer cruising Australia's 'Little Florida' mangrove swamps? Or a mosque built by Albanian tobacco farmers?

The Far North of Queensland is packed with more surprises than you are likely to find in years of travel. The climate is so delightful, the way of life so friendly, peaceful and relaxed that a tourist is tempted to join the ranks of former doctors, lawyers and accountants who have thrown up frenetic city life and 'gone troppo' up north as skippers and deck hands, scuba instructors and motel managers.

As you explore the area, you find artists, potters and sculptors who have also 'dropped out' to live in communities in rainforest, island or isolated inlet.

A simple tourist like me tries to pack in as many fascinating scenic attractions as possible, while finding time to beachcomb on white sand beaches fringed with palms—even do a spot of fishing.

Island buffs come because Cairns is the gateway to the many beautiful islands of the Great Barrier Reef. Millionaires come for the marlin fishing—Lee Marvin, the American actor, for instance, comes most years for the season. The Cairns marina is crowded from September to December with luxury boats while owners—deep sea fishermen—boast of their battles with giant marlin in the Game Fishing Club.

Despite its modern shopping centre and first-class hotels, Cairns still has a sleepy, old-fashioned air, very beguiling to southerners like me. Wooden houses with corrugated roofs are perched on stilts like cranes. The wide streets are lined with flowering trees—orange, apricot, pink, purple, red bougainvillea; pink and cream frangipani, flaming red hibiscus, orange poinciana, pink cassia, and yellow cascara trees cloudy with 'golden rain'.

You can see Cairns in a day but it takes at least a week or two to explore all the surrounding attractions.

I used to love strolling along the park esplanade where what was once beach is now mud flats due to forest logging. It's a great place for viewing bird life, including pretty lorikeets and pelicans. On the Esplanade, past the jetties, you find Reef World, an aquarium. Launches to Green and Fitzroy islands leave from the jetties. So do reef-fishing and diving trips and the showboat paddlewheeler which does the Everglades cruises.

Cairns has many other attractions for tourists—Laroc, a factory producing coral jewellery, which shows visitors an audio-visual story of the Great Barrier Reef, the Flying Doctor Service, the School of the Air at Edge Hill (which radios lessons to kids in the outback), The Waterworks with its tunnels of water, the Botanic Gardens, and a little museum in the shopping centre.

Cairns, on Trinity Bay (named by Captain Cook in 1770), was established as a port of entry for customs purposes in October 1876, after gold was found on the Hodgkinson River and there was a rush of prospectors from the Palmer goldfields.

Cooktown, the port for the Palmer, was a long way from the Hodgkinson area so, in July 1876, miners sent out a party to cut a track from the mining town of Thornborough on the Hodgkinson, to Trinity Inlet. They got as far as the top of the range overlooking Trinity Inlet when illness forced them back.

They returned in September via Cooktown this time, and journeyed on to Trinity Inlet by boat, cutting the rest of the track inland from the coast. The mining field, after a brief period of prosperity, faded out but Cairns grew and prospered over the years.

It used to have a colourful area known as the Barbary Coast, but most of the old hotels have disappeared.

Like most tourists, I took the hour-long rail trip to Kuranda, possibly the prettiest railway station in Australia. The scenic little steam train, with its polished wooden carriages and red seats, chugged up the steep thirty-four kilometres of line between Cairns and Kuranda, providing stunning views across Freshwater Valley to the canefields of Mt Whitfield and the Coral Sea and Green Island.

The rail line was hacked with pick and shovel through virgin jungle, bridging deep gorges. It took four years to build. Fifteen tunnels had to be cut through the rocky mountains. It was finished in 1888. The journey is slow enough to allow passengers time to admire wildflowers and ferns—even to pick them if this was allowed.

We passed pretty Stony Creek waterfall, then stopped at Barron Falls, a magnificent sheet of water which plummeted into the gorge, so that passengers could take photographs. We also stopped at Jungara, the site of a large military hospital during the Second World War.

The rail journey ends at Kuranda station with its hanging baskets and banked potplants of ferns, staghorns, orchids, and other tropical plants and shrubs.

At Kuranda you can visit the Honey House and sample Queensland honeys and on Sunday mornings an open-air arts and crafts market is held.

Some people do the train trip independently and return by the same train but others, like me, combine it with a coach tour of the fertile Atherton Tableland, with its crops of maize and peanuts, dairy farms with red volcanic soil, rice growing and timber mills.

We passed through Mareeba with its Albanian mosque, a centre of tobacco growing, and through Tolga to Tinaroo Dam, with its Barron Gorge Hydro-Electric Station. You can fish, swim, boat, or water ski here. The scenic lookout provides a perfect spot for a picnic lunch.

Inside the beautiful tropical rainforest of Lake Eacham National Park is a jade green crater lake, Lake Eacham, with a lovely walk around its shores. You can fish, feed the tortoises, watch blue birds flitting through the bush.

In the rainforest you can sometimes catch a glimpse of white-tailed rats, tree-climbing kangaroos, possums, black dingoes, wallabies, tiny rat kangaroos, lyrebirds, scrub hens, and cassowaries, which look pretty with their blue and black plumage, but can kill. They sprint at forty kilometres an hour through the forest and can outrun the fastest runner. Many early settlers met their deaths this way.

Lake Barrine, the twin-crater lake, has 800-year-old giant kauri trees growing near by. You can take a four kilometre cruise on the lake exploring hidden bays, and having a close-up view of rainforest with glimpses of tortoises, herons, platypus, eels, bush turkeys and perhaps an amethyst python. You can take a ten-minute walk in the rainforest or a six kilometre walk around the lake foreshores, watching out for leeches.

Many returned servicemen will remember doing their jungle training in Atherton and going on dates with nurses at the hospital there.

We stopped to view a curtin fig tree, over 1000 years old, within a 5000-year-old rainforest.

We returned to Cairns via the Gillies Highway, the 'Alpine Way of the Tropics', with spectacular views over three valleys and mountains. The highway descends through tropical rainforest, drops 927 metres to sea level within fifteen kilometres of curving mountain road with 245 dizzy bends.

In the old days Goldsborough Valley had gold diggings. Nowadays there are cane farms on the Mulgrave River.

It is nearly dusk and blue mist wreathes the towering mountain ranges and the river is a smudgy brown ribbon in the emerald green valley.

We passed Walsh's Pyramid, the tallest single mountain in Australia, the village of Gordon Vale, which holds races up its 914 metre high hill for charity (the record is an hour and thirteen minutes).

From the Gillies Highway we rejoined the Bruce Highway and returned to Cairns.

The fifteen tonne paddlewheel steamer, *Louisa*, takes tourists on a smooth water cruise of the Cairns Everglades. It is thought to be one of the first vessels to have arrived in Cairns. It was owned by William Ingham who, in August 1875 (two months before the Port of Cairns was declared) left his unsuccessful sugar venture on the Herbert, and took his wife and two-year-old child in the erratic paddlewheeler to Cairns.

The swashbuckling Ingham did a lot of exploring around the district, but eventually settled down to run a regular boat service between Cairns and Smithfield. He established the first sawmill in the district using a boiler he towed behind the *Louisa* from his sugar plantation, to power the steam-driven cutting saws.

The *Louisa* sank in Trinity Inlet during the terrible cyclone of 1878, but Ingham refloated the vessel and went back in to business.

The enterprising Ingham then went into the bêche-de-mer trade, but still had itchy feet. He decided to sail the *Louisa* to New Guinea, where he was given a government position. It was to prove a tragic decision.

In December 1878, while on patrol in the Louisiade Archipelago, his native crew threw him overboard. He swam back to the *Louisa*, laughing at their high spirits. But laughter turned to cries of terror, as they chopped off his hands as he tried to climb aboard, then jumped into the sea and dragged him into the boat to be eaten.

The cruise explores Trinity Inlet, named by Captain Cook, who explored the bay by ship's boat on Trinity Sunday. It passes Admiralty Island and then, if the tide is high, steams up Wright's Creek, where an ark built of mangrove logs is beached on a bank. It took an eccentric Canadian named Moody five years to build the ark and he died before it could be launched.

You can sometimes glimpse crocodiles sunning on the mud

flats at low tide, and water fowl, pelicans and night herons, blue cranes, white egrets and giant see eagles.

Green Island, a marine national park twenty-six kilometres north-east of Cairns, is a popular spot for a day tour. Cruises leave Cairns jetty in the morning and return in the afternoon. The island has an underwater observatory where visitors can see beautiful coral gardens with giant clams, anemones, rainbow-coloured reef fish. There is also a marineland Melanesia, with grotto pools, an aquarium and a collection of primitive Papua Nuiginian art.

Other attractions are coral viewing in glass-bottomed boats, walks in the rainforest, reefing at low tide, swimming and snorkelling. There is hotel accommodation on the island.

Green Island has an interesting history. It was named by Captain Cook, whose ship the *Endeavour* ran aground on the reef at the present site of Cooktown, during his voyage of exploration in 1770 to observe the transit of Venus from Tahiti. His journal records a 'low green woody island'—but he actually named it after Charles Green, chief observer and astronomer in charge of the *Endeavour*.

Early in the 1870s Green Island became the headquarters of bêche-de-mer fishermen who used Aboriginal help in gathering and drying the slugs. On two occasions they turned on their white masters and slaughtered them. At least seven white men and a Malay were massacred in the 1870s.

In the 1880s a colourful adventurer, 'One Arm Yorkey', otherwise known as George (Yorkey) Lawson, a bêche-de-mer fisherman, came to the island with his Jamaican companion, known as John the Baptist. After a lifetime of adventuring throughout the Pacific, Yorkey died peacefully on Green Island aged sixty eight.

Organized pleasure cruises to Green Island began in 1890 on the local coaster, the *Zeus*. A regular transport service was started in 1928 by Charlie Hayles and his son, Blake Hayles, still operates it.

Fitzroy Island is another popular spot. It was charted over 200 years ago by Captain Cook and given the family name of the Duke of Grafton, first Lord of the Treasury and acting premier of England when Cook began his voyage in 1768.

Since then it has been a navigation aid, refuge, watering hole, bêche-de-mer station, temporary courthouse, quarantine station, Aboriginal feasting ground, mission and offshore picnic spot.

After Captain Phillip Parker King, on a survey of the east coast in the early 1800s, declared it a safe anchorage with plenty of water and wood, it became the main stopping place for ships travelling north to Cape York.

Later, coconut, banana, pawpaw and rubber plantations were established and, during the early 1900s, an Aboriginal mission. In 1943 the lighthouse was erected to guide allied shipping through Australian minefields during the Second World War.

Today its beautiful beaches, cool green rainforest with orchids and ferns, butterflies and birds, attract visitors. They can scuba dive, para-sail, fish, windsurf, swim, walk to the lighthouse, view coral, enjoy beach barbecues.

A Sydney double-decker Atlantean bus, with destination 'Randwick', was the unusual conveyance which took me the sixty-seven kilometres to Port Douglas, to join a cruise to the Low Isles on the *Martin Cash* (named after a Tasmanian bushranger). The top deck of the bus gives tourists a wonderful bird's-eye view of the magnificent coastline, even if the ride is a bit rocky.

The small hamlet of Port Douglas is renowned for good restaurants, and celebrities. Home owners include singer Peter Allen, and actress Diane Cilento. There are panoramic views of Four Mile Beach from Flagstaff Hill (formerly Island Point). Down on the jetty, Ben Cropp's Shipwreck Museum displays its treasure trove—'pieces of eight' found in Australia and the West Indies during pirate times, and reconstructed historic ships and their cargoes.

Port Douglas has only two hotels now but in the 1873 gold rush heyday there were about twenty. The port was named after John Douglas, then premier of Queensland.

In the late nineteenth century, Port Douglas was the port for the Palmer goldfields. Coastal boats and Cobb & Co. coaches ran cargo and passenger services to the town.

The streets were busy with horse and bullock teams. After the sugar industry began in the Mossman area about 1900, a tramway was built from Port Douglas to Mossman. The port then had a school, hotel and two each of churches, banks, bakeries, butchers' shops, saddlers and blacksmiths, as well as ten stores, three carpenters and a cabinet maker. A joss house and fourteen licensed premises were well patronized.

It is hard to imagine such a bustling town when you look at the sleepy hamlet today. In 1904 the main street had shady verandas on each side, but the road was so muddy that long-skirted ladies paid twopence to enterprising lads to carry them across in sedan chairs.

In 1911 a cyclone destroyed most of the town.

The Cook Highway came through to Cairns in 1935 and in 1958 the last boatload of sugar left the wharf. Port Douglas had long been superseded by Cairns.

The *Martin Cash* leaves from Princes Wharf for the hour trip to the Low Isles. It was originally built for ferry service when the Derwent Bridge in Tasmania collapsed, to ferry people across the Derwent. It was sold, after the service was discontinued, to skipper and present owner, Jim Wallace, who left the rat race in Sydney to start a tourist service to the Low Isles.

It is a relaxed one-hour trip to the larger of the two islands, which has a lighthouse, but no inhabitants apart from the lighthouse keeper's family. We swam, snorkelled and viewed the coral in a glass-bottomed boat.

Another popular tour combines a visit to Mossman, the sugar town, with Port Douglas and visits to the Australian Bird Park and Hartleys Creek Wildlife Reserve and Crocodile Farm. It passes a monument to the teamsters who, in the late nineteenth century, drove their horses, mules and bullocks through the Great Dividing Range along the Old Bump Road—so named because the road was so bad that wagons had to go up in convoys so that teams could be unhooked and harnessed to each wagon in turn to help it up the steep grades.

Mossman has quaint old wooden buildings, mango trees and a little train which takes tourists on tours of the canefields and towering sugar mill.

Picturesque St David's Anglican Church was first dedicated in 1899 when the district was part of a vast diocese which stretched to Carpentaria, the Northern Territory and the islands within Torres Strait.

On our return journey to Cairns, we called at the crocodile farm where Garry Zillfleisch, the owner, gave an entertaining, but terrifying, performance hand-feeding his crocodiles. We weren't sure whether the crocs' sudden rushes at Garry were part of the act, or whether this time Garry would meet his Waterloo.

The pioneers may have had it tough opening up the Far North, but the modern tourist is reaping a lot of enjoyment from their efforts.

PEOPLE

AGGIE GREY— JAMES MICHENER'S 'BLOODY MARY' OF THE SOUTH PACIFIC

WITH a red hibiscus flower tucked behind her ear, Aggie Grey danced to the island music, her hips—and handbag—swinging wildly.

'Faster! Faster!' she called to the band, her red seed necklaces whirling, as the audience went wild, whistling and yelling for more.

That was in 1936. Aggie was on board the liner *Oronsay* bound for a holiday in the United States. Someone in the ship's audience murmured: 'There goes Bloody Mary of the South Pacific.'

Now in her eighties, Aggie Grey still dances on special occasions with a red hibiscus tucked behind one ear. The audience at Aggie's Hotel in Apia, Western Samoa, still go wild.

Aggie is probably the best-known character in the South Pacific. She has even had a stamp issued bearing her portrait. She's had Pope Paul IV around for breakfast, partied with author James Michener, and hobnobbed with stars like Gary

A farmer and his wife, belongings piled on a wooden ox cart, take a rest in a beautiful valley in Central Turkey. Wooden carts are still the main means of transport in remote areas.

These old men of the Bontoc tribe having a gossip may look as if butter wouldn't melt in their mouths, but they may be reminiscing about the head hunting exploits of their youth in the Northern Philippines.

The 'Island of the Saints', the tranquil Greek island of Patmos, with its white cubist houses, terraced slopes and charming harbour, seems an odd place for St John the Evangelist's horrific vision of the Apocalypse.

The street musicians of Katmandu make a living by entertaining passers-by with their plaintive songs accompanied on wooden violins, with rhythms marked by finger clicking.

Cooper and Marlon Brando, and anthropologist Margaret Mead. Three-star generals from the United States have stayed at 'Aggie's'.

I wanted to talk to Aggie about the 'Bloody Mary' legend while I stayed at her hotel. (In his *Tales of the South Pacific*, which became the smash hit musical (and film) *South Pacific*, Michener supposedly based his character on Aggie.) I was told: 'You don't interview Aggie Grey, you request an audience.' Aggie, it seemed, was a national attraction like the Tower of London, or one of Japan's 'Living Treasure' artists.

I first caught sight of Aggie at a *fia fia* or night of festivities held regularly at her hotel. The hotel's servants, a flock of young boys and girls, were on stage in the *fale* native hut, set in the hotel's tropical gardens.

They gracefully danced, singing the songs of Western Samoa. Aggie's pretty grand-daughter danced, but Aggie stole the show, abandoning herself to the music.

Later, she sat majestically in a high-backed 'throne' surrounded by relatives and courtiers. It was then that I requested an 'audience'. I finally managed to meet her and found her to be a very down-to-earth woman with a delicious sense of humour and twinkling blue eyes.

'Ah, that Bloody Mary legend,' she sighed. 'No, I don't believe I am the original of Bloody Mary. It all happened because of a disagreement with an American author called Willard Price.

'He came here to write about the islands and wanted to stay at the hotel, but he wanted special treatment—a separate little house away from the other guests, so he would not have to eat with them. I told him I didn't have enough room. He was very angry.

'Later he wrote a book, *Adventures in Paradise*. He wrote that, "as for Aggie Grey, hotel manager of Apia, Western Samoa, she would make a good prototype for Bloody Mary". But the legend grew. There was that incident on board the *Oronsay*.' Aggie's eyes sparkled.

'It was the ship's gala night with 1200 at the party. We paraded, and the band played the Fijian song 'Isa Lei' as I came on. I was dressed in tapa cloth.

'And I danced, and the crowd went wild and yelled like lunatics. That night I danced till dawn then ate steak and eggs for breakfast. The next morning the steward knocked and said: "Your tea, lady."

'He kept fiddling around opening the porthole and I knew he wanted to say something. Finally, he asked: "Mrs Aggie Grey ... aren't you Bloody Mary of the South Pacific?"

'I said: "Not as far as I know."

'He said: "But everyone is saying you are—it's in a book in the ship's library and people are queueing up to read it."

'I asked to see it and it was *Adventures in Paradise*. By the time the ship arrived in Vancouver, newspaper headlines were screaming, "Bloody Mary is here".'

But the more famous literary Bloody Mary was of course the wily Tonkinese lady in Michener's *Tales of the South Pacific* which later became the musical (and movie) *South Pacific*.

And Michener certainly knew Aggie well. During the Second World War he served in the Pacific as a correspondent and many were the uproarious nights he and his cronies spent at 'Aggie's', then a nightclub. It later became the first hotel of substance in Apia.

Michener would send a message ordering 'steak, eggs and dancing for sixteen'. Aggie would rustle up the Samoan ladies. The Americans would bring the whiskey—alcohol was scarce during the war—and the party would continue until dawn.

'Michener never danced,' Aggie recalled. 'He just sat watching everyone. He was the one who christened my place 'Aggie's' and the name stuck.'

'Aggie's' became one of the best-loved spots in the South Pacific for homesick American servicemen. Twelve thousand of them were stationed in Western Samoa.

Did she ever ask Michener if she was Bloody Mary?

'Yes, but he was very non-committal. After all, the character was Tonkinese. He said that if I was, it was only the nice part of the character. I was unhappy about being called "Bloody Mary", but my children thought it was very funny.

'I was born Agnes Genevieve Swann, and father nicknamed me Aggie. He was a very stern Englishman from Surrey and never spared the rod, but it made us better children.'

Aggie married Gordon Hay-McKenzie, the manager of the Union Steamship Company, after the First World War. The shipping agency was taken away from a German firm when

Germany lost the war and their colony of Western Samoa.

Her husband died, leaving her with four children and not much money. She started a nightclub, the Metropolitan, in the 1930s. After five years of widowhood she married again, one Charles Morton Grey. He too died, leaving her with another three children, and nothing in the bank.

'I had to support the children, so I started another club,' Aggie said.

And that's how Aggie became famous. The American servicemen poured in and her fame spread. After the Second World War, Aggie decided to enlarge the club and turn it into a hotel.

'Friends said I was mad, there weren't many tourists, but I was looking ahead.'

For her contribution to tourism, Aggie had a stamp issued in her honour. Gary Cooper stayed at 'Aggie's' while on location for the film *Return to Paradise*. Marlon Brando loved 'Aggie's'.

'The stamp was a surprise,' Aggie said.

'I was in bed with the flu and my son Alan came in to my room and said: "Would you sign these papers please mother?"

'They were 200 first-day covers with my picture and people had sent them in for my signature. Alan asked: "Aren't you lucky to have your own first-day cover stamp?" '

When Pope Paul IV visited Apia, Aggie received a message to come and cook breakfast for him at the presbytery. She and her daughter-in-law, Marina, rose to the occasion.

Today Aggie has handed over the hotel's reins to her son, Alan. But she still takes a vital interest and can be found morning and evening sitting in the garden.

The hotel is run boarding-house style. Huge tables groaned with food served by twelve boys. The three meals a day are gargantuan and there is also afternoon tea.

At 'Aggie's' you were welcomed with flowers. The gardens, alive with birds, were filled with flaming hibiscus, pink frangipani, red ginger and autumn-toned crotons. The rooms were decked with hibiscus and frangipani strung on spikes. A fresh bunch of bananas was hung in the garden each day in case guests got peckish.

The gardens, as lush as a Gauguin painting, sported wooden

statues of gods, a huge swimming pool and a vast hut for entertainment. Free movies, lavish feasts, barbecues, dancing and singing were held there.

The walls of the open-air bar were studded with shells and the rooms strung along the perimeter of the gardens were equipped with home comforts like ironing boards and irons, refrigerators and air-conditioning. The rooms were homely but comfortable and completely unlike those of the big international hotels.

Aggie's fruit and vegetables were grown in her gardens high in rainforests of the island's interior. A typical meal might consist of prawns in tomato sauce, fruit juice, curried meat, prawn casserole, salmon–cheese casserole, steak and vegetables, rice pudding, pineapple cake and coffee.

On Friday, 31 October 1975, Aggie celebrated her seventy-eighth birthday with a 300-guest feast. The party was as lavish as ever and Aggie danced as though her years had not in the slightest way dampened her enthusiasm for life.

'I don't mind getting old,' she said, 'as long as I can still remember all the good times and my feet don't grow too tired for dancing.'

Today (1986) Aggie is still alive at eighty-eight, and, from reports, still dances occasionally. I treasure a letter she wrote me after I sent her a copy of my interview (published in the *Australian Women's Weekly*), in which she said it was the only truthful account of how she became 'Bloody Mary'.

MOTHER TERESA—
THE WORLD'S BEST KNOWN NUN

THERE'S only one nun in the world who has been given the title 'Padma Shri' by the prime minister of a nation, and received the Nobel Peace Prize.

Her name is Mother Teresa, a woman of great simplicity and humility who has become world famous for her work among the poor, the starving, the dying—first in India, then in Tanzania, West Africa, Brazil, Venezuela, Amman, Sri Lanka, Italy and Australia.

In Australia her order works in Melbourne and among the Aborigines in Bourke.

Indira Gandhi gave her one of India's greatest honours, the title of 'Padma Shri' (Lord of the Lotus). She won the first Pope John XXIII Peace Prize. Pope Paul VI gave her a car he used during his visit to India. She raffled it to raise $60,000 to set up 'Shanti Nagar' (Town of Peace), where 400 leper families live.

That guru of the West, Malcolm Muggeridge, journeyed to India to make a television documentary on her work, shown in Australia and England under the title 'Something Beautiful for God'. Several books have been written about her.

There's an old song called 'Love Is My Reason for Living'. It could well be Mother Teresa's motto.

I met her on a visit to India, before she had become quite as famous as she is today. I was lucky to catch her at the orphanage she set up in Delhi. She is often in Calcutta, or overseas visiting one of the charitable institutions run by the religious order she founded. With her very busy life, she was only able to see me at 7.30 a.m. for an hour.

A small, gentle woman dressed in a plain white cotton sari with a blue border, a small crucifix on the shoulder, what struck me most was the warmth of her smile, her air of serenity and the most vivid blue eyes I'd ever seen. She had an aura of palpable goodness which you find in people who have become totally absorbed in caring for others.

How did she feel about her award from Mrs Gandhi?

'It's a wonderful thing—a title given to people who have done something special for the people of India. Being a Catholic and a missionary in India, I realized the Government appreciated our work very much.'

Are all the legends about her true?

Like the story of how she found a leg sticking out of a garbage can in the slums of Calcutta and on further investigation found a dying woman. She carried her to a hospital. When refused admission because it was overcrowded and the woman was obviously beyond help, Mother Teresa sat down and refused to budge until they admitted her.

Or the story of how she took over a pilgrims' hostel in the Temple of Kali, Goddess of Destruction and Patroness of Calcutta, for the sick and dying she collected from the streets. The legend goes that she was threatened with death by some Hindu fanatics who said they would return to kill her the following day, if she was still there.

She replied: 'If you are going to kill me, why not now?'

But one of their own priests lay dying, unable to find a bed in the crowded hospitals. Mother Teresa took him in and the opposition vanished.

When I reminded her of the stories I'd heard, she just smiled gently and said: 'That's all a long time ago.'

Born Agnes Gonxha Bojaxhiu in Albania in 1910, Mother Teresa grew up in Skopje, now in Yugoslavia, became a Loreto nun and arrived in Calcutta at the age of eighteen to teach in a Catholic school run by the order, St Mary's High School for Girls. Immediately behind the high walls were the slums of Moti Jheel.

In 1946, appalled at the poverty, disease and the dying crowding the streets of Calcutta, she sought permission to leave her convent to live and work in the nightmare world of the Calcutta slums.

In 1948 approval came from Rome. She put aside her Loreto habit to adopt the simple white sari and went to Patna to study the diagnosis and treatment of the sick with the Medical Missionary Sisters there. She set up a religious order, the Missionaries of Charity, in 1950, when she was forty. It now has at least 240 convents in sixty-three countries.

Her first efforts were in Calcutta. Determined that human beings would not die alone on the streets but in peace and with human dignity, she set up the first Home for Dying Destitutes in the Kali Temple in the Kalighat district in 1952. 'My main aim is to feed the hungry, clothe the naked and give shelter to the homeless, in whom I see Christ,' she said.

Thousands of her slum children are sponsored for their education by families in India and abroad, including Australia.

At the time of my interview, 1970, local Indians supported 35,000 lepers and the 150 to 170 people who at any given time occupied beds in the Calcutta Home for Dying Destitutes.

Calcutta has a reputation for fear and violence. Its slums are among the worst in the world. Of its population of over six million in 1970, one-third were refugees.

Mother Teresa worked in the very worst areas without fear.

'We have never been attacked or stopped from doing anything. People no longer die on the streets of Calcutta. Now
the public are more conscious that refugees may be sick and
have nowhere to go. They take them to hospitals or bring
them to us.

'The problems are tremendous. Accommodation is scarce
and there are not enough jobs to go around.'

It was once said of Calcutta that municipal authorities drove
through the streets each morning to collect the bodies of
those left after the street sleepers had risen. The remainder
were those who had died during the night.

With so much suffering around her, wasn't it a temptation
to succumb to despair, to feel that the efforts of a few indi-
viduals were lost in the sea of misery?

Mother Teresa said: 'I have no reason to despair. I can
only do what God wants me to do and no more. Others may
look at the big numbers. I look at only one person at a time.
I can give that person as much love and care as I can. If
I look at the thousands, I know I can do nothing. If I can
help one soul to die like a human being, it is all worth while.'

Mother Teresa made little of her early difficulties: 'After
all, I had been in India a long time and I knew the people.
It was not so difficult to get started. Divine Providence is
much greater than our little minds realize and will never
let us down.

'Money comes in somehow. We started building a Town
of Peace for leper families near Calcutta with the money
brought in by raffling the Pope's car.'

Once, she walked the streets of Calcutta slums looking for
a home. When I met her, there were fifty-nine centres in
Calcutta alone. There were dispensaries, mobile clinics,
schools, feeding stations, shelters for the homeless, homes
for the dying, and for unwanted children, cripples and lepers,
both in India and abroad.

There are now thousands of nuns, Indian and foreign, in
convents founded by her order throughout the world (including
one in Melbourne and one in Bourke, New South Wales).

In 1963 the Missionary Brothers of Charity was founded,
providing religious brothers to carry on her work.

Her motto is, 'Let the people eat you up.'

In Delhi there is a shelter for the homeless at the Kashmiri

Gate and a mobile leprosy clinic stationed near Delhi's top tourist attraction, the Red Fort. Then there is the Home for Children at which our interview was conducted.

From abroad comes help in the form of clothing, medicines, money and sponsorship for education of her children. Many children have been adopted into families in India, Europe and Canada. Many overseas volunteers, including Australians, work with her nuns.

'Our work is for everyone—we help them make peace with God. When there's a death, the Hindus take the dead Hindu, the Muhammadans the dead Muhammadan.

'I see great hope for India. It has a special contribution to give the world. People here have not become engrossed in the material. India is not a poor country, it is rich in natural resources.

'If we could learn how to use them, India would be able to feed other countries. At present we can't help much, but in the years to come India will,' she said with conviction.

'Even a tragedy like the Bihar famine had its good side. People came and dug wells everywhere and the difficulty was solved. Now there'll never be famine there again. The Government is planning and trying to get things done.'

Indians are very hospitable people, she said.

'When you ask help of people who have not much themselves, they give you so much more. They know what it is to do without. Pandit Nehru's teaching was to receive a guest with love and kindness.

'So many people in the world are sharing in our work. They realize that God is putting his love into action by using simple means like our Sisters.

'The only hope of the world is through love. People are realizing more and more that God is close to them. That's why they do works of love.'

Mother Teresa found time to take me to meet the well-cared-for babies and young children in the neat but sparse nurseries and playrooms. She would pick up a screaming baby and calm its cries within seconds. Children are starved for affection and cuddling, she said. What they need above food, clothing and shelter is love.

Love fuels the spirit of this saint of the slums.

AUSTRALIAN PAINTER — DONALD FRIEND ON BALI

ON a moonlit tropical night in Bali, crowds of coffee-skinned children crowded around an open-air theatre roaring with laughter at the antics of rustic peasants, a grotesque monster and an enormous frog.

I watched the frog come into the audience, making froggy noises, his huge protuberant eyes searching out the faces, while the flutes accompanying his dance grew louder and more exciting. He stopped in front of the round-faced man with slighty protuberant eyes framed in black-rimmed glasses, seated at the table next to mine.

Slowly the man rose and began to imitate the frog, his hands moving slowly to the music, head nodding and eyes taking on the thrusting look of the animal. As he finally sank back laughing, the crowd applauded his performance.

The face looked familiar. I searched my memory and up floated a name to match the face. Donald Friend, one of Australia's most famous painters.

After such an interesting encounter, I determined to meet and interview him. Enquiries revealed that he was in Brittany painting but expected back soon. I decided to call at his home in a rather isolated part of the island and leave a message requesting him to contact me on his return.

I went there by sea in a fisherman's sailing boat.

A heavy swell drenched me and I emerged dripping wet, barefoot and dishevelled onto the beach, ignoring a sign that only invited guests were welcome. Through the beautifully carved stone gateway I entered a paradise-like garden lush with green foliage and guarded by stone Balinese gods.

Instead of the servant I had expected to meet and take my note, there was the painter, huddled in a blanket, reclining on a cane lounge on the veranda. Accepting the fact of a totally unknown visitor, he explained that he had returned a little earlier than expected.

'Call back on Sunday at five,' the hospitable painter invited. Apart from the sea route which I did not fancy trying again, the only access to his home was by appallingly rutted roads.

I ordered a bemo, a small taxi-truck seating six. It did not arrive, though a young Balinese lad on a bicycle did. Not being dressed for riding a pushbike, I walked with him to the nearest village where, he said, the bemo would be waiting.

There was no sign of it. It had gone to the town of Den Pasar, some eight kilometres away, and there was no other bemo in the village.

It was now 5.15 p.m. and I saw my interesting interview with Donald Friend evaporating. But, just when the situation grew critical, along came a Balinese boy on a motor bike. My young guide hailed him joyfully, took over the bike and, with me riding pillion, went racing and bumping along the dirt track while trees streamed past, the setting sun whirled and sank and I clung on frantically.

At last a white sign pointed down a side lane. It bore the legend 'Mr Donald Friend'. The Balinese never call him anything but the full 'Mr Donald Friend', pronounced in a slightly sing-song voice.

We came to a thatch-roofed Indonesian-style house set in a beautiful garden, facing the reef-bound sea. Like all Balinese gardens, it had its stone gods, mysterious statues with offerings of flowers and fruit set before them and huge red hibiscus tucked behind their ears.

A small boy of about eight years, dressed in red shirt and bright yellow sarong, with a small gold, red and yellow cap perched on his head and yellow frangipani tucked behind his ears, appeared to conduct me to the house.

The side facing the sea had no walls, it was just a huge roofed veranda, living room downstairs, bedroom and studio on a platform upstairs.

Donald Friend rose to greet me. He wore a comfortable, faded sarong and pale blue T-shirt. He lived like a prince. Six or so small Balinese boys whom he called 'the children' waited on him like the page boys of medieval times. He was surrounded by hundreds of beautiful art objects, some very ancient: stone statues of gods, carved mythical creatures and animals were ranked around the room.

Each statue had been gaily dressed by the boys with red hibiscus and yellow frangipani tucked behind ears and placed on tops of heads.

The gods of Bali are considered people and always wear

flowers. On festivals they are decked in gala clothes, usually black and white checked sarongs. Often ceremonial brocade umbrellas shade them.

Donald Friend was very aware of living in the world of spirits that is Bali.

'Some objects, very ancient and venerated through time, take on a "magical" quality derived from age and the emotions of people who have held them in reverence,' he explained.

Pointing to the exotic statues of birds, animals and gods, he commented: 'They are part of my living room and, as such, lose much of their "power" but, if you take just one statue and put it by itself in an art gallery, it would have a strange and powerful "presence".'

While I inspected a lovely statue of a girl riding a goose, Donald Friend spoke in Balinese to one of the boys who disappeared briefly, reappearing with a *kris*, a Balinese sword.

Incredibly beautiful, the blade was intricately carved, hammered out from a sheet of iron interlaid with meteorite. The handle was a carved ivory 'guardian' of the *kris*, a primitive, fierce-looking creature, god or man I knew not. It had something of the same quality as the terrifying creatures carved on the prow of Viking ships.

It was twelfth century and was owned by one of the first two rajas appointed to rule Bali after its conquest by Hindu rulers. The kris belonging to the other raja was acquired by a Dutchman and Donald did not know where it was.

Donald showed me another seventh-century *kris* which had baroque style jewels studding the 'guardian'.

While I inspected precious books, a *kris* or a statue, the little bank of Balinese boys, a work of art in themselves, sat chattering quietly in the corner. But, at a look from Donald, they came forward to replenish our glasses of vodka, lime and ice or fetched a proud possession for my admiring gaze.

One small boy had asked for a day off. He wanted to dedicate his school books to the goddess of wisdom on Saraswati Day, her feast day. On this holy day nobody was allowed to read or write. Holy books and literature were honoured and offerings of fruit and flowers made to the *lontars* (holy books).

Donald showed me a glass case of archeological finds from Central Java which stood near a beautiful wall screen composed of dozens of linked, ornately carved wooden temple hangings.

Another wall was papered with faded woven material painted with figures of Hindu mythology illustrating the Hindu calendar. The house was crowded with books, art objects, flowers, simple cane furniture. Upstairs lay an unfinished painting of village dogs. He was also writing the text for a book of reproductions of his paintings.

He was an excellent writer and had quite a few books published. I felt bound to ask about his next literary project: 'Are you going to do a Somerset Maugham and reveal the scandals of the island?'

'Not on your life. I live here,' he said with feeling. It was a book about war and peace set in a South East Asian country which could be somewhere around Vietnam.

He demonstrated his wonderful skill as a raconteur, with fascinating stories of Balinese life.

One anecdote concerned the Bali Beach Hotel, a huge luxury resort, set down on a Balinese beach (Sanur). He said it was a different world to the Balinese.

He had been thinking of taking a break from work, perhaps a holiday overseas, when he heard of a competition to name the romantic little rotunda built at the end of the pier by the Bali Beach Hotel. The prize was a free weekend at the hotel, as good a break as a trip, since it was literally another world set down in Bali. He entered the competition, naming the rotunda with an Indonesian name which meant a combination of moonlight and sea, and won hands down.

He duly set out for the hotel with eight small Balinese page boys in attendance. Balinese children have the aplomb of adults and are not easily confused. But the page boys were entering another world. Electronic doors flew open as they approached. The lift made one small boy seasick and the final wonder was Mr Friend picking up the telephone and shortly afterwards huge dishes of icecream appearing! This was indeed 'magic'. His prestige with his staff had never been so high!

I asked how he managed to acquire so many exquisite Balinese works of art.

'I see some in the small villages. People know what I like and village women often bring me pieces, although it is sometimes rather annoying when they crowd around selling things when I'm trying to paint.'

The disturbance is nothing to that created by visitors. He

had become something of a tourist sight and many tourists wandered into his garden, thinking he had a gallery, hence the notice beside the stone gateway from the beach.

'I like visitors, but not the casual dropper-in,' he explained, showing his visitors' book which had names from all over the world, among the last, one from Covent Garden Opera House.

I had heard it said if he liked a visitor, he would talk for hours. If not, he managed to disappear promptly.

We talked on many subjects—Aldous Huxley's books with their ideas on the qualities of life, art critics, some of whom Friend considers destructive and biased against any kind of art to which they are not personally committed.

Friend considers a lot of modern art banal. Great art, he said, had universal themes which were interpreted by artists throughout the ages—for example, mother and child.

The understanding of the viewer and his interpretation of the painting also changed from generation to generation so that art was never static.

Constant re-evaluation meant that the work of art acted as a medium for continual contact between painter and viewer, yet the universal theme remained the same, he said.

'Art should communicate on the highest and most permanent possible level. It should deal with basic human experiences and be so packed and concentrated in the expression of that experience that it can be understood differently by each question. Its reinterpretation must differ from age to age, just as the world of the Old Masters and Bach and Beethoven has.

'The force or belief that goes into a work of art, the magic quality that makes it last forever and keep giving the same message with different variations on its theme to every generation that sees it—that's what's incredible. If a work is great, the centre is simple, the application universal.'

In Bali, everyone is an artist, Friend said.

'It is like Europe in the Middle Ages and early Renaissance. Their art is dedicated to the glory of the gods and they live a community life—harvesting the fields together, participating in village projects.

'In Bali, if a painter has vision and succeeds, his art belongs to the community.'

In Renaissance times, Balinese artists had princely patronage. 'Now the princes have had the rug pulled from under their feet, few are rich in money and their feudal powers have been cut away, but they still have the island's respect.'

Each village had its own gamelan orchestra, dancers, painters, carvers and craftsmen. Even flower arrangements were beautiful works of art. If art could be divided into 'high art' (gallery art) and 'low art' (woven into everyday activity), then it was 'low art', but he thought the distinction arbitrary. He had no superior status in Bali as a painter.

'Now, if only I were a superb dancer, then perhaps I would be considered special,' he smiled.

I mentioned the nonsense art of the Dada School. Friend had actually seen the famous fur-lined teacup of Marcel Duchamp. He admires Marc Chagall immensely.

Here, on lush Bali, he did not miss the amenities of 'civilized' life.

'European amenities are mostly machines and I can't deal with them—television sets, that sort of thing. Here we have all the essentials—electricity, hot water, a gramophone. If you have twenty people to do things for you, you don't really need an egg-beater.

'I like a life in which one can have leisure and not be interrupted by the telephone. I like living among people who haven't yet lost their original civilization.'

On Bali, foreigners were accepted but not quite considered 'real' people. Their ancestors' ashes had not been scattered on the sea to return to water, air and earth and they were obviously not reincarnated from their ancestors, as Balinese believe they are.

The Balinese could be considered to live lives of strong conformity, yet they are really more individualistic than many Westerners who were brainwashed by advertising and pressured to acquire household gimmicks.

The main disadvantage of Balinese life was the lack of good medical care. Friend told me of an incident where the husband of a woman tourist died suddenly on Bali. The local doctor gave a death certificate with cause of death stated as 'over-eating'. He could not be persuaded to change the diagnosis.

The local authorities would not accept such a certificate.

The widow couldn't get an airline to ship the body home without the necessary papers.

Meanwhile, with no air-conditioning in the morgue and hot tropical weather, things were not getting any easier as time went by.

After going to endless lengths to get some sort of official papers, they finally managed to ship the body home as a 'bale of cotton' or some such object.

A rather macabre story, but it illustrated the problem, Friend said.

Balinese life could be likened to that of the medieval Christian community with its accent on religion and similar social organization. The Balinese have come to terms with the idea of death. A funeral is a joyful occasion, because the spirit returns. The West, said Friend, had not come to terms with the idea of death.

Bali's magical world of gods and spirits had made Friend a willing captive in an earthly paradise, at least temporarily.

He returned to Australia in 1981 and now paints and writes in his home in Sydney.

BORIS LISSANEVITCH—
MINE HOST
AMONG THE HIMALAYAS

KATMANDU, capital of the tiny Himalayan kingdom of Nepal, abounds in colourful sights and exotic people.

One of its most fascinating characters is plump, genial, blue-eyed Russian, Boris Lissanevitch, whom everyone calls 'Boris', of the Yak and Yeti Bar.

Even before I left Sydney, I had heard of the legendary Boris. He was one of the first Westerners to settle in Katmandu and he soon achieved fame as manager of the Royal Hotel, the first hotel to accommodate tourists when Nepal opened to the West in 1955.

He was one of the three most interesting men in Katmandu whom I wished to interview. The others were famed Jesuit and authority on Nepalese lore, Father Moran, who was one of the first Westerners allowed into Katmandu, and the ruling monarch who was shortly to visit Australia on a State visit. Boris, the only one I succeeded in interviewing, proved a fascinating character.

His first hotel, the Royal, a former palace, was fashionable in the early days. Don Carlos of Spain and Princess Sophie of Greece stayed there on their honeymoon. King Leopold of Belgium stayed there, enjoying the beautiful antiques and colourful furnishings. Peers and peeresses, the famous, and jet setters flocked to the Royal.

Nowadays the derelict hotel is closed.

When I met him, Boris was presiding over the warm and welcoming Yak and Yeti Bar with its roaring fire, gleaming shields on the walls, tartan fabrics and lovingly salvaged antiques.

He greeted me at the Yak and Yeti, dressed in a bright Hawaiian shirt and slacks. We enjoyed a delicious lunch of Russian bortsch, beef stroganoff and lemon soufflé—the kind of menu you would expect of a White Russian émigré.

Gimlets (gin, lemon and ice) were served before lunch. We had Danish beer with the food and Benedictine liqueur with the fragrant coffee. Strange fare to find in a remote Himalayan kingdom, but Boris was nothing if not resourceful and had been known to bring in Canterbury lamb from Hong Kong as part of his accompanied baggage.

Boris's life story read like the script for an adventure movie.

'I started my career as a cadet in the White Russian Naval School,' he began.

'The Communist revolution had broken out and the Reds captured Odessa, where we were stationed. Red soldiers were checking documents on every corner, arresting and shooting members of the White Army. I could not escape from the barracks.'

A friend, the ballet mistress for a local company, came to his rescue and gave him a certificate stating he was a member of the ballet and so he escaped.

A year later he left Russia to join Diaghilev's Russian Ballet Company, which was setting all Europe by the ears with its brilliant, exciting performances. He stayed with the company until Diaghilev died in 1929, when he joined the equally famous Massine and appeared at La Scala in Milan.

'After that I decided to turn to acting in England. I played the Devil in the religious play *The Miracle* staged by brilliant director, Max Reinhardt. The production starred Lady Diana Duff-Cooper, a famous English socialite and beauty, as a nun. Glen Byam Shaw, who went on to become a director of the Royal Shakespearean Company at Stratford-on-Avon, played dual roles of a mad prince and a cripple.'

When the play ended its tour Boris could not get a permit to stay in England.

'I was travelling on a League of Nations Certificate for Refugees and it was a hell of a job getting a visa. My wife and I began dancing in casinos and music halls.'

Then, in 1933, came an invitation to dance at the Taj Mahal Hotel in Bombay.

'It was eleven days by ship from Genoa, Italy, to India— land of mystery and the end of the world in those days. We were fascinated by the East and when the contract finished, stayed on, dancing and touring, for three years,' he said.

Boris and his wife still had the status of displaced persons so, to qualify for British nationality, they decided to stay on in India to establish British residency.

'I opened a nightclub in Calcutta. It was the first club in India to admit both British and Indians. Most clubs then had an all-Indian or all-British membership.'

Boris's naturalization papers came through in 1937, but by then he did not want to leave India.

'I wanted to put the club on its feet, but then the Second World War started.'

When the King of Nepal, King Mahendra Bir Bikram Shah Devi (the present King's father), visited Calcutta for heart treatment, he became friendly with Boris. At that time he was not reigning, but when he did ascend the throne he sent Boris an invitation to visit Nepal. He and his wife went there in 1951.

'I fell in love with Nepal and stayed,' said Boris.

What was the appeal of an isolated little kingdom in the Himalayas to a cosmopolitan man who had travelled the world and met the rich, the famous, the artistic?

Boris's blue eyes, deep set under bushy brows, twinkled:

'It was the attraction of the "Mysterious East"—you know, that "green eye of the little yellow god" Kipling mentions!'

When Boris and his wife arrived in Nepal, the entire Western community in Katmandu consisted of the staff of three at the British Embassy—the Ambassador and the First Secretary and his wife; a Swiss geologist, Tony Hagen who worked for the United Nations and who had covered a total of 14,000 km on foot in the Himalayas; and a Jesuit, Father Moran, who had opened the first Christian school in Katmandu.

'If my wife went to market, the women would pinch her legs to feel her stockings, which were quite a novelty,' Boris said. 'There were no European clothes. Even green vegetables were scarce. We sent to Calcutta for most things.'

Boris became manager of the Royal Hotel when it opened in 1954. The first group of tourists ever to enter Nepal arrived in 1955. They were a group of Americans who came on a Cunard line S.S. *Caronia* cruise to Bombay, arranged by Thomas Cook. From Bombay some flew to Kashmir and some to Katmandu.

'These cruises were like a club of American ladies who had divorced five husbands, buried another four, and spent their lives cruising the world and buying presents for grand-children,' Boris explained.

'Thomas Cook were always looking for new places for them to explore. I'm sorry in a way that I started the tourist ball rolling, but tourism was inevitable and Nepal certainly needed it. There were only two money-raising occupations here— agriculture and tourism. Heavy industry is impossible because Nepal is land-locked and the cost of transport is prohibitive. People should see Katmandu at once,' he added. 'In three or four years tourists will have changed it.'

Boris was fascinated by the art and music of Nepal. The whole country was a living museum. Houses and courtyards transported you into the fifteenth and sixteenth centuries. You simply walked in and looked around. People welcomed you, introduced you to their families, and gave you tea or *sakshi*, the local distilled liquor, or a sort of beer called *chang*, made from rice or maize, he said.

The country had a rich repertoire of folk music. The street singers in traditional costume sang to the accompaniment of musicians playing folk airs on rough wooden fiddles. The children clicked fingers and teeth to accentuate the music.

I, too, loved the art and music of the country.

'Nepal has wonderful tourist potential,' said Boris. 'The Nepalese are hospitable, honest and happy. Nepal must be the only country in the world where a woman can go anywhere by herself at any time. My wife goes to paint in the hills on walking tours of two or three weeks. She takes just a few coolies and is quite safe.'

(I am not sure that the same would apply today with drug trafficking going on throughout the East.)

Nepal has an unusual link with Australia. Fifty years ago a Prime Minister of Nepal, Maharaja Chandra, had a wife who suffered from tuberculosis. He heard that eucalyptus was good for the disease and imported Australian gum trees and, to add some colour, bottlebrush. They still grow in Nepal.

The Yak and Yeti Bar was a former palace that once belonged to a prime minister and the portrait gallery showed paintings of various prime ministers, their wives and mistresses.

A big mural depicted Boris and his wife riding an elephant, and a yak, a yeti (Abominable Snowman), and lions and tigers painted in ancient Nepalese style.

Boris knew how lucky he was. He was one of the few men who had found their Shangri-La, and was perfectly happy to live out his life among the snow-clad mountains and colourful people of the exotic kingdom of Nepal.

Since my visit, in 1970, Boris has opened a successful restaurant and the Yak and Yeti Bar has become the popular Yak and Yeti Hotel. Nepal is no longer a remote destination. The Chinese have built a road to the old mountain region of Pokhara, a centre of Buddhism, and another to the border with Tibet, which travellers have now begun using.

When Boris finally goes on his last great journey, Nepal will lose one of its most famous colourful characters.

THE BOY ABU

EARLY morning in a Southern Indian fishing village. A delicious time when the day's freshness has not yet become the searing, effort-corroding heat of mid-morning.

A time to sit at my observation post, a simple village restaurant, and watch through the open window the life of the village unfold.

The breakfast menu is uncomplicated—fish straight from the sea, *chapattis* (Indian bread) and tea. Through the long slatted windows the view encompasses the sweeping circle of beach and the turquoise, pungent, swelling sea. Gently waving rollers with the occasional treacherous dumper to catch the unwary.

Out there the rough plank fishing boats are bobbing. To the visitor it is a simple world—of beauty, grace and rhythm. The sun always shines, there is fish in the sea and coconuts on the trees.

Groups of small barefoot school children clutching slates and swinging books go by—bright, shiny faces and bright coloured cotton skirts and blouses or shorts and shirts, long glossy plaited braids or bushy short back and sides. Three incredibly graceful women in long pink, red and green skirts balance baskets on their heads as they glide by my backdrop view of green coconut trees and blue water.

Earlier I had watched the fishermen hauling in their nets. Lines of men pulling in long ropes hand over hand—singing to give rhythm. Long narrow fishing smacks headed out to sea. Always grace and rhythm.

Now it is 9.30 and I watch the coconut workers. There is a grove of trees beside our beach hut. The men have shinned up them, collected the coconuts and husked them on a sharp spike. Now they begin loading the fruit into huge nets, so heavy they take four men to lift. Each net is hoisted onto one man's head, the bearer steadies himself for a moment, then with enormous burden, canters off with long loping graceful stride, every leg muscle straining, pelvis swivelling to balance the heavy load.

Further along the beach he dumps his coconuts, then strolls casually back arms swinging, the empty net sitting neatly folded on his head. The men are naked except for a sarong from waist to above knee in green or grey, and white striped cotton.

Around the communal well a man and his young son are filling shiny brass water pots. Black crows perch on the ledge of the restaurant. The stream of children with bundles of books and billycans of food, thin legged and bare footed, frolic past. Some small boys carry coconut loads instead of books—not for them the privilege of learning to read and write.

The mango lady and her pretty small daughter of the flashing eyes and big bright smile hover nearby with baskets of green juicy mangoes. Yesterday we bought quite a few and she is not letting her quarry out of sight.

It is a humid, sticky day and we swim lazily in the warm salty lagoon-bound surf. Forgetful of the prevalent hookworm I run barefoot over the scorching sand.

Suddenly the temple bells start ringing and the mournful sound of the conch shell blown by the temple priest signals the start of the temple *puja* ceremony. All over India these ceremonies are held to give thanks, petition gods or celebrate festive days.

I decide to go to the temple and that is how I meet Abu. On my way, the sound of the bells suddenly stops. The temple, I had thought, was through a grove of trees. Just as I hesitate, a small boy materializes at my elbow.

Like the Cheshire cat in *Alice in Wonderland*, he does not appear all at once—first huge brown flashing eyes full of mischief, then a smile which lights up his face like a Christmas tree, revealing a mouthful of dazzling white teeth, a polished ebony face and finally the neat brown small body of a ten-year-old.

'Hallo, mem-sahib—where are you going? I will help you.'

A child of beauty in a soft, graceful village paradise.

So Abu became my guide. And, with his first few steps, any impression of child-like grace disappears. Abu is crippled. One leg is much shorter than the other, his back is twisted, but he manages well enough, throwing out his legs in an ungainly fashion like a young foal and hopping nimbly over rocks.

Today, he explains, is the feast day of the elephant god, Ganesh, son of Shiva the destroyer. On this day the priests open the tabernacle door and reveal the garishly coloured half man–half elephant statue for followers to worship.

In front of the altar stand offerings—flowers, coconuts, holy water, incense and multi-coloured garlands. The garlanded priest says: 'The ceremony was just a small one, already

over. Come back in the evening for the big *puja*. You will
receive much *prasad*, many coconuts and bananas.'

He gives me a coconut as a foretaste of the feast (*prasad*
or holy food) to come.

Abu lopes off beside me until we reach the tea stall where
the owner of the tea shop kindly lops off the coconut top
with a huge flat knife, so I can drink the sweet milk. Surrounded
by an audience of small children, I divide up the coconut
and share it with these sweet, shy children, noticing how
they politely take the smaller pieces.

At the nearby shell stall which sells little animals and
figurines, flowers made of shells, and shell necklaces, I meet
Abu's parents while Abu finishes licking out the coconut.

It is a hard living and customers are few, they tell me.
Job opportunities are limited—either working with coconuts,
fishing or selling seashells. The villagers are very poor and
their diet consists mainly of bananas, rice and coconuts. I
give Abu a small notebook and a little money for his trouble.

He is one of ten brothers and sisters. I talk with an older
brother (about thirty I would say, but it is hard to tell age
as malnutrition retards growth). Abu is a bright youngster,
quick at learning and speaking a little English, he says. He
seems surprised when I guess Abu's age as ten—he is actually
fifteen.

Abu has one leg longer than the other. When he was three
years old, both legs were broken in a fall. He now has knock
knees and a twisted spine, and has to throw both legs out
to move in an ungainly gait.

The child listens to all this intently, but when I ask gently
about his legs, his face clouds over and he becomes quite
downcast. He stares at the ground, and looks about to cry.
I wonder how many years of heartbreak, false hope, teasing
by other children, and despair of a normal future lie behind
the instant sadness. The brilliant sun of his smile has disappeared behind a dark cloud.

His brother's set face warns me to say no more in front
of Abu.

Later I ask what his future holds. Abu has told me he
wants to be a fisherman. His brother said it was unlikely
he would achieve his goal. Unless he got help, his back would
worsen. He would never be strong enough to haul in fishing
lines or shin up coconut trees.

I buy a lobster for about forty cents from Abu's father who cooks it. I only want one for lunch, but he has brought three hoping I will take them—it means a week's earnings.

I pack my things and wait for the bus to the city. It does not come. Becoming worried I will miss my plane, I ask the villagers what time the local bus is due. They say perhaps five, perhaps six, perhaps not at all.

Just as I am losing hope, a taxi appears, dropping off a load of Indian holidaymakers. My travelling companions, a young American student Robert, and an American mother and daughter I had met up with earlier, are still in the cottage, intending to leave later and catch the night plane.

Abu comes to my rescue again. Off he goes hopping briskly to ask the tourists to let me share their taxi. Proudly he rides back in the taxi waving to the children and shouting, 'Look at me, Abu, riding in a taxi'; the old cheek and gaiety are back.

He is still waving as our taxi disappears. I wonder what will become of him—one small child among India's millions. Our lives have touched briefly then each returns to a separate world. To what purpose?

Of course, I tried to help Abu. I wrote to Indian welfare agencies, social workers, volunteer health workers I knew from Australia, hoping I could set up some medical help, but all to no avail. I got not one reply. I wrote to Abu's family but even they did not reply.

Back in Australia, I asked an Indian official what more I could do.

'What is one child among so many children like Abu?' he shrugged.

MYSTERIES

THE WHIRLING DERVISHES OF THE ANCIENT TURKISH CITY OF KONYA

THE small city of Konya lies buried deep in Turkey's vast primitive inland. The country is wild and cold, scattered with mud huts roofed with straw and aswirl with dust raised by lumbering bullock carts.

Shepherds huddle in tent-like skin coats watching thin sheep graze on a scrubby flat arid country broken by the outlines of strange derrick-like wells with long wooden poles dangling wooden buckets.

Rugged mountain formations of red and orange rock and brown and silver streams edged with rustling yellow-green poplars relieve the vast stretches of flat, grey country.

At night temperatures fall below freezing and camping out can be a rugged endurance test as we travellers on our way from Europe to India by bus found. But it is worth any hardship. The country is fascinating in its multi-coloured mountain and river scenery, its exotically garbed people, and its legends.

This is the country of the Whirling Dervishes sect whose founder's tomb lies in the city of Konya. Legend has it that

Perseus slew Medusa at Konya. The town's name means 'icon' or 'image'. It was the terrible image of the dead Medusa whose head Perseus hung on the city gate which gave it its name.

Through the market place with its veiled women in baggy pants and its carts loaded with farm produce, past the scurrying boys balancing tea trays of tinkling glasses, we followed the labyrinthine narrow streets leading to the thirteenth-century shrine of Mevlâna Celâleddin Rumi, founder of the local sect of Whirling Dervishes, whose members seek union with the Infinite by whirling to strange music.

Mevlâna was no mean poet. Here's how he wrote of the flute's melody: 'Listen to the flute, its complaining, it tells of separation.'

His tomb, encased under a shiny sea-green tiled tower next to a magnificent mosque, adjoins the Dervish Museum.

Here, with recorded 'whirling' music piped into the high-roofed chamber, and clouds of incense mingling with the hypnotic oriental beat, it is not hard to imagine the Kubla Khan-like world of the Dervishes.

Their huge conical hats swathed in turbans, and wearing embroidered cloaks and gowns of silk and satin during rites, they sit on rich silk pillows. The rooms are lavishly filled with treasure—beautiful wall decorations, the sacred books of the Holy Koran, brass hanging lamps, exotic musical instruments, soft, deep, intricately patterned carpets.

When the Dervishes meet for their ritual, they form a 'quasi-mystical circle', silent praying, 'There is no God but Allah and Muhammad is His Prophet', as they slowly begin turning.

Gradually they raise their arms and extend them at shoulder height with the left hand turned towards the floor, the right one raised, the head inclined over the right shoulder and the eyes closed.

They dance for joy, revolving ever more quickly to the flutes, violins and small, soft drums. While his brethren intone the prayer to Allah, the 'Zikr', the leader or *Sama Zan*, signals what distance apart the dancers must be during the dance. The priest (or 'shaik') watches the hypnotically whirling Dervishes.

Suddenly the musicians call out the salutation, 'Oh Friend', the music stops instantly and all bow solemnly to the shaik.

After a pause, the whirling recommences. The dance is said to symbolize the harmonious movement of the spheres in the Universe.

Around and around they whirl until time has no meaning for them. They are caught up in the frenzied beat of drums, the wail of the pipes and the monotonous chanting of hymns. They whirl into ecstasy and fall exhausted in a trance.

The Dervishes, or Sufis as they are also known, derive their name from the Persian word for 'poor'. *Dar* means 'door' and *vish* means 'spread'. The poor who had no home stretched themselves at night across doorways to sleep. The Dervishes gave up their worldly goods to feed these poor. Their aim was their own spiritual perfection and union with God by emotional experiences such as whirling, and mental and physical discipline.

The Sufi doctrine of Divine Love was a powerful influence on Islamic writing, especially the mystic poetry of Persia, Turkey and Muslim India.

The Whirling Dervish leaders changed the course of history, stirring up revolt against tyranny. One such leader or 'Mahdi', Muhammad Ahmed Madhi of Sudan, defeated British and Egyptian forces in the 'Holy War' of 1881, the forerunner to Sudanese independence.

Nowadays, the Whirling Dervishes sect is banned, but here and there, in remote and primitive parts of Turkey, the dancers still whirl endlessly into ecstasy, seeking absorption in the Divine.

Tourists may find it difficult, if not impossible, to see the dance of the Whirling Dervishes, but they can do the next best thing—visit Konya's Dervish Museum where the story of the Dervishes is brought brilliantly to life.

THE HOUSE OF
JIMMY THOMPSON

SOMERSET Maugham would have loved the strange happenings surrounding the owner of the picturesque Thai house on a *klong* (canal) in Bangkok.

No doubt he would have woven a web of intriguing plots

and counterplots to explain the mysterious disappearance of
its owner, millionaire 'Thai Silk King', Jimmy Thompson,
and would have come up with a neat solution to tie all the
threads and explain the red herrings. Maugham, who unco-
vered and wrote about many family skeletons in the Orient
and South Pacific would have nicely rounded off the story
to the reader's satisfaction.

In real life, it just didn't happen that way. Oh, the circumstances were incredibly strange, the red herrings were
there, the plots suggested. But it all added up to one of the
world's most intriguing unsolved puzzles—the Case of the
Disappearing Millionaire.

It all began in 1967 when Thompson closed the door of
his picturesque Bangkok home and set off on holidays, to
disappear without trace from a holiday cottage in the Cameron
Highlands in Malaysia. Today tourists flock to his beautiful
house and gasp at its magnificent collection of sixteenth-
century Siamese paintings, old Chinese procelain, Burmese
and Khmer statues and art objects of carved wood and stone
dating from the sixth century.

It was here I stumbled across his story. A tourist in Bangkok,
I was intrigued by the portrait of Jimmy Thompson, a sophisticated face with a touch of humour about the mouth. It bore
the imprint of a colourful, witty personality. With fresh flowers
set before the portrait, it looked almost like a shrine. You
felt its owner could walk in any time.

Indeed Thompson, an urbane Noël Coward-like character,
loved to entertain lavishly in his rich and sumptuous Thai
house with his lifetime's collection of antiques from all over
South East Asia. Celebrities who had enjoyed his hospitality
included Prince Michael of Greece, Senator Robert Kennedy,
Tennesse Williams and Somerset Maugham.

It should have been a happy house. In accordance with
Thai tradition, Thompson had taken great care to placate
the spirits.

When the house was built—from a combination of several
old Thai houses, including a palace and a nineteenth-century
village house transported down river by barge—the priests
used a horoscope to decide on the auspicious day to occupy
the new home.

Both Brahmin and Buddhist priests purified the house,

sprinkling sandalwood powder, gold leaf and holy water, and twining a sacred cord around the corners of the house.

The first daily bowls of food and flowers were offered to the spirits dwelling in the miniature Spirit House in the garden.

On the auspicious day, Thompson moved in, even though his new home was without electricity or running water.

The door stoops had been raised to prevent evil spirits (which travel in straight lines) from entering the house.

Thompson was later to declare: 'I have been very happy here and I have no intention of moving unless something unforseen happens to this place.'

Something unforseen did happen, but not to the house. Thompson, the man who revitalized the Thai silk industry, the collector of fabulous treasures, was to vanish without trace. All efforts to solve the mystery of his disappearance have failed.

Thompson's life was almost as fantastic as his disappearance. Born of a socially prominent family in the United States, he attended an exclusive preparatory school, graduated from Princeton University, and went on to study architecture at the University of Pennsylvania. Although he never took his degree he later practised as an architect in New York City.

The man born 'with a silver spoon in his mouth' inherited over a million dollars from his aunt. He invested it with his American banker.

He didn't get much chance to practise as an architect before the Second World War broke out and he became a captain in the United Stated Army, serving in the office of Strategic Services, the wartime intelligence unit which later became the CIA, in Africa, Europe and South East Asia.

The war ended when he was about to parachute into Thailand with the Free Thai movement.

As part of the American Mission after the war, he helped rid Thailand of the remaining Japanese. This involved trips upcountry where he became fascinated with the beautiful silks the villagers wove.

He was then in his forties, divorced, with no ties. He fell in love with Bangkok and decided to make it his permanent home.

His interest in building led him to accept a commission

to rebuild the famous Oriental Hotel, on the River Chao Praya (River of Kings), for the expected post-war influx of tourists.

But he kept thinking of the exotic shimmering silks he had seen in the villages. He had watched the villagers weaving and had bought some materials.

There were few weavers and standards varied from village to village, but Thompson saw the potential. He took a suitcase of samples to New York to show an old friend, Edna Woolman Chase, then editor of *Vogue* fashion magazine. Her verdict— fabulous! She and her fashion experts encouraged Thompson to set up a company, which he did.

He imported Swiss dyes, created fashion designs for the export market and gathered together 200 local weavers. Some of them, together with American and Thai friends, bought stock in the new company. Thompson kept twenty per cent for himself and fifty-one per cent was Thai-owned, which made the company eligible to own land.

Business boomed to such an extent that imitators sprang up and there were eventually over 154 silk companies in Bangkok exporting Thai silk to over 105 countries.

As Thompson prospered, his interest in antiques deepened. He ranged the countryside collecting Khmer and Burmese statues, ancient Siamese painting, carved wood and stone. He housed his growing collection in the Thai house on the Big Naga (snake) *klong*.

He made a will leaving his house and its contents and stock in his company to the Siam Society, a non-profit organization under royal patronage, which encouraged interest in South East Asian art.

Thompson then made one of his most thrilling discoveries. He found five ancient limestone heads in a dealer's shop in Ayudhya, the old royal capital of Thailand. He added them to his collection in the house on the *klong*, now a private museum.

But the Government Fine Arts Department promptly confiscated the heads. Thompson was upset and bewildered. He knew that Thai treasures were being taken from the country because there were no protective laws, but his treasures were already housed in a private museum which he had willingly left as a legacy to his adopted country.

Much upset, Thompson altered his will to leave the house

and contents to his nephew, Henry B. Thompson III, a New York stockbroker, but with the verbal condition that it became a museum for the Thai people.

Henry's mother (Thompson's sister) was later to be murdered under mysterious circumstances. Her killer was never found.

Thompson had lost confidence in the Siam Society, which had not been able to help him retain his treasured statues.

That's how things stood when he accepted a holiday invitation to join friends in the Cameron Highlands of Malaysia.

On Good Friday 1967, he joined his old friends, T. G. Ling, a Malaysian doctor of medicine, his American wife who was an antique dealer, and Mrs Connie Mangskau, in Penang. They then motored to the Highlands and settled in Moonlight Cottage, which belonged to the Lings.

Twice before, the same four had met to spend Easter together at the cottage. But this time was different.

The first strange thing to happen concerned the driver of the cab shared by Thompson and Mrs Mangskau. He turned into a garage—for repairs he said—and asked the couple to transfer to another cab, sharing it with two unknown Chinese men. They refused.

They reached Moonlight Cottage without further incident in the original car but, as events turned out, they could narrowly have missed a kidnap attempt.

On Easter Sunday the whole party went to church, then drove up the mountain for a picnic, returning about 3 p.m. The garage attendant later reported seeing a caravan of five cars bearing Thai license plates going up the road to the Highlands at three thirty that afternoon. Such traffic was unusual on a Sunday.

Everyone, except Thompson, then took a nap. Dr Ling, who couldn't sleep, heard what he took to be Thompson's footsteps on the garden gravel path, and concluded that he was taking a walk.

That was the last time Thompson was heard of. He simply vanished.

At five thirty p.m. the mysterious five-car caravan was seen descending the mountain road. Was there any connection with the disappearance? None was ever proved.

One of the biggest searches ever known in Malaysia was

mounted for Thompson. It involved the Malaysian Army, United States support troops, helicopters and trackers with police dogs. School children and tourists joined in, combing the jungle for days.

Even the local aborigines, the Sakai, joined in. They knew every inch of the jungle, but found no trace of Thompson.

At first he was thought to have been killed by a tiger, but the Sakai found no evidence of it—no broken twig, sign of buzzards, or any activity, no bones.

Friends began to hope it was a kidnapping and offered a reward of US$25,000—but nothing came to light.

There were stories that Thompson was being held for ransom by a gang in the Highlands who would turn him loose if Charles Sheffield,* Thompson's export assistant in his multi-million-dollar silk export company, would identify him.

Sheffield flew to Malaysia and took part in the melodrama, running to and from checkpoints, but it was all in vain.

Thompson, according to Sheffield, had been friendly with a former Thai prime minister, who had been forced out and fled the country to live in The People's Republic of China. Some people thought he had summoned his old friend, Thompson, to join him for unknown reasons.

A mystic who tried to locate Thompson kept murmuring a word which sounded like the ex-prime minister's name, 'Pridi'.

For the next eighteen months people came to Sheffield with theories. Thompson had been kidnapped by a Chinese gang, they said. He had been executed by Communist guerillas—hidden by a terrorist band who were hiding out in the Highlands—held in Communist China for his know-how in the silk industry.

Because of his past conection with American intelligence (he had served with the Office of Strategic Services during the Second World War) stories of political plots became common. It was even rumoured that he had been a CIA agent, but American officials denied this.

Then Peter Hurkos, a Dutch mystic from America, arrived

* My thanks to Charles Sheffield, who provided much of the information in this chapter in an interview with me.

in Bangkok. He was famous for his work on the Boston
Strangler case. He visited Thompson's house, felt his belongings and looked at maps. He asked if Indonesia's President
Sukarno had ever been in the house. It so happened that
he had been brought there once when Thompson was out
of town.

Hurkos talked to Thompson's acquaintances in Bangkok.
He then went to the Cameron Highlands to get what he
called 'the vibrations'.

In a trance he said he could see Thompson walking to
the foot of a hill where thirteen men in jungle-green uniforms
captured him and took him to a place which Hurkos identified
as a village in Cambodia (now Kampuchea). At that time,
neither the Thais nor the Americans had diplomatic relations
with Cambodia, so it was difficult to check out this story.

Many people did not believe Hurkos, but friends and business associates wanted to. They made discreet enquiries in
Cambodia because nobody could go there officially. They discovered nothing.

Then on 30 August 1967, just five months after Thompson's
disappearance, the brutally battered body of his wealthy
seventy-four-year-old socialite eldest sister, Mrs Katherine
Thompson Wood, was found in Wilmington, a town near
Philadelphia in the United States.

It was never discovered why her two huge watchdogs let
in the intruder. Her papers and jewellery were untouched.
No link with her brother's disappearance was ever discovered.

The search for Thompson then intensified. Witch doctors
and clairvoyants got into the act. A Portuguese Jesuit brother
suggested that Thompson was at a spot near Penang.

Brigadier-General Edwin F. Black, a friend of Thompson,
flew to the Cameron Highlands, but found no trace of him,
dead or alive.

Then Richard Noone, British SEATO officer, who knew
the customs and dialects of the local tribes, searched the
Malaysian jungle, accompanied by a North Borneo Border
scout and a witch doctor. Even they failed to find a trace
of the missing man.

The secrets behind the baffling mystery of the Disappearing
Millionaire will probably remain unsolved forever. And tourists, like me, will continue to be intrigued by the enigma

An industrious little girl of Northern Thailand's Meo tribe does fine embroidery destined for sale.

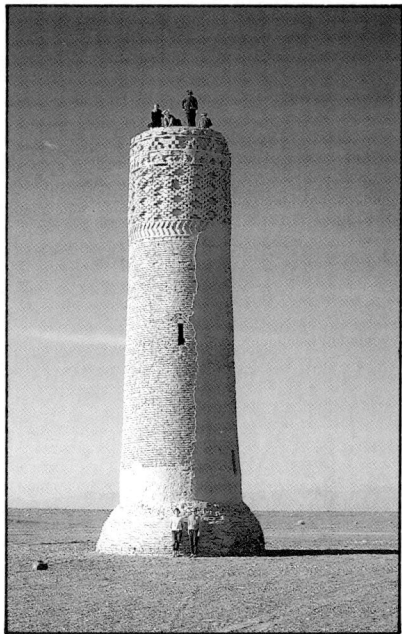

In the desolate wastes of Iran's Great Sand Desert travellers rely on this fire tower's brightly burning beacon at night.

Children in the traditional South African Zulu village, Phezulu Kraal, wear little but colourful beads and interesting expressions.

This thirteenth century shrine of Mevlâna Celâleddin Rumi, poet and founder of a sect of Whirling Dervishes, lies in the Turkish city of Konya where, legend has it, the hideous dead Medusa's head hung from its gate.

The Zulu warrior has just finished his blood-curdling war dance and the woman is about to demonstrate pot-making in Phezulu Kraal. Feathers and beads, often in intricate designs are traditional ornaments.

which lies behind the smiling portrait in the house by the *klong* in Bangkok.

THAIPUSAM—
TRANCE IN SINGAPORE

TRANCE happens in many countries of the East and some in the South Pacific. In Sri Lanka I watched a woman give a strange cry and fall—taken by the spirit. The temple attendants carried her out and a priest dashed holy water on her face. Was it the hypnotic power of the insistent drums or the clouds of incense which induced her trance?

In Fiji, firewalkers tread fiery pits without being burned. They too are enchanted—by magical rites of preparation. In a Singaporean Chinese temple, Chinese spirit mediums demonstrate their religious fervour by slicing tongues and piercing flesh without pain or injury, in honour of the Monkey God. In Bali, young girls in trance dance in perfect unison the complicated movements of a temple dance they have never learned.

To the Westerner, trance is one of the strangest mysteries encountered on travels to exotic countries, whereas the people of those countries, living in a magical world of spirits and demons, take it for granted.

In Singapore, trance is part of many religious festivals. Let's join the crowds at one such celebration—Thaipusam.

The temple courtyard is crowded with thousands of devotees whose monotonous chants rise with heavy clouds of incense and smoke from burning joss sticks. As religious fervour rises, pilgrims fall into a dream-like, almost drugged trance. These are the men who will endure what seems to the onlooker, gruesome torture, in order to give thanks to the god, Subramaniam, for favours, or to expiate sins.

The scene is the Perumal Temple in Serangoon Road. Tourists watch in horror as a temple attendant pierces toungues, foreheads and cheeks with silver needles or spikes, usually trident-shaped silver (the trident is the emblem of the Hindu god, Siva). Fish hooks are inserted into thighs, upper arms and other parts of the body. Small pots, lemons, coconuts and other weights are hooked on. The devotees, dressed in a yellow loin cloth and smeared with sacred ashes, feel no pain and the wounds do not bleed. The trance state enables mind to subdue body.

Then the kavadi, a metal arch, decorated with peacock feathers (reminders of the bird upon which Lord Subramaniam rode), flowers and tassels, is slipped over the shoulders, and spikes driven into the flesh of the chest. Every movement will tear the skin.

Devotees believe that carrying the kavadi will please Lord Subramaniam, the younger son of Lord Siva by celebrating his victory over the demon, Taraka. Subramaniam, as leader of the divine army, is considered the model of bravery and power. His battle symbolized the struggle between good and evil and final victory of good.

Weeks of preparation precede the procession of the kavadi bearers. A strict fast is observed from the beginning of the month called Thai, the tenth month of the lunar calendar when the full moon passes in front of the star Pusam, giving the name to the festival, Thaipusam. During this time devotees must abstain from meat, alcohol, and sexual contact, not shave, nor use any cooking utensils used by others, and sleep in a mat on the temple floor. For the twenty-four hours before carrying the kavadi, they maintain a strict fast.

The festival lasts for two days. On the first day the image of Lord Subramaniam leaves its home in the Chettiar Temple in Tank Road, in a silver ceremonial chariot drawn by two bullocks and followed by worshippers, for the Vinayakar Temple, with a stop at the Sri Mariamman Temple in Chinatown on the way.

Having paid his respects to his older brother god, the elephant-headed Ganesa at the Vinayakar temple, Subramaniam returns in procession to his own temple, passing the business houses of the Chettiars on the way. ('Chettiar' is the name of a caste of money lenders and merchants who originally came from Southern India.)

In the past it was customary for only Chettiars to carry the kavadi on the first day, but nowadays any man may volunteer for the fearful ordeal. Women and boys may also carry the kavadi, but only men may have their skin pierced.

The evening of the first day, crowds gather at Perumal

Temple, the starting point for the procession, to watch the kavadi carriers prepare. The carriers take up positions in the courtyard and throughout the night spiritually prepare themselves for their ordeal next morning. At daybreak they take a purification bath, in readiness for the final preparations in the temple.

Then, cheered by thousands of shouting worshippers, the kavadi bearers join the procession. In Tamil, kavadi means an offering and refers to the gifts of the faithful to the temple, in thanksgiving for favours. Later, the highly decorated kavadis became the traditional gifts. Gradually, the idea of penance for sins was added and sharp steel spikes, silver needles and razor-sharp fish hooks began to be used. Thaipusam was a day for keeping promises made during the year—either in thanksgiving or penance—to Lord Subramaniam.

Thousands of Hindu worshippers and tourists jam the procession way, watching while devotees whirl and dance, with shrieks of religious ecstasy, under the painful weight of the kavadi, while stall holders and hawkers do a roaring business.

The scene looks gruesome to Western eyes, but certainly colourful. The elaborate kavadis are decorated with palm leaves, flowers, images of the gods, bells, and beads, peacock feathers and tinsel. The brass pots tied to the hooks are filled with fresh milk. Each bearer is accompanied by musicians and supporters who pray and shout in encouragement.

The parade passes two temples where coconuts are broken in honour of the gods before reaching Chettiar Temple. Here worshippers pour milk over the image of Lord Subramaniam and receive milk and food in return. After prostrating themselves before the Lord Subramaniam's statue, devotees are relieved of the kavadi and their gruesome implements of torture—spikes, needles, fish hooks. Temple priests apply lemon juice and ashes to the bodies of the carriers to prevent infection.

Miraculously there are no wounds and the kavadi bearer is physically none the worse for his ordeal. Spiritually he feels wonderful. The god has been pleased and placated. He can return to the workaday world cleansed of sin and debt-free for favours received.

THE JON FRUM
CARGO CULT—VANUATU'S
MYSTERIOUS RELIGION

ON my arrival on the Pacific island of Tanna, an airport notice greeted me: 'When God sets up his Kingdom, hear amazing fulfilment of Bible prophecy.' It was a sample of things to come in the island home of the mysterious Jon Frum cargo cult and many other religions.

Tanna is one of the eighty jungle-covered islands which make up the republic of Vanuatu, formerly called the New Hebrides, situated in the Pacific about 2250 kilometres northeast of Australia. Its scenery is paradisiacal and its inhabitants lead a colourful life, keeping to ancient ways but deeply influenced by the various Christian missions on the island.

It is a land where wild horses roam to White Grass Plains. Magnificent and temperamental, they fight to the death to decide leadership. Its volcano, Yasur, rumbles and smokes, spewing grey ash. In one village I found a *kermesse* (French fête) in progress. Practical prizes for the raffle were: first prize a bull, second a radio, third a shovel and fourth iron roofing sheets. Many village men still wear only penis coverings called *nambas*, made from banana leaves, calico or other materials, and the women grass skirts. Lap laps are kept for special occasions.

Perhaps the strangest custom to visitors is the island's cargo cult. There are many versions of how the strange belief came about and the first appearance of the island's mythical saviour is uncertain. The whole subject is shrouded in mystery but most islanders agree that Jon Frum promised to bring the white man's 'cargo' (envied Western goods) and to free the Tannese.

My driver, Joe, gave this version.

A native was exiled to a remote village by Seventh Day Adventist missionaries after upsetting them by taking two wives.

In revenge, he declared he had had a dream in which he saw an American, called Jon Frum, who said he would return with lots of Western-style gifts such as refrigerators, beds and bedding, associated with white men's comforts.

News spread like wildfire. People were told to give up sending their children to school, to avoid church services, and to wait for the coming of the Messiah, Joh Frum. Almost overnight missions were deserted, cattle destroyed and money thrown in the sea. People believed that if they destroyed everything the Europeans had given them, Jon Frum would send them free shiploads of cargo from his own El Dorado.

Although the administration imprisoned the leaders, the cult quickly spread. Then, in 1942, Americans arrived to build aerodromes and naval bases and their affluence led the islanders to decide that Jon Frum was an American.

In 1951 a Tannese called Nampus returned to Tanna after release from prison, wearing a cast-off American medical orderly's jacket with a red cross. He announced that Jon Frum had given him the cross and it became the cult's symbol. Red crosses were erected all over Tanna. Many islanders believed in the cult and refused education.

When I was in Tanna a few years ago, tourists were forbidden to visit the Jon Frum village, partly because there were arguments going on between it and other villages as to who owned the volcano. It all started when one village decided that visitors should pay a fee. The squabble was unsolved and, at that time, no one was allowed to visit the volcano.

Perhaps frustration with the conflicting Christian religions had influenced the natives to turn to the cargo cult.

Bob Paul, who owned the local store and the tourist cottages where I stayed, and had farming interests, told a slightly different version.

A villager from South Tanna dreamed in 1941 of a visit by Jon Frum who promised that, if the people would destroy everything the white man had given them, he would send shiploads of cargo free. Missions and plantations were destroyed, cattle killed— but still the 'Messiah" did not come.

Americans, however, did, to fight in the Pacific. Vast stores of building materials and goods such as Coca-Cola, jeeps, and weapons poured into the islands as Americans built bases. The Tannese believed that, surely, this was the promised cargo at last. The belief seemed confirmed when American Negro GIs arrived and they decided that Jon Frum was obviously an American.

Another popular legend has it that an American warplane flew over Yasur volcano in 1940, making a mysterious emergency landing on the sulphuric-smelling, ash grey plain. Here the pilot unloaded a quantity of war material before departing after introducing himself as 'Jon Frum'.

Yet another version tells of a Messiah who would free the Tannese from French and British colonial rule and the Christian missionary influence. The islanders would take up the old customs such as circumcision ceremonies, kava drinking, sorcery and traditional singing and dancing.

This version has Jon Frum speaking from beneath a banyan tree in 1938 with great wisdom, and promising cargo.

Frum is said to appear in kava-induced dreams. Many Tannese believe he will return bringing rich cargo, despite government attempts to discredit the cult, and 14 February is set aside for Jon Frum Day celebrations at a village centre for the cult at Sulphur Bay. Certainly the cargo cult has given the islanders a nucleus of nationalistic feeling, in a land where independence from French and British colonial rule arrived only a few short years ago.

FIJIAN FIREWALKERS OF BEQA

THE stones of the fire pit are white hot—even a handkerchief tossed on them bursts into flames—yet the firewalkers of Beqa walk unscathed across them.

Tourists standing by feel the scorching heat from the stones and shield their faces, but the tribesmen seem to possess some magical power which protects them from burns.

Of the Fijian population only the Sawau tribesmen from certain villages on the island of Beqa, off the Coral Coast of the island of Viti Levu (the island where most tourists go), possess this incredible ability. Although the ceremony is put on by several tourist hotels as a 'sight', it never loses its power to mystify.

There seems no rational explanation. Even the firewalkers cannot explain it. They do know, however, that failure to observe the taboo associated with preparations could spell disaster. For two weeks before the event, participants may not have any contact with women, nor eat coconut, at the risk of suffering severe burns during the ceremony.

Villagers dig a large circular pit, and line it with large stones, thirty to forty centimetres in diameter. Six to eight hours before the ceremony a huge log fire is built over them. When all is ready, men of the village in colourful garb prepare the fire pit. Armed with long green poles, some of which have loops of strong green vines lashed to their ends, the young men clear the burning logs from the stones, chanting as they work together, 'O-vulo-vulo'.

A long tree-fern called *waqa-bala-bala*, said to contain the Spirit God, is then laid across the pit. Following this, a large vine is dragged across the stones, levelling them and preparing them for the firewalkers. The leader then jumps on to the stones and takes a few trial steps to test their firmness. Bundles of leaves and long swamp grass are placed round the edge of the pit. Just before the firewalkers appear, the long tree-fern is adjusted to point in the direction from which they will come.

The village men, their preparations finished, surround the fire pit, leaving only a small gap for the firewalkers to enter. The leader gives a great shout, 'Vuto-o', the signal for the firewalkers to approach the pit at a brisk run.

The tree-fern is quickly removed and the firewalkers enter the pit in single file, walking fearlessly on the white-hot stones. A handerchief is tossed on the stones and bursts into flame, yet the tinder-dry tree-fern leaves forming the anklets of firewalkers don't ignite. Nor do the firewalkers suffer a single burn.

Ceremony is still observed as bands are carefully removed and buried in the fire pit together with four special baskets of roots said to take the place in the pit of the performers.

The pit is then covered with earth and left for four days, when it is opened by the firewalkers and the baked roots taken out, ground and mixed with water. Taro roots are cooked in the liquid and eaten by firewalkers.

INDIAN FIREWALKING

The Indian population of Fiji also have their firewalkers, whose ancestors came from South India bringing with them religious traditions and ceremonies.

Once a year, under a full moon, a firewalking ceremony is held to honour the goddess Kali, the Supreme Mother (Mother Goddess) of Hindu mythology.

Men, women and even children take part in firewalking. Sometimes participants carry babies or young children over the fire, in fulfilment of a vow or to petition help to cure a sick child.

Before the firewalking ceremony, devotees spend their time in worship and meditation, concentrating their minds on the spiritual, and remaining in the temple for ten days.

They bathe in the sea or river to cleanse themselves then return to the temple to the beat of drums and chant of worshippers.

In the temple their bodies are pierced with skewers or needles, they are dressed in yellow robes (the Mother Goddess's favourite colour) and yellow thread is tied around their wrists. Red is painted between eyebrows, ashes spread on the head and a yellow powder smeared over the body, a symbol of power and riches.

The fire pit is lit at midnight before the day of performance—about twenty to forty tonnes of firewood is used to provide the burning coals.

Under the direction of the head priest who leads the walk, the performers, grasping a three-pronged spear (said to destroy the evils of lust, greed and anger), tread the fiery path. As they walk they call on Lord Vishnu who was said to help Kali slay demons.

The wounds inflicted by spikes and needles do not bleed and, as with the Fijian firewalkers, the soles of their feet are not blistered. Spirit has again conquered body.

PLACES 2

IRELAND—ISLAND OF SAINTS AND SINNERS

'TIS a darling of a day,' said the old Irishman with the leprechaun face.

It was pouring rain, but when I pointed this out, he simply smiled and said: 'But 'tis a soft day with real Irish mist.'

The old man's reply was typical of the quixotic charm and poetic temperament of the Irish. It's a country where the visitor feels instantly home, where every face is signposted 'welcome' and, if you have an Irish name, the response, as the song goes, is: 'If you're Irish , come into the parlour.'

In no time at all, everyone is trying to work out if you're a Harrington from Cork or an O'Malley from County Mayo, over a jar of whisky, in a dim and cosy pub, while the fiddler plays a jig in the corner.

From the green wooden hills of Wicklow to the stark, desolate grandeur of Connemara's landscape of stony mountains and wild shore (the Irish had a battle cry, 'To Connemara or death'), Ireland is incredibly beautiful.

Like most visitors, I arrived in Dublin first. The city's poetry, wit and wisdom have been immortalized by writers such as

Oscar Wilde, George Bernard Shaw, W. B. Yeats, Robert Brinsley Sheridan, Brendan Behan, James Joyce, and Jonathan Swift—all born in Dublin.

Colourful plays were produced in the old Abbey Theatre, which burned down, and Irish plays by, among others, O'Casey, Synge and Brendan Behan are still performed in the New Abbey.

Dublin was a kaleidoscope of experiences—strolling along the quays of the River Liffey, browsing in the little antique shops, a fiddler's jaunty jig in a small pub, street vendors wheeling prams full of fruit and vegetables.

The fashionable shops of Grafton Street had tempting buys like hand-knitted fishermen's Arran sweaters, fine Irish linen, Waterford crystal, delicate lace and handwoven tweeds.

Trinity College Library's most famous treasure is the *Book of Kells*, a copy of the four gospels beautifully illuminated by the monks at Kells in the ninth century.

If you have an Irish name, it's fun to visit Dublin Castle's Heraldic Museum and discover your family heraldry. Our family's (on my father's side) was a lizard and a green holly tree—I didn't discover the significance.

But it whetted my appetite to visit Belmullet on the West Coast in County Mayo, the birthplace of my paternal grandfather, according to family tradition. (I later discovered it was some kilometres from Belmullet in a village called Ardmore.)

Crossing Ireland by car was sheer delight. The country was rich emerald green, a panorama of white-washed, thatched cottages with blue smoke curling from peat fires, donkey carts, wayside shrines, and picturesque stone walls.

Gradually the scenery changed to wild moor, bog with stacks of cut peat drying for fuel, stark hills with stone boulders and tranquil lakes reflecting still clouds. Drivers were generous with lifts (we were hitch-hiking, my sister and I).

Crossing a bridge I noticed several stones sitting on the railing and part of the stonework at one end missing. The driver explained that it was a 'musical bridge'. People scraped the stones along it to produce musical notes. The stonework was missing because of a legend which said that bad luck would dog the steps of anyone who replaced them.

We were not far from the 'fairy forts', once used as underground refuges from marauding neighbours. Reputed to be the haunt of fairies, local children were warned not to go near them.

My driver said: 'Of course I don't really believe in fairies—or pixies and leprechauns—but 'tis better to be sure than sorry!'

Belmullet turned out to be a tiny village on the futhermost point of Mayo overlooking the Atlantic. By evening, with a huge moon rising, it looked beautiful in its lonely setting of moors, water and hills.

In the main cobblestone square an old lady in a long black dress and shawl sat beside a donkey with two panniers full of seaweed for sale. The main street was paved with rough pebbles and lined with little stone houses.

Behind lace-curtained windows, the curious eyes of women peered at the strangers. Children surrounded the car.

We put up at a local home and had a wonderful tea of farm fresh eggs, crisp bacon, delicious soda bread and 'tae' with a drop of whisky to keep out the cold.

A visit to the priest's house produced no trace of our ancestors. The name was not even registered in parish records and the graveyard revealed no clue in the headstones.

So, next day we set off for Galway Bay, passing encamped gypsy caravans with tinkers mending pots and pans around fires.

We came to the mountain, Croagh Patrick, where St Patrick had fasted and prayed for Ireland in A.D. 441.

My driver was keen to stop so I could climb the 790 metre mountain—preferably barefoot—because it was a day of annual pilgrimage.

'You must go for the good of your soul,' he urged.

'You'll never regret it and you'll have something to talk about for the rest of your days.'

He accepted my refusal with good grace.

We passed the fifteenth-century Round Towers, built as a defence against fighting neighbours. The only entrance was by ladder which the defendants climbed. They then drew up the ladder and poured boiling oil on their enemies below.

We didn't see the sun go down on Galway Bay but we climbed over the stony beach, enjoyed the panoramic view and admired the Claddagh rings on sale in little shops. They are a folk design consisting of two hands holding a heart, surmounted by a crown, and were exchanged in marriage by fisherfolk in the Claddagh district. They are still given as love tokens.

Our next stop was Killarney and a walk through the wooded estates to see the shining lakes, then on to romantic ruined Ross Castle which sat in flower-strewn meadows.

The Ring of Kerry turned out to be an enchanting coastal road down to Dingle, where beehive stone cells stood along the coast, once the retreat of monks who meditated there, and on to Slea Head where scenes from the movie *Ryan's Daughter* were filmed.

Blarney Castle was nearly my undoing. Determined to kiss the Blarney Stone and so gain the gift of eloquence, I climbed out on to an iron grating over a sheer drop, wriggled my feet into position, hung with my face under the rock and dizzily kissed the stone.

'Are you mad? Would you be trying to kill yourself?' shouted an attendant, who rushed up out of breath. Having explained that my way was not the right one, he insisted I do it again, this time with two men holding my feet and lowering me down.

As a reward for my persistence, he told me about the first man who kissed the Blarney Stone. He was the owner of the castle and had a terrible stutter. He rescued an old witch from the lake and she told him to kiss the stone which he did with the witch holding his feet. His stammer immediately disappeared (probably from fright).

But he did gain eloquence and even talked Queen Elizabeth I into withdrawing Ireland's heavy taxes and granting many favours. But, when another Irishman tried the same approach, the Queen said: 'I'll have no more of your blarney!'

The delightful resort of Youghal with its pounding surf and soft green and silver country once had Sir Walter Raleigh as mayor. He planted potatoes and introduced tobacco. When his servant saw smoke coming from his nostrils, he rushed to throw a bucket of water over his master.

Through the fertile country of Dungarvan, with its panoramic mountain roads and shining aquamarine sea, we came to Arklow and the Vale of Avoca, and stopped to see where 'the bright waters meet', and so back to Dublin.

I did not find my ancestors, but I did find the Ireland of

poets, saints and heroes. I drank dark Guinness in snug pubs before roaring fires, stayed in old inns, talked to brown-shawled women on lonely shimmering beaches and watched patient anglers in tweed hats beside mountain streams.

I discovered that Ireland is really emerald green and full of shamrocks and blarney—not to mention musicians playing ballads on fiddle, guitar, banjo, whistle and kitchen spoons; that truck drivers crossed themselves as they passed a church and diners in restaurants said a simple grace before meals.

All in all, there was a lot to be said for having more than a touch of Ireland in my veins.

RISHIKESH— HOLY TOWN ON THE GANGES

QUITE early one morning we drove from Dehra Dun through the Himalayan foothills of Northern India to the holy town of Rishikesh. Famed throughout India as the hallowed place where the sacred Ganges River comes down from the Himalayan foothills, the town is a centre of pilgrimage, its river banks crowded with ashrams.

Perhaps its greatest claim to fame in the Western world is that the Beatles' guru, Maharishi Mahesh Yogi, has his ashram here.

It was pleasant travelling in the early morning freshness before the fierce heat of an Indian summer day turned the car to a furnace.

We drove through forests aswirl with diffuse mist as the pale sun penetrated its thickets. Monkeys chattered from trees turned autumn shades of orange and yellow by months of scorching heat. Green parrots rose in clouds and a somnolent elephant tethered in a wooden shelter lazily swung his trunk.

We passed wandering *sadhus* clad in saffron robes walking to the sacred place, and a small brown boy flying a purple kite.

A notice posted at the road toll barrier listed charges for an interesting variety of traffic: 'Land lovers (Rovers I assumed), camels, bird-in-cage, pig-ups (tip-trucks perhaps?), elephant, horse and cart.'

We took breakfast at the famous Choti Wallah's (*choti* means 'little' and *wallah*, 'the owner or person in charge'), choosing from piles of sweet syrupy cakes.

My companion, an Australian-trained nurse and volunteer health worker in India, Anne Young (now Anne Boyd), ran the hospital and leper colony at 'Raphael', the International Centre for the Relief of Suffering (supported by the Ryder-Cheshire Foundation) home in Dehra Dun, a nearby hill station in the foothills of the Himalayas.

Ann chose her favourite dessert, *gulab jamon*, rings of fried sweet batter in syrup, and *lassi*, a salty sweet milkshake of buttermilk.

My breakfast consisted of curry and *chapatis* followed by *rabri*, a dessert made from sweetened condensed milk. We bought a handful of *barfi*, a rich fudge, from the vendor squatting among piles of exotic coloured cakes and sweets, great pans of boiling sugar for brown sugar cakes, and simmering vats of curry. This was all washed down with lime soda (too late I realized the bottle had a marble top). We had been warned to stick to Coca-Cola or beer and make sure the tops were proper commercial ones. Some drinks were made with unsterilized water from the river, we had been told.

(By the time I reached Katmandu, my next destination, my 'Delhi Belly' which resulted from the Choti Wallah's stop, necessitated a visit to the missionary hospital. But that's another story.)

Meanwhile the 'Choti Wallah' himself had taken up his stand outside the restaurant, drumming up business. His strange appearance attracted customers like flies to honey. The little shopkeeper was about ten years old, painted all over in pink body paint decorated with silver designs. His only garment was a pair of bright yellow baggy pants. His head was shaved except for one thick topknot which, swirled and painted pink, stood up like a unicorn's horn from the middle of his head. He looked supremely bored by the staring crowd.

Rishikesh is divided by the sacred Ganges. Ashrams and shrines straggle for kilometres along both banks. Pilgrims can cross by a swinging suspension bridge or a free ferry provided by the ashrams. Thick, sluggish sacred carp crowd the river, fat with feeding on blessed puffed wheat which pilgrims buy by the bag from the shrine priests.

Leading to the bridge was a line of wailing beggars thrusting out deformed limbs for our compassion. Their tins rattled with coins. Pilgrims gained blessings by giving alms and temple beggars could sometimes do quite well.

Anne stopped to talk to one voluble lady in the Hindi she had acquired since working in India. The animated conversation ended with the leper lady shaking her head decisively.

Anne explained: 'I thought I recognized her, she was a patient in our leper colony. I asked her why she ran away with another patient's husband and asked her to come back and be looked after properly in the colony. But she replied that begging was much more fun!'

At one stage the leper colony had quite a begging problem. Patients insisted on having an annual holiday, as staff did. They disappeared for a few weeks and, later, it was discovered they had been on a 'working' holiday. Begging brought in a little pocket money until the colony strictly forbade it.

Rishikesh is a pretty town, backed by forests. Through it runs the silver-green river fringed with sand, pebbles and rocks. Pilgrims crowded garish pink, yellow and orange painted shrines and ashrams. Tourists peeped in at the blue-faced god, Krishna, doll-like deities robed in splendid garments, altars decked with peacock feathers and silver paper and brightly coloured statues illustrating the tales of the religious epic, the *Ramayana*, and verses from the *Bhagavad-Gita* (the Lord's Song).

Pilgrims—many of them had spent a lifetime's savings on the journey—crowded river banks, washing away their sins. A woman dipped a naked screeching baby with a shaved head in the stream while its father looked on approvingly. Then she gave it the breast to pacify its shocked anger. With one hand she casually threw puffed wheat to the fat carp jumping out of the water to snap it up.

Clad only in white loin cloths, European hippies in uncomfortable-looking poses sat meditating on rocks or doing yoga exercises. In town they wandered in and out of shrines dressed incongruously as Sikhs, pilgrims or holy men, ostentatiously Eastern.

The purple bougainvillea rioted in ashram gardens. Meditation and peace apparently compensated for early rising and forbidden comforts of smoking, meat eating and sex.

Stalls sold fruit, vegetables, sweets, Hindi books and magazines. An orange-clad holy man leaned against a red pillarbox listening to a wandering flute player. The leisurely omnipresent sacred cow scattered the devout before it. It knew it had right of way over all traffic.

Through the forest, a few kilometres from town, we arrived at the Maharishi Ashram set in pleasant gardens and aswarm with black-faced monkeys. A disciple told us the yogi was travelling abroad, then launched into a lengthy explanation of transcendental meditation. He apologized for his fellow disciple, an Australian teacher, who was too busy meditating in one of the ashram's underground caves to meet us.

We also visited a downtown ashram. In return for a small donation, wooden holy beads were placed around our necks, a blessing given, our foreheads dotted with red powder and a bag of puffed wheat to feed the sacred carp thrust on us. The gardens were full of glass cases containing statues of gods, heroes and holy men, illustrating Hindu mythology, including some stomach-turning incidents.

Down by the ferry wharf where the thickest knot of pilgrims concentrated, sellers of brass and copper containers for holy water plied their trade. The balloon vendor held aloft a string of blue, red, pink and yellow globes, giving a fairground atmosphere to the holy proceedings.

Bells rang, conch horns sounded, holy chanting drifted from temples on clouds of pungent sweet incense. But the sun was growing ever fiercer, the ferry waited, and we left the holy city for the more pukka atmosphere of the former colonial hill station of Dehra Dun.

PERSEPOLIS—
ONCE THE CEREMONIAL CAPITAL
OF THE WORLD

WE had journeyed across the hot, dusty desert of Marv-Dasht on our way to Persepolis, almost a day's journey from Isfahan, a city of wonder to the ancient world.

Suddenly, like a mirage, a huge platform of rock rose towering out of the plain, with the magnificent backdrop of the purplish 'Mountain of Mercy', the Kuh-i-Rahmat.

The ancient Iranian capital of Persepolis is theatrical — like a huge stage set for some magnificent spectacle, as indeed it was when ancient kings presided over ceremonies of tribute from captive tribes.

This ruined city of Persepolis was once the ceremonial capital of the world conqueror, Darius the Great. The ruins are still known as the Throne of Jamshid, a mythical hero from India, who was transformed into an Iranian cult figure. It is solemn and imbued with a sense of mystery. The presence of ancient kings and old ceremonies of tribute lingers.

I could hardly wait to jump out of the bus and climb the platform. It was only an hour until dusk. The golden glow of sunset had bathed the ancient stone in a soft mellow glow. A forest of tall columns soared upward. I solemnly mounted the broad staircase. It was not a place to hurry. At the top of this monumental stairway of one hundred steps was the Gatehouse of Xerxes, guarded by winged bulls with human heads.

Persepolis is built on a man-made terrace hewn out of rock, with the blocks joined by iron dovetailing, and is approximately 457 metres long by 30 metres wide and from 8 to 20 metres high.

The city was built by world conqueror, Darius the Great, in the sixth century B.C. as a fitting setting for ceremonies of national importance, where the captive people could come to bring tribute and pay obeisance to their emperor.

It was occupied temporarily on occasions of national splendour and no expense was spared in building this city as a setting for an invocation by the whole nation led by the king-emperor, who took his kingship as of divine right from the god, Ahura-Mazda.

Persepolis was the capital of the first World Empire and one of the most magnificent cities of the ancient world.

I entered the Gatehouse of Xerxes and passed through into a square hall with four columns and three doorways and then on into the huge square — the 'Apadana' or Great Hall of Darius and Xerxes. Scattered around were huge fallen heads of mythical animals, of lions, horses and unicorns, which had toppled from their place as capitals on top of towering columns.

I sat astride an enormous double-headed horse, then climbed a ceremonial staircase to gaze at curly-haired Persian and Median officers carved into the stone. Dressed in long, pleated robes, with wavy beards, their enormous eyes seemed to stare into mine. Stairways and walls were covered in bas-reliefs depicting the captive tribes — Medes, Assyrians, Babylonians and Greeks.

Remnants of the city's former glory persisted in the soaring fire-ravaged columns, the winged colossi and the beautiful sculptures. Persepolis was a sacred place of national tradition, representing the achievement and power of the king.

The Spring Festival (now called Now Rouz— 'the new day') was held here, when the gods were implored to give fertility and abundance to the kingdom. It was here that the former Shah held his official coronation celebrations, because of its evocation of ancient Persian glory. (Now Rouz is still celebrated by Iranians on 21 March, with dancing, feasting, and festivities to welcome spring.)

Persepolis was built by the combined efforts of the Empire. Begun by Darius I (The Great), it was continued by his son, Xerxes. Egyptians, Carians and Hittites worked together with Babylonians. The Ionians and Lydians carved the stone, Medes, Egyptians and Carians who were the best goldsmiths worked the gold-leaf decorations. Babylonians made the mud bricks.

The stone carvers were paid the least, silversmiths did somewhat better and goldsmiths had the best wages, paid partly in cash and partly in goods. Women and boys did much of the gold and silver work. The workers lived in little mud huts below the huge platform; the nobles in larger, better houses — but the city of Persepolis was reserved for the royal family and their servants.

Materials came from all over the Empire. The timber for walls and ceilings was of Lebanese cedar and Indian teak; the gold came from Lydia and Bactria and the precious stones, such as emeralds, turquoise and lapis lazuli from Turkestan, Afghanistan and Uzbekistan.

The ruins of Persepolis were rediscovered at the end of the fifteenth century. It was not the capital of the Achaemenian Empire. Capitals had included Bablyon, Ecbatana (modern

Hamadan — called the fortress), and Shushan or Susa, which was the palace of Darius (Persepolis was for ceremonies).

It was from these capitals that the emperor ruled his kingdom. A stone-paved road was built from Susa though the mountains to Persepolis, which was originally called 'Para' by the Persians, but later 'Persepolis' by the Greeks.

The Achaemenian Empire, led by Darius, had hoped to bring peace and prosperity into the world they conquered. Darius said that he 'loved righteousness and hated iniquity'. He maintained, 'It is not my will that the strong should oppress the weak ... God's plan for the earth is not turmoil, but peace, prosperity and good government.'

His predecessor, Cyrus, King of Persia, had annexed Babylon and delivered the Jewish people from the fifty-nine-year-old captivity. Cyrus was convinced that God had charged him to build a temple at Jerusalem and the Jews were returned there to build their temple. Cyrus's kingdom stretched from the Aegean to the Ganges and from the Nile to the Oxus River. It was Cyrus who chose the site of Persepolis as a magnificent setting for the emperor to receive tribute from captive nations. His successor, Darius, carried forward the work.

As I sat on a pedestal, the sun lit the tall columns, the huge heads of mythical animals, and brought to life the bas-reliefs depicting captive tribes bringing tribute for the Spring Festival.

There were Scythians in pointed hoods, Assyrians in Phyrgian caps with chin straps, shepherds from Bokhara, Persians, Babylonians and Parthians. Some carried sheep and jugs; others led oxen. Camels and giraffes joined the frieze. Arabs, Indians and Greeks marched in procession. Here were portrayed the foot soldiers, the royal guard of Medes and Persians, cavalry officers, archers and charioteers.

The huge carved plain gradually darkened as dusk filled the valley. The mountains grew golden and Persepolis took on the colour of flame.

Once it had burned with a fierce conflagration when Alexander the Great, who captured the Royal City, put it to the torch, destroying forever the pomp and pageantry of the Royal City.

He massacred the men, enslaved the women and plundered

the treasury. Perhaps he was avenging the sack of Athens.

The mountains turned rose, then finally purple, as night descended.

We made camp at the foot of the great rock platform, lit our cooking fires, then spread our stretchers under the star-filled sky. Persepolis by moonlight was still a magical city.

I rose early to climb the double staircase leading to the Audience Hall. Perhaps Persepolis is seen best at dawn, when there is a wonderful clarity of light. Fascinating carvings show the king fighting with a bull, a lion and some mythical beast. Others show him shaded with a ceremonial umbrella held by an attendant.

The Winter Palace had only ruined doorways and windows, but the Palace of Xerxes had bas-reliefs showing servants going about their daily duties. There were ruins of the royal harem, the guards' quarters and the treasury. Walls were carved with the figures of Achaemenian guards and a huge lion of iron devouring the symbol of Assyria, the bull.

The tribute bearers, the courtiers and soldiers marched step by step with me, etched in scale on the wall of each stair. Darius was seen with the crown prince, Xerxes. Palace officials greeted a Median visitor and guards stood to attention. The Persians wore little caps which had influenced the design of the national hat of Persia, called the *pahlavi*. The *pahlavi* gave its shape to the former Shah's crown, called the Pahlavi Crown. Medes wore little round helmets which were the forebears of the headgear worn in the province of Persia called Azerbaijan.

Persepolis, with its marvellous evocation of the Persian Empire of Darius, is quite unique — perhaps one of the Wonders of the Modern World.

About five kilometres from Persepolis, is the burial place of kings at Naqshi-i-Rustam. Here, near the Zoroastrian Fire Worshippers' Temple, are the tombs of four great kings — Darius the Great, Xerxes, Artaxerxes and Darius II. Their tombs are carved high on the cliff face. They have been despoiled and were no longer open to the public but, even from the outside, they were impressive.

The tomb of Darius bore the inscription:

'I am Darius, the great King, King of Kings, King of lands

peopled by many races, King of this great, wide earth, son of Hystaspes, the Achaemenian, a Persian, son of a Persian and Aryan of Aryan descent.

'By the grace of the God Ahura-Mazda, these are the provinces which I have conquered afar. I have governed them; and they have paid me tribute. What I have commanded they have done; the law which was mine was imposed upon them; Media, Susiana, Parthia, Aria, Bactria, Sogdiana, Khwarezmia, Drangiana, Arachosia, Sattagydia, Gandhara, India, the land of the Amyrgioi Scythians, the Scythians with the pointed hats, Babylonia, Assyria, Arabia, Egypt, Armenia, Cappadocia, Sparta, Ionia, Skudra, the Scythian lands away from the sea and the Ionian lands away from the sea, Africans, Ethiopians, Magians and Karkhians.

'Said the King Darius: Ahura-Mazda, when he saw the earth in commotion, gave it to me. He made me King. I am King by the grace of Ahura-Mazda.

'If you think the lands dominated by Darius be few in number, then look upon the image of those who support my throne. Then shall you know them, and you shall learn that the lance of the Persians has ranged far afield, then shall you know that Persia has fought her enemies far afield.'

Has there ever been such a proud boast in death? But, alas, even for emperors, the glory of the world passes and they return to dust.

ISRAEL—
ALL THINGS TO ALL PEOPLE

ISRAEL is a country of startling contrasts—modern cities and nomadic goat-herd tribes, Arabs in traditional costume, girls in bikinis, Franciscan monks and bearded Orthodox Jews in the garb of nineteenth-century Eastern Europe.

It's a country that's all things to all people—the land of Moses and King Solomon's Temple, of Jesus and his followers and of Muslim holy places such as the rock on which Abraham prepared to sacrifice his son, Isaac. This is the very rock from which Muhammad rode to heaven astride his famous steed, El Burak. And this same stone, within the Dome of the Rock, is, according to Jewish tradition, the foundation stone of the temple.

Like Greece, Israel is part of our Western cultural heritage and, no matter what your religion, or lack of it, you can't help feeling excited to come 'home'. Israel is both exotic and familiar, an exciting journey following in the footsteps of prophets and saints, emperors and conquerors.

History comes to life in Israel, whose story began almost 4000 years ago when God called Abraham to go into the Land of Canaan. In the years which followed, Hebrew patriarchs and prophets, invading armies of Assyrians and Babylonians, Persian kings, Roman emperors, Crusaders, Saladin and Napoleon have all come this way.

It's not surprising with such a history that there is so much to see—Roman ruins, Crusader castles, places of pilgrimage for Jews, Christians and Muslims alike—and the crowning glory of magnificent Jerusalem.

You can stay on a kibbutz, float like a cork in the salty Dead Sea, follow in the footsteps of Jesus in Galilee, sample the hot springs in Tiberius, relax in Tel Aviv, Herzliyya or Netanya on the Sunshine Coast, or Eilat on the Red Sea, visit Mount Sinai and St Catherine's Monastery where Moses is said to have received the Tablets of the Law.

From London I caught an El Al flight to Ben Gurion airport at Lod, the international airport, half way between Tel Aviv and Jerusalem, a distance of forty-five kilometres. At London airport I was interrogated as to where I had spent the previous night and whether anyone had a chance to get at my baggage. My hand baggage was searched (I had remembered to keep my camera empty of film and the films in a plastic bag in my cabin bag for easy inspection).

I was touched on my arrival to see an old woman get off the plane, take her first steps on Israeli soil and, overcome with emotion, weep as she knelt and kissed the ground.

From the airport I took a *cherut*, a metered taxi which is a community cab taking up to seven people. I could have taken an airport bus to either Tel Aviv or Jerusalem.

There is an inexpensive bus network throughout Israel but the few trains are rather slow. The train journey between Tel Aviv and Jerusalem through the mountains is quite pleasant, however.

Israel was an easy country in which to travel independently. English is widely spoken, people are very helpful and a lot of exploring can be done on foot because each area is packed with tourist attractions. You don't have to join a package tour unless you really want to. Security is very apparent with checks at entrances to public buildings, theatres and cinemas. I was careful not to wander alone at night and to make sure I was out of the old city in Jerusalem by dusk. I dressed modestly by any standard, but was still plagued by Arab touts when alone.

Eating in Israel was quite an adventure. Of course Jewish restaurants are kosher, which means they serve either dairy products such as milk and eggs, plus vegetables and fish, or meat meals which exclude dairy products. Hotels often had two dining rooms, one for meat meals, the other for dairy dishes. Certain foods were excluded by Jewish dietary laws.

Israeli breakfasts are enormous. You choose from a buffet of soft and hard cheese, cold salted fish, eggs, salads, yoghurt, cereal, croissants, sweet pastries, and toast.

I sampled typical Jewish dishes such as gefilte fish, blintzes, chopped liver and chicken soup. Kosher restaurants were of course closed from Friday evening until sundown the following day for Shabat (Sabbath). A few remained open, but you had to buy your meal ticket before Shabat.

I also enjoyed eating in Arab restaurants, sampling Middle Eastern ('Oriental') cuisine which is similar to Lebanese. Not long after you sit down the table is covered with a variety of salads which may include cucumber in yoghurt, pumpkin salad, fried eggplant and eggplant with sesame sauce, humus, a paste of chick-peas with olive oil, and flat bread for wiping it all up.

Next, stuffed vegetables appear—vine leaves, eggplant, artichoke stalks, carrots, green peppers and courgettes stuffed with rice, and kubeh (a meat ball coated with cracked wheat).

This was followed by shishkebabs (chunks of spit roasted meat), roast lamb, lamb chops, lamb testicles (!) served with steaming rice.

Those who had any room left could hoe into baklava made with nuts, almonds, dates and honey, and tiny cups of Turkish coffee spiced with cardamon.

Seafood restaurants also abounded, especially on the coast.

Shopping was fun. Leather goods (including coats and hand-bags) attracted up to thirty per cent discount for overseas visitors. Other good buys were furs, women's fashions, textiles, pottery, diamonds, jewellery of gold, silver, precious and semi-precious stones, straw items, Eastern antiquities, native hand-work, hand-blown glass, arts and crafts. Unusual pottery and ornaments were on sale at artists' colonies in Jerusalem, Jaffa (Tel Aviv), En Hod in the hills of Carmel and Safed (or Zefat).

It was also fun to shop in the narrow alleyways of bustling bazaars, remembering to bargain.

There was no lack of entertainment. Israel has three ballet companies—the Israel Classical Ballet and the modern dance groups, the Bat-Sheva Dance Company and the Bat-Dor Dance Company, which perform in main cities and in kibbutzim. The Israel Philharmonic, the Haifa Symphony Orchestra and the Israel Broadcasting Symphony Orchestra give regular per-formances. There are many nightclubs, rock, jazz and folk groups in main cities and resorts, and folklore evenings of song and dance are presented regularly in Jerusalem, Tel Aviv, Haifa and Tiberias.

My journey began in Tel Aviv, from where I travelled by car up the coast to Caesarea, Haifa and Acre. I then turned inland to Nazareth, Safed, the Sea of Galilee area, the Jordan, Jericho, Massada and the Dead Sea, finishing up in Jerusalem for a week.

Tel Aviv—it means 'Hill of Spring'—combines a modern city and beach resort with the old city of Jaffa (also called Yafo), claimed to be the oldest port city in the world. Japhet, son of Noah, gave it a Hebrew name meaning 'beautiful'. The Greeks linked it with Jopa, daughter of Aeolus, ruler of the winds. Under King Herod and the Romans, Jaffa lost its supremacy to Caesarea.

The best hotels, including the luxurious Sheraton, where I stayed, are along the beach front where you catch the sea breeze.

Old Jaffa is mentioned in the Bible as the port from which Jonah set off on the voyage which landed him in the whale's belly.

After the whale threw him out at Jaffa, he boarded a boat for Ninevah. Jaffa was an ancient port when Solomon brought the cedars of Lebanon to build the temple in Jerusalem.

It is also where the apostle, Peter, brought Tabitha back to life, while staying in the house of Simon the Tanner. The lovely old church, St Peter in Jaffa, commemorates the miracle and the pulpit shows scenes from the life of St Peter. Jaffa was also the port of the Crusader Kingdom of Jerusalem.

The old city has been renovated to look as it did in Turkish times. Colourful old stone houses where artists, painters and actors live, antique shops, art galleries, speciality boutiques and arts and crafts shops enliven its cobblestone, narrow, winding streets. At night crowds flock to its restaurants and night clubs.

No visitor to Tel Aviv should miss the Nahum Goldmann Museum of the Jewish Diaspora, situated on the campus of Tel Aviv University. It tells the history and culture of the Jewish race in stunning audio-visual displays, including documentary films.

Diaspora means 'dispersion' and the museum deals with the history of the Jewish people after they were scattered throughout the world. Exhibits include models of synagogues of various countries throughout the ages, family life and religious ceremonies.

I found the Weizmann Institute of Science at Rehovot, about an hour's journey from Tel Aviv, interesting. The home of the first president of Israel, Chaim Weizmann, is located here in beautiful gardens. Much research of world importance is carried out at the institute.

Tel Aviv's other attractions include the Shalom Tower— for a panoramic view of the city, Carmel market, Carmel wine cellars, and Jaffa's picturesque flea market.

In summer you can attend concerts under the stars, folk singing and dancing in the parks. 'Coffee music evenings' with coffee and light refreshments served, are held in front of the old city hall.

Tel Aviv's fine eating places include several fish restaurants at Jaffa and restaurants such as the Yemite and the Zion which serve Oriental food.

Further north, past the attractive seaside resorts of Herzliyya and Netanya, is the ruined Roman city of Caesarea on the Mediterranean. Here Herod the Great built a magnificent city and named it Caesarea in honour of the Roman emperor.

Later it became the seat of the Roman procurators of Judea, including Pontius Pilate. It was once the leading maritime city in the eastern Mediterranean, but declined after the Muslim conquest, until the Crusaders took it over and fortified it.

It was very pleasant strolling around the remains of Byzantine and Crusader buildings including a cathedral, the Roman theatre, the main Crusader gate and the arched second century Roman aqueduct. The theatre is used for concerts, ballets and plays during the annual music festival.

You can stay at Caesarea in a luxury hotel or at a moderately priced beach colony run by a kibbutz.

Further along the coast we detoured to visit the artists' village, En Hod, in the Carmel Hills.

About sixteen kilometres on, the Carmel Hills area with its white houses and green parks becomes a dramatic background to the port of Haifa. From Panorama Road on the hill, there are sweeping views of the city and harbour, including the gold dome of the Bahai Shrine. If time permits, it's worth a visit to the Church of the Carmelite Monastery and the little cemetery where Napoleon's soldiers who died of plague are buried. There are also many fine museums.

Across the bay, we found the old walled city of Acre (Akko) with its ramparts, minarets, spires and domes. Acre was once the Crusaders' capital and you can visit the Knights' Hall in the underground Crusader town and walk on top of the ramparts.

The Ahmed El Jazzar mosque, with its relic of the hair of Muhammad, was built by Ahmed the Butcher, who also built the fortress on top of the city and fought against Napoleon. (The fortress was later used as a prison by the British.)

I enjoyed a stroll through a couple of ancient *hans* (early Eastern inns) and the bustling Oriental markets, and along the 'Beach of Purple', which takes its name from the days when the Phoenicians extracted the famous purple dyes from sea creatures found here. Fish restaurants such as Abu Christo (Father of Christ) and Ptolemais line the waterfront.

We turned inland and south, to Nazareth, a small hill town mid-way between the Mediterranean and the Sea of Galilee, and a centre of Christian pilgrimage since the sixth century. It also has the largest Arab population in Israel.

Wandering through its bustling bazaars, watching Arab children astride donkeys and veiled Arab ladies haggling over their purchases, it was easy to believe that the town was unchanged since the boy Jesus lived here. Tradition says He preached in a still-standing synagogue in the bazaar.

The tourist mecca is the Basilica of the Annunciation with its murals by artists of other countries. I liked the madonna mural by Australian painter Justin O'Brien, which featured a lyre bird and flannel flowers. The grotto beneath is the reputed site of the Angel Gabriel's message to the Virgin Mary.

Nearby, St Joseph's Church is said to be the site of the carpenter's shop.

Not far from the Basilica, near the Nazarene Milk Bar, was a coffee shop which had some of the best Arab coffee and pastries I have ever tasted.

Another surprise was the Frank Sinatra Brotherhood Centre.

From Nazareth you can explore Kafr Kanna (Cana), where water was miraculously turned into wine; Mediggo, site of Armageddon, Mount Tabor, which saw the Transfiguration of Christ, and Naim where Jesus raised the widow's son to life.

Further north, we visited Safed (Zefat), capital of Upper Galilee, a charming, ancient hillside town, with twisting cobbled lanes and alleys in the Old City. Here the mystic Jewish tradition of Cabbalism began and is still practised. The artists' quarter and the remains of the Crusader Castle are also worth a visit.

I stayed overnight at the Ayelet Hashahar Kibbutz Guest House, near the excavation at Hazor, and enjoyed a talk and film on kibbutz life. It is an ideal centre for tours to the Upper Galilee, the Tiberias area and the Golan Heights.

Kibbutz charges, depending on standards and location, vary from very cheap to quite reasonable. Convent and hospice accommodation is even cheaper. Some rooms even have private baths. And the Ecce Homo Convent in the Via Dolorosa in Jerusalem has magnificent rooftop views of the Old City.

Next day I explored Galilee country—the Valley of Genassaret, Tapego, the site of the miracle of the loaves and fishes, Capernum where you can see the ruins of the house

of Peter the Apostle's mother-in-law, where Jesus stayed, and
the synagogue where He preached.

The Mount of Beatitudes is surely the world's most peaceful
spot. The colonnaded modern white Italian chapel which
crowns the mount overlooks a tranquil landscape of wheat
fields, cypress trees and fields of purple flowers, down to
the sparkling blue Sea of Galilee.

The Chapel of the Beatitudes and the pleasant garden are
cared for by Franciscan brothers and the simple pilgrim hostel
is run by Italian Franciscan nuns. It is very inexpensive and,
I was told, served excellent food. You could also lunch there,
if you booked ahead.

Tiberias, built 2000 years ago by Herod Antipas, around
the magnificent baths and hot springs, was named for the
Roman emperor. The hot springs are still famous and I enjoyed
a mineral bath followed by a swim in a pool overlooking
the Sea of Galilee, then a delicious lunch by the shore, at
the Galei Kinnereth Tiberias Hotel. Unfortunately, St Peter's
fish, found only in the Sea of Galilee, was not on the menu.

Tiberias is also a good centre for touring the Galilee.

Next stop was the River Jordan where John the Baptist
preached. We continued south to the oasis town of Jericho
where the walls came tumbling down, and to the weird-looking
caves of Qumran where the Dead Sea Scrolls were discovered
by a wandering shepherd in 1947.

We stopped overnight at Moriah Dead Sea Spa Hotel and
next morning I sampled the hot sulphur baths, then swam
in the salty Dead Sea, the lowest spot on earth 400 metres
below sea level where, try as I would, I couldn't turn over
on to my stomach to swim. It is impossible to sink in a sea
where the 'icebergs' are of salt.

The country is a beautiful primeval lunar-like landscape—
a desert of craggy slopes of the Judean Hills and deep canyons
with an occasional oasis such as En Gedi where the young
David hid from the wrath of King Saul.

I took a look at the En Gedi Kibbutz Guest House which
was reasonably priced and set in pleasant gardens.

A few kilometres south we found the hilltop fortress-palace,
Massada. The once luxurious palace refuge of King Herod,
it is perched on the cliff top and reached by cable car or
winding footpath (a stiff climb). An early morning or late

afternoon visit is wise—the sun is too hot at midday, when I visited it. From the summit there are magnificent views of the pink mountains of Moab and the blue waters of the Dead Sea. Here, three years after the fall of Jerusalem, the Zealots—nine hundred and sixty-seven men, women and children—held out against the power of Rome for three years, then committed mass suicide rather than be captured.

Jerusalem, my last stop, is possibly the world's most interesting city. I stayed for a week, first at the luxurious King David Hotel, then at the smaller, delightful American Colony Hotel in the Arab area.

I found myself returning again and again to the old walled city with its eight gates, entering either through the Jaffa Gate, guarded by the Tower of David, or the Damascus Gate.

Near the Jaffa Gate, the Christian Information Centre provided information and organized interesting walking tours of the Old City and religious sites. Tourist information centres also provided advice on tours by foot or bus.

Joining an American archaeology professor staying at my hotel (and waiting for his students to arrive to dig at Caesarea) I explored the Old City. We visited the fabulous Dome of the Rock Mosque with its gilded dome and blue mosaic walls, the El Aqsa Mosque, the Wailing Wall (western wall of the Temple), the Way of the Cross (Via Dolorosa) and the Basilica of the Holy Sepulchre.

On Mount Zion, David's Tomb, the Jewish Museum, the Room of the Last Supper, the Dormition Church (site of the Virgin Mary's assumption to Heaven) and the Church of St Peter Gallicantu (St Peter in Chains) are the main attractions.

I sat having coffee at the Intercontinental Hotel overlooking the Old City and watched the setting sun turn the ancient buildings to gold, and lights like points of candle flame come on.

On Friday evening I walked to the Wailing Wall to see the pious Jews gather to pray at this holy spot—men at one end, women further along.

I took a bus at the Damascus Gate and got out on the Mount of Olives to visit the various churches, the Garden of Gethsemane, the Place of the Ascension and the Kedron Valley on foot.

I visited the Holy Land Hotel with its interesting scale model of ancient Jerusalem at the time of the Second Temple in its grounds. Mea Shearim, the orthodox Jewish quarter, was also fascinating, with its strictly observant Jews in traditional Hassidic garb, many small prayer-houses, synagogues and Talmudic college, and an open-air market.

I took a bus to Mt Hertzl for sightseeing but it took a long time to get around—a coach tour would have been easier.

At Hadassah Hebrew University Medical Centre on Mt Hertzl I found the splendid stained glass windows created by Russian Jewish artist, Marc Chagall. I went on to the John F. Kennedy Memorial and Peace Forest, then the Museum of the Holocaust, Yad Vashem, which is approached along a tree-lined Avenue of the Righteous Gentiles, a tribute to those who helped save Jewish lives during the Holocaust. The museum was the saddest experience of my visit, as friends and relatives of those lost wept as they remembered the Holocaust.

The mountain overlooks the pretty suburb of En Kerem, worth a visit for the Church of the Visitation, Church of John the Baptist, and Hospice of the Sisters of Zion.

Bethlehem was only nine kilometres to the south of Jerusalem, easily reached by bus. Here I found the beautiful Church of the Nativity, over the traditional site of the grotto of Jesus' birth. From the church, the bells ring out at Midnight Mass on Christmas Eve, proclaiming Christ's birth to the world. Outside the hillside town, shepherds still watch their flock in the Shepherd's Field.

Having done all that, I had only exhausted a fraction of Israel's fascinating sights, but like General MacArthur, 'I shall return.'

NORTHERN LUZON—
ANCIENT TRIBES AND THE
RICE TERRACES
OF A LOST CIVILIZATION

THE wrinkled grinning old men of the Igorot tribe perched like crows on a low tree branch outside the *ato*, the men's council house, looked harmless enough. It was hard to believe that, in their youth, they had set out on headhunting expeditions from this *ato*.

A pile of the unlucky victims' skulls were buried right under my feet.

The old men sat smoking their little metal pipes, and grinning as if butter wouldn't melt in their mouths. They wore G-string loin cloths, woollen jumpers and straw pageboy hats perched on the backs of their heads.

I was told that headhunting still survives in Bontoc, a Filipino mountain town of northern Luzon, but that it was mainly revenge killing when a member of the Bontoc Igorot tribe has been killed. Further north, in more remote provinces, it was a different story, the guide said.

When the red coral tree bloomed, the headhunters used to set out to raid rival tribes. Sometimes the hunt was a test of courage for a man about to be married. The severed head was a wedding gift for the future father-in-law and the bridegroom delivered it in a special headhunter's basket to prove his manhood.

Before an expedition, the rituals were observed. Pigs and chickens were sacrificed and the gall bladders examined for good omens. The enemy was attacked in the darkness of pre-dawn. As soon as a man fell to a spear, he was decapitated and the head placed in the *sangi*, the basket the warrior carries on his back for this purpose. Back at the village, heads were hung on poles and a chicken sacrificed to the spirits.

The previous day I had set out from the sophisticated luxury of Manila's Intercontinental Hotel on what sounded like a pretty primitive journey.

I packed slacks and blouses in a basket, loaded my airline bag with camera equipment, cosmetics and first-aid supplies,

selected a shady straw hat and saved my breakfast rolls to
eat on the 1500 kilometre journey north.

I had been to the central mountains of Turkey, the deserts
of Afghanistan, the remote regions of Iran, and was mentally
well prepared for a rattling old 'rabbit' bus to transport me
north. But my transport turned out to be a streamlined, air-
conditioned coach with a pretty uniformed hostess. My carefully gathered provisions stayed in my basket. The very reasonable fare included snacks and soft drinks.

I was due for lunch in Baguio, the mountain resort known
as the Summer Capital of the Philippines, six hours later.
The bus left at 7 a.m. I reclined in my window seat which
Mel, a lanky American, had insisted I take so I could 'watch
the view'. Mel knew it by heart. He had been journeying
to Baguio for many years on holiday from Okinawa where
he worked as an engineer with the American air force.

The passing parade was reminiscent of every highly coloured
postcard I had seen of the Philippines. Buffalo-drawn peddlers'
covered wagons swayed along the road loaded with straw
baskets, woven cane furniture and every conceivable straw,
bamboo and rattan household article. Farmers sat astride
caribou (water buffalo), wearing bright blue shirts, black pants
and wide-brimmed straw hats, jogging their rope reins.

The sense of space was overwhelming. Lush green rice
paddies stretched to the horizon. The sky seemed so high
that the curve of earth seemed caught in a glass bell jar of
incredible smoky colours. The sky was ribboned in pale pink,
soft turquoise blue, misty mauve, grey and cream. We passed
a broad, smoothly sweeping river along which chugged canoes
with outboard motors and a lazy paddle steamer puffed out
the odd cloud of smoke.

The smell of burnt sugar cane hung over the lush green
sugar-cane plantations which grew as tall as a man, where
burning was taking place. Lines of colourfully garbed country
folk moved in rhythmic lines planting rice.

We passed Mary Jane's Store which, like its many little
wayside stall counterparts, sold everything from soap and
biscuits to candles and rope. Men squatted in village streets
preening their prized fighting cocks. Christmas lanterns hung
from shop fronts (in the Philippines Christmas celebrations
last for six weeks).

The wooden houses were built on stilts for extra coolness and perhaps protection when the rains came.

The town of Angeles looked hardly a town of angels. Not far from the American Clarke Air Force Base, it was a rather tawdry mixture of 'Topless à Go Go', gambling dens, nightclubs and cocktail lounges, with slum shacks on the outskirts.

We sped in our air-conditioned glass cocoon through seared yellow wheat fields, past pools of purple water lilies, through the town of Carmen Rosales with its open-air shops and traffic tangle of bicycles, trishaws, *jeepneys* (colourful jeep buses) and cowboy movie posters for *Bandolero*, *Crazy Joe*, and *Life and Death*.

Then the purple-hazed foothills with their coconut palms, rioting pink bougainvillea and white frangipani gave way to racing mountain streams and autumn-coloured croton bushes. We wound up into an alpine world of pine trees and tall yellow sunflowers, to Baguio.

The resort is famous for its cool climate, parks and markets, schools of weaving and silver craft and its Igorot tribal community which does primitive carvings. But Baguio's main claim to fame is that it is the gateway to the mountain provinces with their fascinating primitive Igorot tribes—the Ifugao, Galinga, Apayao, Bontoc and Bengets, and what has been described as the eighth wonder of the world, the Banaue Rice Terraces.

These terraces were hand-carved from the mountain before the time of Christ by a migratory people believed to have come from South China or Indo-China. They took more than 2000 years to build and, placed end to end, would reach more than half-way around the world. The Ifugao tribe still carefully hand cultivate these rice terraces which are irrigated by a system of bamboo pipes bringing water from mountain springs.

After lunch at the first-class Pines Hotel, I left Baguio by car for Banawe, to arrive the following day. We had to reach our overnight destination, Mount Data Lodge, four hours' journey winding around tortuous, largely unsurfaced roads, before night descended on the mountains.

Ominous dark clouds hung over the magnificent mountain ranges, trailing mist along the pine-clad mountain tops. It was sombre, brooding, solitary country. At the bottom of a ravine a sapphire-blue river glowed. White lilies starred the mountain side.

We wound higher and higher until it seemed we were approaching the roof of the world. Dark-skinned mountain women with long jet-black hair hanging down their backs, wide-brimmed straw hats, and babies strapped to their backs, looked like South American Indians.

Some mountaineers from a logging camp squatted outside their huts smoking metal pipes, while a man leading a pig on a string strolled by. Children in faded cotton dresses and pullovers came leaping for joy down the mountain road. A primitive wayside cross was decked with a woven, fibre grey rose.

Rain and fog made visibility poor and we had several near collisions with mountain buses and jeeps. But, just as night fell, and it would have been too dangerous to continue on the hairpin bends, we drove up to the lodge.

I was the only guest and sat sipping a gin and tonic before a roaring log fire, looking at the headhunters' baskets, part of the hotel's collection of Igorot artifacts. There were old cooking pots, wine jars, antique Chinese plates brought up from the lowlands, mother-of-pearl necklaces used as money to barter for essentials like salt, and mysterious wooden idols with secret, savage expressions. Many Igorots are now Christian but still worship carved idols.

The comfortable lodge was run by the Government as a stopover hotel on the way to the rice terraces. There were all kinds of interesting places to visit from the lodge—Kabayan with its ancient mummies, Salinas with its salt springs and Sagada with its primitive burial caves. With no time to visit them all, we were making the next morning for Bontoc, the town centre of the Igorots, a headhunting tribe which still lived much the same way as it had done for hundreds of years.

I woke to darkness and cold. The mists had closed in and the lodge seemed isolated and eerie. After a breakfast of scrambled eggs, tea and toast served by friendly, cheerful servants, the day began to look brighter.

After a few hours' journey through villages of galvanized-iron-roofed huts and red-roofed wooden churches, and fields of green vegetables, the first terraced rice field cascading down the mountains came into view. Not far from Bontoc we came across some burial caves with coffins made from hollowed-out trunks of trees.

Then came the parade of the Igorot tribal people, trotting along the road. The men wore G-string loin cloths. Their strong, sinewy thighs and legs were bare. Some had woollen pullovers and pudding-shaped knitted caps. Others wore small woven straw 'page-boy' caps. Bachelors wore them turned towards the front, married men perched them on the back of their heads. Matches, pipes and odds and ends were kept under the cap in place of pockets.

The ladies wore wrap-around, gaily coloured striped woven skirts with fringed belts, and cotton blouses. Their hair was bound with beads, their arms bare and intricately patterned with tattooed designs. Both men and women smoked small metal pipes. Some carried wooden sticks and shovels to dig the fields.

Our first stop was at the Weaving Co-operative in Bontoc. It was a simple hut with several long looms. One woman sat on the floor at one end of her loom, while a second woman with coloured balls of cotton in a plastic dish ran up and down the length of the room passing the cotton under the loom. The Igorots are justly famous for their weaving and the intricately embroidered bright red, green, yellow, purple and black skirt lengths are very beautiful and sell at a reasonable price in the Co-op's store.

But it was the women's tattooed arms which fascinated me. From wrist to shoulder they were a mass of finely worked blue-black designs, done partly for decoration but also as an initiation test. Girls without tattoos were barred from celebrating festivities and the village people spat on them in contempt. Women were tattooed all over their breasts, necks and arms, the patterns taking the place of clothes. Women were naked from the waist up.

Tattooing was a painful process which took a day. Metal needles or the spines of trees or animals were used to scratch in a mixture of soot. The wounds take up to a week to heal and sometimes infection sets in and women run a high fever.

My guide, Bong Cawed, was one of the new generation of Igorot tribesmen. A handsome, educated young man in a broad-brimmed 'cowboy' hat, he managed the Cawed Hotel in the township of Bontoc. His modern dress of slacks and shirt was a complete contrast to the old men in their G-string loin cloths, woollen pullovers and page-boy hats called *fallaka*, and often decorated with beads, boar's teeth and red feathers.

I wanted to explore the men's house, the *ato*, which had a galvanized-iron roof, walls of stone, grass and sticks plastered with dried mud to close the cracks, and no window. The entrance was very low (about a metre high) and narrow. Glancing nervously at the old men perched on their branch, I asked Bong if a woman was allowed in this all-male village stronghold. He said it was quite all right, so I concertina-ed my head and legs and crawled crab-like, sideways through the entrance.

Like the other young boys, from the age of seven Bong had slept in the *ato* where he received training in obedience, discipline and tribal laws and customs. The *ato* is also used as a council house and a public dormitory for unmarried men, widowers and married men who have had a quarrel with their wives and spend the night away from home.

From here headhunting expeditions set out after suitable ceremonies and animal sacrifices. The warrior who claimed a head was given the jawbone as a souvenir. Often he used it as a handle for the gong he played in festivals and which is named after the decapitated man. He is also entitled to have a special design tatooed on his chest.

Inside it was quite dark, but I made out the traces of a fire. It must get very smoky without a chimney, but Bong said the men got used to it. Everything was designed for warmth. In a space about 1.5 metres by 2.2 metres a series of wooden benches made of planks took up most of the room. The men and boys slept packed like sardines, lying on their sides with legs drawn up under their chins to save space.

Apart from being a public male dormitory (visitors also are put up here), the *ato* is a meeting house where the men of the tribe spend their leisure time weaving straw baskets or hats, smoking their pipes and talking of village matters. Sometimes they babysit with their children while the mothers finish the chores.

The council which meets in the *ato* used to accept or reject war challenges from rival tribes, declare war and sue for peace.

Nowadays (1986) it still decides the activities and rituals of the village, fines and punishes offenders against tribal law.

Outside the *ato*, where the old men squatted on their haunches, is the *pak-ko*, a leafy tree that grows sideways, and here once stood a post where heads from the headhunting expeditions were hung. Now the *tiken*, a mountain plant believed to have magical powers of protection against chest disease, hangs here. The doctor has little place in the Igorot tribal society. If someone falls ill, villagers believe the spirit of a dead relative is angry. Instead of a doctor, an old lady of the tribe is called in to pray and animals are sacrificed to placate the spirit.

Since the dead are buried in the village gardens, only sweet potatoes for pigs are grown. Any vegetables grown in such soil would be considered unfit for human consumption, but fruit on trees is considered a different matter and villagers happily eat bananas, avocados and papaya grown here.

Most villages have a young maidens' dormitory (*olog*) but in Bontoc it had been abandoned and the girls stayed at the mission school. But in other villages the *olog* still played a big part in village life. From the age of thirteen, the marriageable age, girls slept in the *olog* under the care of a spinster or a childless widow. But men were not excluded. Courting was done here and when a couple was betrothed they slept together here. Later they sleep together at a friend's house, then prepare for the wedding by ceremonious bathing in the river. If on their way back to the village they don't meet a bad omen like a red bird or a black snake, then the marriage goes ahead. If they do, it is postponed.

The *olog* looks like the *ato* but does not have fire places. Most *ologs* are built on top of pig pens and the narrow space between is used as a gathering place for the girls and boys before each retires to his or her separate sleeping places.

Divorce is not recognized except in the case of childless couples who may wish for children from another partner. Then, by mutual consent, the marriage may break up. When a man leaves his wife for any reason he leaves everything to her and the children, just keeping his G-string loin cloth.

Bontoc is a good place to stop over on the way to Banaue. A few kilometres further on we left Igorot country and entered Ifugao tribe country, thick forests with timber camps, rice terraces, magnificent mountains and villagers wearing varied headgear—knitted berets with pom-poms, head scarves and straw sombreros. Pink tree orchids grew by the road.

Around a bend we came upon a fantastic sight—as far as the eye could see, the whole mountain had been carved into a cascading series of symmetrical rice terraces filled with mirror-smooth green water like scalloped waterlily ponds.

Over 3000 years ago a Mongolian tribe carved up the mountain into terraces, three times as long as the Great Wall of China. Remains of the Mongolian migration from China or Indo-China suggest it took place in the second millennium before Christ.

These early migrants brought a culture of polished stone, copper and bronze, but a second migration in the first millennium before Christ brought iron, pottery and woven cloth. The Ifugao tribe of Banaue are descendants of these folk, carriers of the terrace culture. They till the terraces using a bamboo irrigation system just as their ancestors did.

Not far from the first-class Banaue Hotel is an Ifugao village where the inhabitants live as they did over 400 years ago in the time of the Spanish occupation.

The journey back to Baguio takes from eight to ten hours. We took a different route, although the roads were said to be worse, through the province of Nueva Vizcaya. It was a long, tiring journey, broken by a picnic on a hillside when my driver, Amado, and I lunched on ham and cheese sandwiches, bananas and Coca-Cola. But the journey was enlivened by Amado's stories.

He came from Lagawe, the principal town of Ifugao, and told me how on a nearby hill General Yamashito signed the Japanese surrender during the Second World War. The rank of the Filipino officer was only lieutenant and Yamashita refused to surrender to a junior officer, so the Filipino was immediately upranked to colonel.

Amado also told me that the former president of the Philippines, Magsaysay, who was enormously popular with the people and had been lost in a plane crash, was still believed by some of the mountain people to be alive, surviving somewhere in the mountains.

The roads were indeed terrible, the car slipping in mud and bumping over rocks and piles of earth, but it was passable, except in heavy rains. The plains which followed the last Ifugao town of Lamat were covered with luxuriant rice paddies, palm trees and vivid flowers. The houses were of neat bamboo or thatched with iron roofs and bamboo fences.

The people of Nueva Vizcaya are Christians and trucks appeared bearing names such as 'St Matthew' and pictures of the Sacred Heart with slogans such as 'I am counting on You.'

Clip-clopping *calesas*, wooden carriages dating from Spanish times, drawn by high-stepping horses, passed by.

Amado used to drive a bus from Manila to Baguio in former troubled times when drunken passengers, hold-ups and stan-dover men made such journeys difficult. Not unnaturally, he prefers driving a taxi. But even that has its hazards. If a driver kills a mountain child, retribution is swift. Even if a chicken is run over, he must pay exorbitant compensation because the villagers calculate its value to include all its possible descendants and their eggs and chicks.

I asked him did the Igorots still headhunt?

'Yes, if one is killed,' he said.

Some years ago a soldier shot a drunken Igorot boy. The Igorots set up road blocks to find the soldier and avenge the boy's death. The authorities, afraid to let the soldier out, kept him confined to quarters.

We reached Baguio that evening and next morning I flew to Manila. In forty-five minutes I passed from the primitive world of headhunters, ancient mountain terraces and tree orchids to the colourful, bustling, Spanish-influenced city of Manila—an incredible contrast.

But the Philippines is like that. Many strange and wonderful worlds lie locked within its 7000 islands just waiting to be explored.

MONTEREY—
STEINBECK COUNTRY,
CALIFORNIA

MONTEREY'S canneries closed after the sardines disappeared from the Bay in the mid forties, but tourism has given Cannery

Row, immortalized in Steinbeck's novel, a new lease of life.

You can't help wondering what Steinbeck's colourful characters—loafers, cannery workers, prostitutes and boozers—would have made of the transformation.

Gone are the sardine fishermen, in hip boots and yellow oilskins, in the days when sardines were abundant and canneries worked day and night.

But you can still get the flavour from the old buildings which remain. There's the weather-beaten frame building where 'Doc' (Edward F. Ricketts) operated his marine biology laboratory at 800 Cannery Row.

Here Ricketts collected sponges, anemones, barnacles and octopi for sale to schools teaching marine biology, and caroused on rough red wine with Steinbeck and other mates.

Wing Chong's market building, now called the Old General Store, still sells everything from fireworks in the middle of winter to Christmas decorations in July.

'Wash hands often. Rinse thoroughly in disinfectant. Prevent fish poisoning', reads an old notice board on the façade.

Dora's bordello (the prostitute's real name was Flora) has been torn down, but Doc's place is now a private club for artists, writers, lawyers and businessmen of the Monterey Peninsula who carry on the tradition of sitting, talking and drinking.

Steinbeck wrote: 'Cannery Row is a poem—a grating noise, a quality of light, a tone, a habit, a nostalgia, a dream.'

Cannery Row today sports fine restaurants, boutiques, a wax museum, wine-tasting room and a merry-go-round.

The Monterey Canning Co. has been restored as a gift shop.

Another cannery is now part of a fascinating restaurant, the Sardine Factory. Its speciality, Monterey prawns, was served at President Reagan's 1981 Inaugural Dinner—a great honour, as only a handful of top restaurants were asked to provide a special dish.

The restaurant has a nautical atmosphere with portraits of local sea captains, and a model ship above the big, open log fire. Scenes for the Clint Eastwood film, *Play Misty*, were filmed here. It is famous for its pasta and a secret recipe for abalone chowder.

We ended a fine meal with 'flaming sardine'—hot coffee laced with allegro liqueur and lemon peel, flamed.

One room of the restaurant (which can seat up to 1220 people) used to be the cannery cafeteria. An original menu on the wall reads: 'Cake 10 cents, chilli beans 15 cents, stew 20 cents, soup 10 cents.'

About US $50,000 worth of fine wines is stacked away in the cellar, including an 1897 Château-Latour at US $4000. Customers can bid for the restaurant's wines at auction or, if they prefer, can keep a supply of their own favourite bottles in the cellar.

Wildlife is another great attraction of a visit to Monterey. Whales love the area and you can see them at close quarters between December and April on a cruise from Fisherman's Wharf. The cruise also provides close-ups of birds, sea lions and sea otters.

The sea lions, with their bristling moustaches, enjoy sunning themselves at the base of Fisherman's Wharf, barking as they lie in wait for the fish tidbits thrown by tourists.

Point Lobos is the place to view the cute sea otters—those 'teddy bears of the sea'.

It's fun to stroll down Fisherman's Wharf with its takeaway seafood, fish markets, Italian and seafood restaurants, souvenir shops and boat marina. Charter boats are available for fishing trips.

Monterey Bay Aquarium takes its exhibits from local waters, including salmon, bonito and several species of sharks. You can also get close up views of harbour seals and marine birds. The forty-million-dollar complex follows in the tradition of Doc Ricketts and Steinbeck (who started out to be a marine biologist) and who both loved sea 'critters'.

The aquarium is located on the oceanfront side of Hovden Cannery, once Cannery Row's largest sardine cannery, and gives visitors a chance to enjoy the marine life of Monterey Bay, one of the richest and most diverse marine areas in the world.

Monterey's colourful past adds much to its charm today Many old adobe buildings (adobe is sunbaked mud and straw) have been carefully preserved.

Monterey was discovered by Spanish sea captain, Sebastian Viscaino, in 1602, and claimed for King Philip III of Spain. Father Junipero Serra established a mission in 1770, and Captain Gaspar de Portola a *presidio* (fort), garrisoned with troops.

Mexican rule replaced Spanish in 1821, in 1846 the bear flag of California flew, and a few years later, the Stars and Stripes, when California joined the union.

The best way to explore Monterey's fascinating past is by taking the four-kilometre Path of History walking tour (maps from the tourist department). It is part of the Monterey State Historical Park.

For a one dollar fee you can visit nine historic buildings and do escorted tours through three—usually a choice of the Monterey Custom House, the Stevenson House, where Robert Louis Stevenson lived in 1879 and got inspiration for *Treasure Island*, and the gracious Larkin House where the only United States consul to California lived from 1844 to 1846 (before California joined the Union).

The tour takes you to the spot where Spanish soldiers claimed the land for their king, and for a walk on a footpath made of whalebone.

A totally different experience is the magnificent Seventeen-Mile Drive, with its Monterey cypresses. The picturesque Lone Cypress is a popular spot with photographers.

Monterey provides many sporting activities but, above all, golf, with sixteen courses on the Monterey Peninsula (tame deer roam on some).

The courses include the world-famous scenic Pebble Beach course where the annual Spalding Pro-Amateur Golfing Championship is held.

Festivals include the California Wine Festival, the Monterey County Wine and Food Celebration, Monterey Jazz Festival and Dixieland Monterey Festival.

Fresh seafood—Monterey rock cod, Bay salmon, abalone, shrimp and squid—and fresh fruit and vegetables from near-by Salinas Valley make eating out a great pleasure. You can enjoy French, Italian, Mexican, Chinese, Japanese, Continental, and American-style meals.

Many movies have been shot along the rugged, superb coastline—one of the most beautiful in the world.

A famous artist once called Point Lobos 'the greatest meeting of land and water in the world'. The Point Lobos State Reserve is a paradise for hikers, cyclers, bird watchers, swimmers, photographers, snorkellers and picnickers. Wildlife abounds: sea lions and others offshore, brown pelicans, the great California grey whales. There are many interesting hikers' trails and more than 485 hectares of sanctuary for 250 species of birds and animals, 300 species of plant life, and 304 hectares underwater to explore. Free walking tours are available.

The area is rich in history—Indians, whalers, ranchers, smugglers, and gold miners have made it their domain.

Monterey is a good centre for exploring other areas. The legendary Hearst Castle, which the press baron once shared with Marion Davis, his mistress, is only 130 kilometres away. Big Sur, a stunning, wild and wonderful 145 kilometres of spectacular coastline, is a short drive away.

Much of this area inland from the coast is wilderness—lush meadows, giant redwoods, forests and mountains where wildlife (deer, red fox and bobcats) abound. I visited a famous inn, the Ventana Inn, furnished with rustic charm and great taste. It had an air of utter tranquillity, magnificent views, and the thunder of distant surf mingled with bird song and the rustle of tall trees. It was an idyllic, if expensive, retreat from the hassle of modern living.

It is a couple of hours' drive from Monterey to Salinas with its memories of Steinbeck, who described it in *The Wayward Bus* like this: 'In the deep spring, when the grass was green on the fields and foothills, when the lupins and poppies made a splendid blue and gold earth, when the great trees awakened in yellow-green young leaves, then there was no more lovely place in the world.'

The Steinbeck House, where the famous novelist was born and grew up, is a charming Victorian house which is now a restaurant serving delicious and inexpensive lunches. Determined that its historic associations would not be lost, a group of enterprising local ladies raised the money to buy and restore it. They formed the Valley Guild, a volunteer organization which owns and runs it. Volunteers staff the gift shop and serve lunches. Any profits go for maintenance and to Salinas Valley charities. The house is also a museum with Steinbeck memorabilia—a remarkable success for local initiative.

The Salinas Public Library is also worth visiting. It has a collection of fascinating Steinbeck manuscripts, various editions of his books, play posters and old photographs.

Carmel by the Sea, on the next bay south from Monterey,

is a charming small town with a romantic atmosphere. At various times a Spanish mission, Bohemian retreat and artists' colony, it still has the air of a sleepy village. The shopping centre—Ocean Avenue, and the small side streets—has quaint boutiques selling pottery, antiques, books, fashionable clothes, over seventy art galleries and many attractive coffee shops.

The village appearance has been maintained by local laws. Shopfront windows must blend with the colonial look, there are no traffic lights, neon signs, parking meters, high-rise buildings, cemeteries or gaols. Tree-lined streets are a fitting setting for pretty cottages with balconies, Spanish adobe-style villas, 1920s 'doll house' homes, courtyards, and the mansions of the wealthy. There are no street lights or pavements in residential areas and homes must have names, not numbers.

A short distance from town, a shopping area known as The Barnyard, started life as a bookshop, The Thunderbird, with an added coffee shop. John and May Waldroup, the owners, wanted customers to enjoy good books, wine and food in a pleasant atmosphere. It grew from there to become perhaps the most beautiful small shopping complex in America. Its cluster of eight buildings was inspired by old Californian barns. Fifty shops and galleries are built on different levels among fragrant gardens ablaze with colour, a windmill and water tower, colourful outdoor patios for enjoying the scenery, charming coffee shops. It is a place to browse, perhaps buy an antique, or beautifully hand-crafted souvenir, some old-fashioned candy, something quaint for your kitchen, an interesting addition to your wardrobe, or sample a variety of food, ranging from Japanese sushi to Americna beef, at the eleven restaurants. The day I was there a string quartet played Mozart in the peaceful gardens. As one *Los Angeles Times* writer summed it up: 'The Barnyard is what shopping centres ought to be.'

The beautifully restored Carmel Mission is well worth a visit. It was built by Father Junipero Serra in 1770, part of the mission trail along the Californian coast. Other missions open to visitors are San Antonio, Soledad and San Juan Bautista. The Tor House, built of granite found along the coast, and the adjoining Hawk Tower are striking examples of local architecture and open to the public by appointment on certain days.

Carmel has an annual Bach Festival in July, with concerts and recitals attracting lovers of baroque music.

I stayed at some wonderful hostelries. My two-level cabana at the Highland Inn, at Carmel, had its own spa, a roaring log fire and luxurious appointments. The magnificent Lodge at Pebble Beach, right on the world-famous golf course, had fantastic views, a vast bedroom with lavish appointments, a massive log fire, wine and cheese waiting to greet me. The quaint Green Gables Inn at Pacific Grove was a half-timbered, step-gabled house, built in 1888, furnished with antiques. Rooms had fresh flowers and fresh fruit, the softest quilts and pillows and pretty, feminine furnishings. It was one of many such charming old inns throughout California. (A directory is available from the tourist department for about fifty cents.) A new luxury hotel, La Playa, a three-storey Spanish-style building set in beautiful landscaped gardens, was being built in 1984.

It is hardly surprising that many stars of film and television choose to live in the area. Clint Eastwood, who owns a restaurant, The Boar's Breath, in Carmel, recently stood for and was elected mayor of the town. I met him when he joined his friend, Herb Caen, columnist with the *San Francisco Chronicle*, Caen's girlfriend Donna Ewald and me, when we dined there.

Novelist Henry Miller, writing of the area, said it all: 'One feels exposed not only to the elements, but to the sight of God . . . a place of grandeur and eloquent silence.'

LANGKAWI—MALAYSIA'S ISLANDS OF LEGENDS

BUTTERFLIES as big as your hand, monkeys swinging from jungle trees and eagles soaring around mountains of marble. They are all part of the magic of the remote, tranquil islands of Langkawi.

If you ever sought a relaxed, peaceful hideaway from civilization, Langkawi is the place.

The group of ninety-nine islands takes its name from the biggest island, Pulau Langkawi. The group lies thirty kilometres west of Kuala Perlis and 108 kilometres north of Penang, at the northern border of peninsular Malaysia.

Langkawi is known for its colourful legends. The strangest concerns the Lake of the Pregnant Maiden, surely a contradiction in terms. Childless couples from all over Malaysia make pilgrimages to the beautiful jade-green freshwater lake set on an island of the same name. Legend has it that a married couple, childless for 19 years, drank from the lake and the wife subsequently bore a daughter.

It is a sacred place and its air of mystery and tranquillity add to the legend. According to a waiter at my hotel, the Langkawi Country Club, a white crocodile lived in its depths. The crocodile is the ghost of a man who wronged others when he was alive. The waiter assured me he had seen the *bomoh* (local priest) call up the white crocodile for a group of tourists from the hotel.

That wasn't the extent of the *bomoh's* powers. He had also apparently called up a dead Chinese boy who had drowned in the lake, which police had dragged without success.

'The upright body rose straight up out of the water, was attached to a boat and taken to land,' the waiter assured me.

The hotel manager, Muhammad Latiff, confirmed that the *bomoh* had indeed located the body, but its upright ascent was a local embroidery of the tale. As for the white crocodile, three workmen repairing a wharf at the lake had seen it, together with two ordinary crocs. When I protested that tourists swam in the lake, I was reassured that legend has it that the crocodiles only attack evil-doers.

Local rumour had it that the Japanese buried a treasure near the lake during the occupation of the Second World War, but it has never been found. There is also a banshee cave full of bats nearby, reportedly haunted.

I took a speedboat to the lake and walked along a path through thick jungle. Monkeys swung from the trees, a huge lizard ran across my path and disappeared, red and black winged dragonflies and brilliantly plumaged kingfishers flew overhead.

The lake, jade green and deep, a slight breeze stirring its waters, had an atmosphere of utter peace befitting its mysterious legends. I declined a swim, not fancying an encounter with the white crocodile and zoomed off in the speedboat through the outer islands to a deserted white sand beach, where I swam in warm, gently undulating water. There were many such deserted beaches and the hotel would pack a lunch, arrange a boat and despatch you to the island of your choice, where you had the beach to yourself for the day.

April is a good time to visit Langkawi because it's the month when villagers go to one of the islands and climb the trees where the bees hive, after the honey. This is also the time when the *bomoh* is asked to call up rain, and the drums are beaten. The sound that once summoned the warriors to war echoes again across the islands.

Langkawi began as a pirate stronghold. It was mentioned in a chart used by the Chinese admiral Cheng Ho when he visited Malacca in 1405. Seventeenth-century records show that Langkawi traded in fine pepper with India, Sumatra, France and Portugal.

Legend has it that the island was under a curse for seven generations after the cruel execution of Mahsuri, a Malay princess unjustly accused of adultery. She proved her innocence when white blood flowed from her body at her execution. Soon after her death the islands were laid waste by Siamese invaders.

The islanders scorched their rice fields rather than abandon them to the invaders and this gave rise to another legend—that the black rice continues to surface after heavy rain. Island tours include Padang Masirat, the Field of Burnt Rice, and it's true that our guide did discover a few grains of charred rice to prove the legend.

Princess Mahsuri's tomb, a white marble monument near a village, is carefully tended by her admirers and is also a stop on the tour run by the Langkawi Country Club.

Some of the island's most beautiful beaches are visited, including Tanjong Rhu beach, shaded with casuarina trees— at low tide you can walk across to the neighbouring island— and the Beach of Black Sand which glitters in the sun, probably from tin ore or an oxide of tin.

The island tour also reveals mountain vistas, water buffalo in rice paddies, pink flowering trees, coconut palm plantations, banana groves, parties of Muslim schoolgirls covered from head to toe with only their little round faces peeping out from head veils.

Langkawi then (1983) had only one tourist hotel, the Langkawi Country Club, which was like an old-fashioned, comfortable guest house, but with first-class amenities. Its air-conditioned bedrooms had balconies overlooking magnificent views of sea and islands. Guests gathered in the evening to sink a few pints and play table tennis and darts, or relax in comfortable cane armchairs in the indoor games area.

The coffee shop-restaurant had roll-up blinds instead of walls so that guests could enjoy a spectacular view of beautiful gardens, sparkling sea, and dreamy mist-shrouded islands. The hotel served Chinese, Malay and European food. At night the seafood restaurant opened and diners were entertained by a local singer and pianist.

There was lots to do. The hotel had a swimming pool, tennis and badminton courts, billiards, fishing boats, sea cruises, picnic trips to beaches on neighbouring islands, sailing boats, windsurfers and snorkelling equipment.

There were pony rides for the children, volley-ball matches between guests and staff. You could hire archery equipment, a push bike or motor bike. The hotel also organized jungle treks, fishing expeditions, picnics and visits to the night market in Kuah Town.

If you felt like being alone, you could organize a solitary picnic on a secluded beach, collect sea shells, swim and tan.

Remote, unspoilt Langkawi is the perfect spot to relax. But if you are an evil-doer, steer clear of the white crocodile.

COCHIN—THE VENICE OF SOUTHERN INDIA

COCHIN, one of the most beautiful cities of Southern India, is like Venice, a network of lagoons, canals and islands.

But, unlike Venice, its islands are emerald green, its lagoons palm-fringed, its backwaters crowded with thatched villages, its sun tropical and its air perfumed with a scent of coconut and cinnamon. It has the beauty of a tropical paradise.

It also boasts a rich and exotic history: Egyptian writers like Ptolemy wrote of the delights of Musiris (the old name for Cochin), the Phoenicians of 3000 years ago traded in ivory, spices and peacocks, and 900 years ago Chinese traders plied these waters.

The ships of King Solomon brought the first Jewish refugees, fleeing after the destruction of the Second Temple of Jerusalem by the Romans in A.D. 70. Cochin, which has always had a reputation for religious tolerance, welcomed them, as it did St Thomas, Christ's companion and apostle, who came to nearby Cranganore in A.D. 52 to preach Christianity on the sub-continent, and the Muslims who made Cochin an early centre of their faith.

If religion was the spur which drove Christian, Jew and Muslim to Cochin, trade was the lure for the seafaring nations of Europe. There was a fortune to be made in spices, tea and coffee.

The Portuguese, under Vasco da Gama, landed in 1498, to be overthrown by the Dutch in 1663, who, in turn, were overthrown by the British in 1795.

This exotic mixture of influences is still apparent in a Dutch palace, Anglican churches, Portuguese forts and Jewish synagogues, in the graceful arc of Chinese butterfly fishing nets, in Chinese dishes sharing Indian restaurant menus, and in the ever-busy deepwater harbour where freighters still come from the four corners of the world to trade in ivory, pepper, spices and seafoods. It all makes Cochin an exciting place to explore.

Orientation begins with a boat tour of the harbour and lagoons by chartered motor boat, small canoe, low skiff with coconut matting roof, or regular ferry boat.

The scene is absorbing. Floating bamboo logs drift down river, ebony-skinned men in shallow canoes squat under huge sun-resisting black umbrellas and orange-sailed wooden boats brim with white turbanned Indians.

Birds hover over fishermen hauling in their catch. The port is filled with freighters loading fish, coconut, pineapples, teak, pepper, tea, coffee, rubber, oils, coir matting and cashew nuts.

Over the water the hot air is tempered by a spice-perfumed breeze. Along the shore the black silhouettes of the Chinese

fishing nets expand and contract as counterweights lower them
into the sea for a haul. Their owners live in temporary huts
built on the platforms which support the nets and take tea
from passing vendors in boats.

The city of Cochin covers a vast complex of islands and
lagoons — the mainland, Ernakulum, the artificial island of
Wilmingdon, made from earth excavated when the harbour
was deepened, the British-built Fort Cochin, Mattancherry,
the Jewish area, and the island of Bolghatty.

In the Jewish area of Mattancherry, women fill water pots
at the wells as they did in biblical times. The faded yellow-
and white-washed houses with red-tiled pitched roofs shimmer
in the heat.

The Jewish synagogue, built in 1568, has China-blue tiles,
white plaster walls and an ornate ceiling of gold squares
centred with blue flowers. The room is lit by white, gold
and blue Belgian glass chandeliers divided by brass columns
and its walls are lined with wooden benches. The ladies sit
for services in purdah behind wooden screens.

Its treasures include copper plates recording the privileges
granted to the Jews by the local maharaja and, in the sanctum,
the 200-year old torah (sheepskin parchment scrolls of holy
writings) surmounted by a golden crown presented by the
local Maharaja of Travancore (now Kerala) in 1805. Its greatest treasures — the two original silver trumpets from the
Second Temple of Jerusalem — were lost. The story goes
that the Levites, who blew the trumpets on the eve of the
Sabbath were running late and the laity usurped the privilege.
In the resulting quarrel the trumpets were destroyed.

The Dutch palace, next door to the synagogue, was in fact
built by the Portuguese who gave it to the Indian Raja of
Cochin in 1555. But it became known as the Dutch Palace
when it was renovated during the Dutch occupation. Its most
historic occasion was the reading, in its coronation hall, of
the Papal Bill of Pope Alexander Borgia, which gave the
western hemisphere to Spain and the eastern to Portugal.

Cochin was the site of the oldest European settlement in
India and the focus for military activity. The Portuguese, the
Dutch and the British all built forts here. Little remains of
the forts, but the military Church of St Thomas, which followed
the fortunes of war, becoming in turn Portuguese Catholic,

Dutch Reformed Church, Anglican and Church of South India, as each conqueror became the loser in the power game, is well preserved.

Vasco da Gama, who died on Christmas Eve 1524, was buried in this church. His memorial is still there, but the body was removed to Lisbon in 1872. The neat rows of pews, and the old-fashioned brown cloth *punkas* (fans) swayed by small boys stationed outside the church windows, are a reminder of colonial days.

Cochin is the home of world-famous Kathakali dancing and regular performances are held year round. The dance is 2000 years old and was traditionally performed all night in the temples. Nowadays, performances are given in a straw-roofed open pavilion and audiences sit on cane chairs under a star-filled sky.

All the parts are taken by men, who begin training at five years of age and continue for fifteen years.

From early times Cochin attracted the explorer and the traveller. When Marco Polo visited it in 1295, the journey was long and dangerous. The modern visitor has it easy with travel by swift, comfortable jet, but Cochin still rewards its visitors with its own special blend of romantic history and exotic beauty.

'ISFAHAN IS HALF THE WORLD'

FOR 400 years travellers have journeyed to Isfahan to wonder at its magnificence — its turquoise jewel-like domed mosques, soaring minarets, ancient luxurious palaces and rich handicrafts.

Muslims, Jews and Armenian Christians mingled with British and Dutch merchants haggling in the bazaars over carpets, spices from India or merchandise from Samarkand and Bokhara. Swiss watchmakers worked alongside Chinese potters and Persian silversmiths. These early travellers to the fabled Iranian city came by mule and camel on trade routes.

Just as I did, they must have gasped at the splendour of the shining blue-green domes, the exquisite aquamarine and amethyst tiles. Isfahan is a 'blue' city, almost a city of the sea, shimmering in the midst of a dry, arid land, south of the Great Salt Desert and east of the Great Sand Desert.

Within easy reach of Isfahan are the fabled ruins of the city of Darius, Persepolis, a city built as a summer retreat for an emperor-conqueror to receive tribute from his captive lands, cities and states. Within a day's journey, too, lies Shiraz, the city of poets, nightingales and roses.

But Isfahan is the greatest attraction. It dates from Achaemenian times but its most beautiful buildings were raised during the sixteenth and seventeenth centuries during the Safavid dynasty, especially under Shah Abbas.

The city is situated in a fertile valley, on the banks of the Zayandeh River. Spared by the Mongols, it is one of the most magnificent cities of the world, famous not only for its beauty, but for its fine crafts, woven rugs, hand-beaten silver, copper and brass, and miniature paintings.

I came to Isfahan by bus on an overland journey from Europe to India. After traversing the long, dusty barren desert areas, it was like coming to a green oasis. It didn't take me long to find the main square. I just followed the sound of hammers beating out copper and brass into pots, pans and table tops. The air resounded with the beat of hammer on metal.

The merchants sat in their shops intricately carving rich patterns on silver. If you liked a platter, bowl or tea glass holder, they would weigh the article on a pair of large scales and so estimate its price, taking into account the amount of workmanship in the beautiful patterns. They would bargain, writing down a price which the customer read, then add a lower price under it. The merchant then wrote a price between the two until finally a bargain was struck.

The bazaar and the main street of little shops were treasure troves. You could watch a miniature painter applying his ancient skill and acquire a tiny miniature on bone or ivory, or perhaps on the shell-like lid of a tiny silver pill box. The jewellery was delicately hand-made, often of silver, with turquoises and emeralds. Persia (now known as Iran) has both emerald and turquoise mines and the domes of the mosques seem to take their colours from the nation's jewels.

A covered labyrinth where you could easily become lost was known as the Covered Bazaar. It was filled with copper pots and pans, huge brass trays of geometric designs, hookahs, inlaid and carved wooden objects and brocades. You could watch the Iranian craftsmen printing the cloths, carving wood or moulding metal.

The heart of Isfahan is the huge Royal Square, known as the Medan or Nasq-e-Jahan. One side is dominated by the Mosque of the Shah, called the Masjid-i-Shah, an immense building with soaring green- and blue-tiled dome and minarets. In front, a shallow reflecting pool mirrored the exquisite tiles of its enormous doorway. On another side stands the smaller, but exquisite, Lotfellah or Lady Mosque, its brown and gold dome glittering in the sun. The third side contains the Ali-Kapi Palace. From its shady terrace, Shah Abbas Safavi and his courtiers watched polo (which originated in Persia), contests with lions and bulls, horsemen shooting with bows and arrows at a golden bowl on a pole, fireworks and processions.

Planned as a market place, a religious centre and a place of public assembly, the square is a rectangle 457 metres by 152 metres. The Ali-Kapi Palace dates from the time of Tamerlane and is three storeys high. Inside, stairways, corridors and halls are decorated with drawings of flowers, animals and figures.

The Covered Bazaar takes up the remainder of the square — a dim, musty place lit with streaks of sun filtered through shafts in the roof. You could become lost for hours in its maze of alleyways, emerging many kilometres from where you entered.

The Shaking Minarets of an ancient mosque lie on the outskirts of town as does the Palace of the Forty Columns — twenty columns reflected in a pool (to make the other twenty), bordered by archaic-looking stone-carved lions and servants supporting water spouts — all surrounded by cool, leafy gardens. It was used as a royal pleasure pavilion and hall of audience and is now a museum of art.

An unusual experience awaited us. With a guide we descended into the bowels of the earth and, as we descended, a peculiar odour became stronger. We eventually came to a cave and the source of the smell, a blindfolded camel which slowly walked in a continuous circle, moving a grinding stone which pressed out oil from cakes of linseed. The stone was attached to a long pole which the animal patiently pushed. The oil ran out into a tunnel, from where it was stored. The cave was lit by artificial light. We felt sorry for the camel and wondered if he ever saw the light of day but, the smell being rather overpowering, we were glad to emerge and take a few gulps of fresh air.

We next visited a carpet factory where tiny children, from six years of age, wove carpets into intricate designs, following a picture of the pattern kept before them. They squatted on benches in a row, their tiny hands working with great dexterity among the threads. They were unbelievably skilful, producing exquisite designs. They attended school for a few hours each day.

I had often wondered how it felt to live in a caravanserai where camel trains once stopped so that men and beasts could eat and be housed on their long journeys. Isfahan had converted a famous seventh-century caravanserai into the superb Shah Abbas Hotel. Sitting in its delightful gardens sipping perfumed tea, followed by clear toffee, we tasted a little of the paradise about which the Persian poets wrote.

Next door to this hotel is the famous Madreseh-e-Madar Shah Theological School, completed in the eighteenth century. It has the most beautiful blue-green dome in Isfahan. Here the Muslim theological students lived and brown-robed priests with white turbans walked by. A long still canal ran through the courtyard reflecting the turquoise archway, the little cells of students, and the yellow, gold and brown autumn leaves. From the minarets the muezzin called to prayer.

The Friday Mosque is Isfahan's oldest. Parts are believed to be over 1000 years old. It is thought that a Zoroastrian, or Fire Worshipper's Temple, stood here originally. It was ravaged by fire in the twelfth century, added to in the fourteenth and fifteenth centuries and is quite a mixture of Iranian styles of architecture.

Each mosque has a reflecting pool which mirrors the glorious colours — not only blue and green, but yellow, brown, mauve and amethyst. Beautiful tiles covered in floral or geometrical designs cover the walls. Depicting human beings was forbidden by the Muslim religion. Much of the decoration consisted of exquisite Arabic writing — calligraphy was considered a great art.

The bridges of Isfahan are a marvel, composed of archways through which water gushes, and little pavilions in which rulers and nobles sat watching the water sports and festivals held on the river.

The two most beautiful are the Shahrestan with its thirty-nine arches, and the Pole Khaju with its long promenades and booths used in the past for entertaining, dancing and music. In the river below, women were washing carpets.

It is the little scenes which lingered in my memory — the public scribe (letter writer) penning a letter for an old, illiterate peasant ouside the modern post office, for instance. (The Shah was then (about 15 years ago) bringing education to the villagers with his Education Corps of young male teachers.) I remember too the main square by moonlight with the sound of camel bells and the sky over the river exploding in galaxies of fireworks. And the crowd of mysterious-looking women draped in their chadors (long cloaks) which covered them from head to toe — one draped fold held clenched in teeth, covering mouth and nose, so that only a pair of huge expressive brown eyes was visible. (In Afghanistan, even the eyes were covered and the chuddar slipped over the head, covering women from top to toe, with only a latticed silk grill over the eyes so that the occupants could see.)

Across the river lies New Julfa, the Armenian Christian quarter where persecuted Christians settled when Shah Abbas, who founded the city as it is today and was most responsible for beautifying it, forcibly shifted the Armenian population of Jolfa (on the border of Azerbaijan) to New Jolfa in Isfahan, to save them from their enemies, the Turks.

Their cathedral looks a little like a mosque. Inside are paintings combining Russian, Italian and Iranian influences. There is also a Museum of Armenian Culture with models in national costume, paintings, church embroideries, bibles and sacred manuscripts.

Shah Abbas may have had more motive than compassion in gathering up the Armenians. They were said to be good workers with a keen business sense. He burnt their town behind them, so there was no turning back.

There were modern public bath houses in Isfahan, where for a small sum you were provided with soap, slippers and a large white towel — to shower in comfort. You could stay at an inexpensive small inn, shower at the public bath house and eat at an inexpensive café. We loved the *chelow kebab*

— broiled meat on skewers served with rice and the special nougat called *gaz* for which Isfahan is famous.

It was difficult to decide what to buy as a souvenir. The Chahar Bagh Avenue tempted with its antiques, art work and handicrafts. We could choose from finely worked brass, copper, silver, jewellery, miniatures, inlaid boxes, rich brocades. I found an artist called Imami, a miniature painter, as were his father and brothers, and chose an exquisite ivory miniature portraying an ancient game of polo played by Persian noblemen (alas, it later disappeared from my Sydney apartment), a small hand-made silver bracelet, some tinkling camel bells (I still have them) and a brass hanging flower pot.

The ancients were right. Isfahan is indeed 'Half the World'.

HOTELS

RAFFLES HOTEL— SINGAPORE'S GRAND OLD LADY

IN Rudyard Kipling's day, Raffles was known as the Savoy of Singapore. Kipling himself stayed there. So did other famous writers—Somerset Maugham, Noël Coward and, according to some experts, Joseph Conrad.

On my last visit I sampled a Singapore Sling in Maugham's suite with a fellow writer, who was staying the night there hoping the old boy's ghost would appear and give him a marvellous story for his newspaper. But, even a couple of Singapore Slings did not produce the apparition, despite the tradition that Maugham's ghost has appeared.

Another Raffles ghost is that of a little English girl. At one stage in its early history, the building which became Raffles was the Raffles Girls' School. In 1974 a guest reported hearing a young girl's voice singing 'Mary Had A Little Lamb'. Staff used to light Chinese temple joss sticks and candles, and burn incense outside room 83 to placate the spirit.

The first ghosts were reported in 1886 before Raffles became a hotel.

Raffles' famous Singapore Sling was created by Ngiam Tong

Boon, a barman in the hotel's Long Bar about 1915 and christened by British planters from Malaya who downed the potent drink as if it were fruit juice.

The recipe is two parts of gin, one part of cherry brandy, with a few drops of Cointreau, Benedictine and Angostura added, and some pineapple, lime and orange juice, topped with a cherry. If anything could make Maugham reappear, we decided, it would be a couple of Singapore Slings.

Five guests hold the record Singapore Sling contest, downing 131 drinks between them in less than two hours.

Writers have always had a strong link with Raffles and thousands of articles about it have appeared in the press worldwide.

Recently two new books came out—*Raffles, the Story of a Grand Hotel* by Ilsa Sharp, and *The Year of the Tiger* by Raymond Flower, written to mark the hotel's centenary in 1986. They follow a long tradition of writers who stayed in and wrote about the hotel. These famous writers are immortalized by photographs in the Writers' Bar, and in suites named after them.

Maugham is said to have written *Of Human Bondage* and *The Moon and Sixpence* sipping a *stengah* (the local name for whisky and water) in the garden.

Kipling wrote: 'Providence conducted me along a beach in full view of five miles of shipping—five solid miles of masts and funnels to a place called Raffles Hotel, where the food is excellent as the rooms are bad. Let the traveller take note. Feed at Raffles and sleep at the Hotel de l'Europe.'

Management used the comment, 'Food is excellent', to promote the hotel, conveniently ignoring the rest—but they also upgraded the accommodation in 1890.

Joseph Conrad normally stayed at the Sailors' Rest Home in South Bridge Road for a dollar a day—whether he stayed at the Raffles Hotel when he became more affluent after he obtained his Master's certificate in 1887 and a ship command seems to be a contentious issue. But he did describe it: 'The straggling building of bricks, as airy as a birdcage...'

Maugham also praised the hotel: 'It stands for all the fables of the exotic East.' During his visits in 1921 and 1925 he and his companion Gerald Haxton used to pick up stories of local scandals over drinks in the bar or dinner with friends.

He was accused of abusing hospitality by ferreting out family skeletons of his hosts, and writing about them. His last visit was in 1959, aged eighty-five, when he stayed in the suite which now bears his name.

Noël Coward was finishing *Private Lives*, perhaps his most famous play, when he arrived with his friend Jeffrey Holmesdale, Lord Amherst, in 1929. Coward mentioned Raffles in stories such as 'Pretty Polly Barlowe', written in 1964, which tells of a young English girl who decided to live it up when her aunt drops dead on a holiday in Singapore. The story was made into a film in 1967 starring Hayley Mills and Trevor Howard and shot in Raffles.

Modern guests have included writers Hermann Hesse, André Malraux, Günter Grass, Leslie Charteris (author of 'The Saint' series) and James Michener.

But writers are not the only celebrated guests. Over the years an endless procession of the famous have stayed at Raffles... world leaders Pandit Nehru, Mrs Indira Gandhi, Lord Mountbatten, Australia's former prime minister, Malcolm Fraser, former British prime ministers, Harold Wilson and Anthony Eden, film stars starting with the early stars such as Charlie Chaplin, Maurice Chevalier, Mary Pickford and Douglas Fairbanks senior, Ronald Coleman, Norma Shearer, Jeannette Macdonald and Jean Harlow; and later, Grace Kelly, Ava Gardner, William Holden, Marlon Brando, and Liz Taylor with Mike Todd.

Charlie Chaplin got a standing ovation from the usually silent rickshaw drivers who clapped and cheered the 'little tramp'—hero of many an early movie they had watched.

Colourful 'characters' as well as the famous abound in Raffles' history. The tale is still told of an old Dutch anthropologist, Professor Pieter van Stein Callenfels—1.9 meters tall and nearly eighty-nine kilograms in weight, who was reputed to drink ten bottles of gin for breakfast each morning. A dozen bottles of beer at a sitting were grist to his mill. He had a gargantuan appetite to match—working right through the menu on one occasion then ordering each dish in reverse!

The professor would sit in curry-stained pyjamas holding court among admiring women whom he treated with lofty disdain. He wore shoes only on great occasions and had his hair cut yearly on his birthday. Sir Arthur Conan Doyle's character, Professor Challenger, in *The Lost World*, is said to be based on him.

Perhaps Raffles' most famous story is of the last shooting of a tiger in Singapore. It was shot under the billiard table by Mr C. M. Phillips, Headmaster of nearby Raffles Institution, who was summoned, still wearing pyjamas and nursing a hangover, to shoot the tiger which had escaped from a circus. A crack shot, he dispatched it neatly, then presumably returned to bed.

Raffles today reflects the images of its colonial heyday. You can still take tiffin in the Elizabeth Grill every Sunday at lunchtime. Trishaw 'boys' (drivers) still wait outside the hotel to take you downtown. The elegant hotel portico, vast vaulted ceilings and spacious marbled corridors hark back to a more leisurely era.

The hotel was named after Sir Stamford Raffles, founder of Singapore. The hotel was founded by the Sarkies family— five Armenian brothers—Martin, Tigran, Aviet, Arshak, and Arathoon, hoteliers from Penang. They were responsible for a chain of grand old hotels in the East—the Strand in Rangoon, the Eastern and Oriental (E. & O.) in Penang, and Raffles.

They were also proprietors of the Crag on Penang Hill and the Grosvenor and Sea View in Singapore.

Martin and Tigran fell in love with a house on Beach Road with a beautiful view of the sea and charming gardens. It belonged to George Mildray Dare whose family had been ruined by his father's business associate's speculations.

The mansion had been a tiffin house serving superb luncheons. (*Tiffin* is an Anglo-Indian word for a light lunch, usually with curry as the main dish, accompanied by side dishes.) It had also been a girls' boarding school. The brothers bought the property in 1886, and turned it into a hotel with forty-eight rooms with private bathroom and veranda, and a billiard room (as necessary as a swimming pool today).

The brothers were all colourful personalities, especially Arshak, who became the friend of millionaires, royalty and diplomats. His party act was to waltz around the ballroom floor with a glass of whisky and soda balanced on his bald head, without spilling a drop—a trick he also performed at the E. & O. Hotel in Penang.

He was a generous man and many an impoverished planter owed his fare home to Arshak.

By 1917 the hotel boasted a motor garage with thirteen cars, and three motor lorries for luggage and goods, although the rickshaws still operated at the hotel entrance. Custom was so good that in 1923 several hundred rickshaw 'boys' fought a pitched battle to decide which of two rival groups was to have rights to this lucrative spot. Police were called in and charged with fixed bayonets. The result: twenty-three 'boys' imprisoned, one killed, several taken to hospital.

Raffles' heyday came in the 'dancing years' of the 1920s and 1930s when Singapore's social life revolved around the hotel. Grand occasions such as St Andrew's Day, St George's Day and New Year's Eve were celebrated in style. Women wore elegant ball gowns, men wore dinner jackets or white 'mess' jackets, known as 'bum freezers'. Few Asians, apart from royalty and the very rich, were admitted. Pomp and circumstance accompanied lavish balls and banquets, which were followed by fireworks.

Guests were waited on hand and foot, usually paying by the 'chit' system—signing for their bills and paying later. Punkah wallahs lay on floors outside bedrooms, a string attached to their toes which connected with a length of cloth suspended from the bedroom ceiling. The 'punkah wallah' pulled the unusual fan by foot, creating fresh currents of air.

In 'Cad's Alley', planters on leave, after a good time, lurked waiting to poach someone else's girl the moment his back was turned.

If a gentleman had the temerity to take to the dance floor without white tie and tails, a uniformed 'buttons' passed him a card asking him to leave. Turning up with a Eurasian or Asian partner was equally frowned on. On one occasion an Indonesian princess, part of an official party, was asked to leave.

In the years before the First World War many European wives joined husbands in Singapore, bringing stuffy ideas on class into what had been a freebooters' colony, where many officials and planters had native mistresses. Any single European nurses, teachers or secretaries were in great demand.

Life was formal but still a certain amount of 'hanky-panky' continued. Arshak Sarkies reputedly told a guest that the only rule was: 'We ring the bell at six o'clock in the morning and you all go back to your own rooms.'

From 1917 Raffles had an orchestra playing each night at dinner and for balls. Jazz musicians and cabaret artists did the circuit of grand hotels in the East. One impressive artist was Boris Lissanevitch who danced at Raffles, with his wife, Kira, in the mid 1930s. Boris was a Russian ballet dancer who had performed with the legendary Nijinsky, and he and his wife did classical and character dances. I had a very interesting lunch with Boris in Katmandu at the Yak and Yeti Bar which he owned and which featured in novelist Han Suyin's *The Mountain is Young*.

The Japanese invasion of Singapore on 9 February 1942 caught everyone napping. The European colony danced on in the blacked-out ballroom almost to the day the Japanese arrived. Staff did manage to save the magnificent silver roast beef trolley and other treasures by burying them in the garden. The Europeans huddled in Raffles, washing lines strung across the ballroom, awaiting their fate. For most it was a prisoner of war camp—for many, death.

The Governor, Sir Shenton Thomas, had ordered all stocks of liquor on the island destroyed and the Raffles manager reluctantly complied.

The Japanese renamed Singapore 'Syonan' meaning Light of the South and Raffles became 'Syonan Ryokan', Light of the South Hotel. Japanese officials took over Raffles and Japanese soldiers drilled in the Palm Court, whirling huge broad-bladed swords around their heads.

When war ended in 1945, Raffles for six months became a transit camp for former prisoners of war who slept six to a room, on floors, and even on the billiard table. Sausages and mash was about the best in food the hotel could produce. There was little to drink. But the 'upper crust' atmosphere was still there and men under the rank of lieutenant-colonel were likely to be turned away.

The joy of returned ex-prisoners of war was recreated in the BBC television series 'Tenko'. Scenes of the women living in Raffles after their release were shot on location in the hotel.

Immediately after the war, Raffles took on a new character, dropping its cosmopolitan air to become a refuge for hundreds of ragged, sick refugees from camps in Java and other islands in the East Indies.

But, by 1946, it was business as usual, as Raffles prepared to open its doors again to the famous and the glamorous, as well as the ordinary traveller.

'Meet you at Raffles' has been a catchphrase for generations. On my next trip to Singapore, I've promised to meet author Raymond Flower in the Long Bar and drink to Raffles' centenary with a Singapore Sling.

THE EASTERN AND ORIENTAL HOTEL, PENANG

THE Eastern and Oriental Hotel (E. & O. for short) in Georgetown, the capital of the beautiful Malaysian island of Penang, is one of a fast-disappearing breed, the grand old hotels of South East Asia.

It was built by Martin and Tigran Sarkies, two of the famous five Armenian brothers who also built Raffles in Singapore, the Strand in Rangoon (Burma) and the Crag Hotel on Penang Hill. They were also proprietors of the Grosvenor and Sea View hotels in Singapore.

In over 100 years of history, sultans and their retinues, planters, tin miners and businessmen have stayed in the E. & O., so-named because it was once two hotels, the Eastern and the Oriental.

In 1884 Martin and Tigran built a hotel facing the Esplanade, which they named the Eastern. The venture was so successful that the following year they opened another hotel, the Oriental, on a plot of land facing the sea.

Further expansion was thwarted when the authorities quashed their plans 'due to lack of available land'. The brothers did the next best thing and combined the hotels.

A third brother, Arshak, took over the running of the hotel in 1891. He wanted a larger, grander hotel and kept up petitioning for land. His efforts succeeded when, in 1922, he managed to buy a large plot of land on which he built the 'handsome and palatial' Victory Annexe.

The Victory Annexe added forty more rooms to the E.

& O. The ballroom and dining room were also expanded and redocorated. For a hotel which started with only thirty rooms and a hall with about a dozen dining tables, the E. & O. by the early 1930s had 120 suites, telephones in every room, a tremendous dome at the entrance, rich carpets, a permanent orchestra, and—a rare luxury in the East for that time— constant hot and cold running water in English baths.

An old booklet entitled 'Sea Ports of the Far East' recorded: 'On the evening of Armistice Day, the firm, after long endeavour succeeded in securing by purchase a large plot of land contiguous to their already extensive sea frontage and on that new area has been erected the handsome and palatial Victory Annexe.'

In the 1920s, the hotel advertised itself as the 'premier hotel East of Suez' with the 'longest front of any hotel in the world' (257 metres). It was bordered by a delightful walk, shaded by whispering palms, gently rustled by the soft sea breeze. But the pride of the establishment was a ballroom built by Arshak in 1903 which became the 'centre of the social life and gaiety of Penang and the neighbouring towns on the mainland'. Every major function, such as the annual St George's Day Ball, weddings, banquets and concerts by visiting musicians, was held there.

The hotel's vast lobby is said to have an echo.

During the 1920s and 1930s dances were held twice a week in the ballroom. They were packed, even though the rules stated that only clean-shaven men were allowed in and the only 'Asiatics' permitted were rajas and *tunkus* (local titled people). Arshak, who had a great sense of humour, was proud of his feat of waltzing around the ballroom with a glass of whisky and soda balanced on his bald head.

He never asked his guests whether they were enjoying themselves. He simply stated, 'You've had an enjoyable stay', before moving on. He would sit over a small *stengah* (whisky and water)—literally 'half and half'—appraising guests, who included Rudyard Kipling and Somerset Maugham.

In 1930 Noël Coward and his friend, Lord Amhurst, stayed at the E. &. O. George Bilainkin, a former editor of the *Straits Echo*, wrote of their meeting with Arshak in his 1932 booklet, *Hail Penang*:

'Arshak, stern, red-faced, with Semitic nose, sat as usual before a small stengah. He looked up and extended his sensitive and critical hand to the visitors. Apparently he liked them. I knew by Arshak's expression whether he approved. He spread his freemasonry sparingly but men who were his friends knew a generosity difficult to match . . .'

Arshak was a famous and beloved character and when he died in 1931, a record crowd turned out for his funeral in Penang.

The Second World War and the Japanese Occupation took their toll (the Japanese occupied the hotel during the war and used it as an officers' mess). The Sarkies brothers' hotel empire never recovered after the war. The E. & O., Raffles, and the Strand reopened, but under new ownership and management. The E. & O. was acquired by a local Chinese family, passed on to the Chan family in 1973 and then to a business group.

The colonial splendour was still very much apparent when I stayed in the E. & O. Wood panels and plush lounges abounded. There was a Sarkies Corner and, above the fireplace, in the plush 1885 Grill and Cocktail lounge, hung a photograph of brothers, Arshak, Aviet and Tigran.

The best bedrooms still faced the sea. Through their vast picture windows I could see the delightful garden with its canon, coconut palm trees and stone sea walls. At night the soothing sound of the waves lapping against the wall and the sighing of wind in the palm trees lulled me to sleep.

I loved breakfasting in the garden near the swimming pool and the spirit tree, with small offerings beneath it to placate the spirits, tables and chairs neatly set out for breakfast. The view from the garden took in fishing boats, distant islands, dark green in an aquamarine sea, sandy beaches, and the faintly purple mountains of the mainland.

Since my last visit, the hotel has undergone extensions with huge tower blocks facing the sea and a helicopter pad on the roof. I hope that the colonial charm and old-world atmosphere have been preserved, and that old Arshak Sarkies would still recognize his famous hostelry.

THE PENINSULA HOTEL, HONG KONG

HONG Kong's most famous hotel, the Peninsula, is part of the colony's history. When closure threatened in 1975, protests poured in both from Hong Kong residents and abroad. Hong Kong was unimaginable without the Peninsula. The hotel was reprieved and renovated.

In 1978 the much-loved 'grand old lady' celebrated her golden jubilee, still attracting the famous and the discriminating traveller with its combination of luxury living and exotic past.

The hotel was built in Kowloon (the mainland side of Hong Kong) as a terminus hotel for overland travellers on the Kowloon-Canton Railway. In the early 1920s Hong Kong experienced an accommodation shortage so acute that visitors often could not find a room.

The Hong Kong and Shanghai Hotels Ltd, which had hotel interests in China, decided to build a first-class hotel. The General Strike of 1925, when the colony was paralysed for four months, held up construction. Then, in 1927, with the hotel finished, but not furnished, it became a temporary home for soldiers of the Shanghai Defence Force sent from Britain to safeguard British interests in Shanghai, following labour unrest and a strike against foreign-owned business, British in particular.

Billeted in the Peninsula, they made the hotel echo to the sound of bagpipes and bugle calls.

It was handed back to the owners later that year, the ravages by troops paid for by the military. It opened at last to guests on 11 December 1928.

The King's Own Scottish Borderers Band and two dance orchestras entertained at the hotel's grand opening, which drew 3000 of the finest of Hong Kong's society. The National Anthem heralded the arrival of the Acting Governor, the Hon. W. T. Southorn and his wife, who took their places on a dais draped by two Union Jacks.

Southorn gave a rousing speech with, strangely enough, the accent on the 'amazing care lavished on hygiene'.

'There can be no place in the world where the diner can

eat his food with a greater faith in the purity of its preparations than in the Peninsula', he declaimed, adding this ponderous testimonial: 'It stands as an outward and visible testimony of the faith which is in us all that the greatness of Hong Kong is in the future and not in the past.'

Those were the days of King and Empire.

The *South China Post* called the Peninsula 'the finest hotel in the Far East'.

It was a gracious nine-floor hotel with a vast, awe-inspiring lobby with huge whirling fans overhead, marble columns and a mosaic floor. It towered over the sleepy little tree-lined village of Kowloon.

The Roof Garden with its windows sporting embroidered valances of green and gold was to become a popular place for tea dances and cabaret shows. A children's dining room featured a décor of nursery and barnyard subjects.

As the bands played, the dancing got into full swing, and the bars did a roaring trade, an American guest summed up the feelings of many: 'It makes me feel like a million dollars— I'd feel rich here even if I hadn't a dime in my bag.'

Prices, even for the times, seemed cheap. Guests were charged US nine dollars a day for a single room including three meals and two teas. Breakfast was a mammoth meal of about twelve dishes.

The Peninsula soon became the social mecca. Couples flocked to tea dances in the Rose Garden Ballroom where admission was US fifty cents, including tea.

The first royal visitor was the Duke of Gloucester, who arrived in April 1929 on HMS *Suffolk* on his way to a state visit to Japan. At the banquet in his honour at the Peninsula, the Kings Own Scottish Borderers Band played 'The Roast Beef of Old England' amid masses of roses and violets.

At the end of the year high society—men kilted or in tail coats, women exquisitely gowned—flung up their heels at the St Andrew's Society Ball with its ancient ceremonies and Scottish pipers, its clan shields and illuminated thistles.

A local newspaper reported the function: 'The scene in the lounge as guests thronged to the lifts . . . was like that of a great hotel in any of the capitals of Europe.' Praise indeed for a colonial celebration.

The New Year's Eve celebrations were even more lavish.

Streamers, balloons and 'A Happy New Year' in electric lights added to the gaiety. At midnight 500 dancers took part in a chariot race between the Old Year and the New Year, with the latter winning by seconds.

At a Christmas Eve ball four tiny suckling pigs tied with blue ribbons were let loose on the dance floor while dancers scurried in hot pursuit to capture a free Christmas dinner. At midnight dancers burst from a huge rose.

Modern dances, especially the Charleston, became the rage, even with Chinese couples who had never danced before.

Entertainers on a circuit of South East Asian hotels included French singers and dancers, a Spanish illusionist, a Portuguese tenor, Russian dancers, and acrobats.

The Lobby became the 'in' place to meet for drinks or afternoon tea. Unofficially, the left hand side was reserved for singles not averse to a little romance, the right for married couples and old friends.

Lavish weddings were held at the hotel. A Mrs Angus was astonished that her 1934 wedding cost only five pounds a head for 125 guests and included flowers, champagne, a buffet with lobster and other delicacies and a wedding cake.

The 1930s saw the first of the Hollywood stars arrive. In 1936 Charlie Chaplin came by ocean liner with Paulette Goddard, the star of his latest film, *Modern Times*. About 100 European and Chinese children crowded on board for a close-up view and signed autograph.

Warner Oland, Charlie Chan in the popular movie series of that name, arrived to gather some local atmosphere for his role. He commented, rather condescendingly: 'The beauty and strangeness of the whole scene is amazing—but you people wouldn't notice that, living in it all the time.'

The hotel had never had it so good and a board member who had considered the hotel a constant financial drain in the early days, prophesied: 'Our white elephant has turned into a swan. I am firmly convinced that as the years go on, the Peninsula at Kowloon will become world-famous.'

Through the thirties the band played on, but shadows were gathering. In 1937 an ominous sign of the future appeared as a flood of refugees from the Sino-Japanese fighting in China sought refuge in the colony, taxing accommodation.

While Hong Kong foxtrotted and tangoed, war in Europe

broke out and business declined in the colony. But Hong Kong residents refused to see the writing on the wall.

When the British Government ordered the evacuation to Australia of the colony's expatriate women and children, people were still convinced that war wouldn't reach the colony. A group of the colony's menfolk met in the Peninsula to protest the Government's action and demand the return of their families.

Petitions were drawn up and letters read telling of 'appalling conditions under which wives were living in Australia'. Many wives complained that rooms allocated were not as big as they had been used to in the colony, and that, due to the White Australia Policy, they were not allowed to bring in their Chinese amahs.

The 'Husbands' Protest' as it became known so influenced public opinion that the Government stopped evacuations although it refused to bring back those already evacuated.

War seemed unreal and social life went on, although blackout drills and petrol rationing were discussed.

As the Japanese attacked Pearl Harbour on 7 December 1941, the lights of the hotel blazed as over 800 guests laughed and danced their way through a gala ball given by the Hong Kong Chinese Women's Club to raise money for the British and Chinese Bomber Funds. Five days later the Japanese swept over the Chinese border into Hong Kong.

The last British troops crossed to Hong Kong Island, and the Peninsula's foreign staff left on the 'last ferry to Hong Kong Island' on 13 December. Left behind were 1200 hotel staff and families and 800 refugees who thought the basement would make a good bomb shelter. The hotel had stocked up with 150 bags of rice, 300 of flour and 60 tonnes of meat and provided two free meals a day.

Rampaging mobs looted Kowloon but the hotel defended itself, locking the doors and throwing heavy articles from the balcony.

Hong Kong fell on 25 December, and the Governor, Sir Mark Young, and General Maltby, Commander of the British Forces, officially surrendered in the Peninsula Hotel to Lieutenant-General Sakai, Commander of the Japanese 23rd Army. The Japanese flag replaced the Union Jack which flew over the hotel.

Over 7000 prisoners of war were interned in camps, suffering terrible privations.

The Japanese changed the hotel's name to the Toa Hotel
(East Asia) and it became headquarters for high-ranking Japanese officers and government officials. Times were hard and
staff endured subsistence living, some even risking execution
to steal enough to eat. In 1942 the Japanese opened the hotel
for business, advertising both European and Chinese meals,
as well as Japanese. Official parties in the ballroom and fireworks displays on the rooftop were held to celebrate Japanese
victories.

When American bombers strafed Hong Kong, the Japanese
mounted a machine gun on top of the Peninsula, the tallest
building in Kowloon, but it had little effect on allied attacks.

On 14 August 1945, the Japanese surrendered. The 'Toa'
sign was torn down and the Union Jack raised over the
Peninsula. The hotel divided up rooms with makeshift par-
titions and filled them with civil servants, military, and former
prisoners of war. There was no wholemeal bread or fresh
milk. One former prisoner of war complained: 'At least we
had vitamin pills and three cigarettes a day for workers in
camp.' Rice was rationed and officials sent overseas to seek
emergency food supplies.

The hotel appealed for the return of china and cutlery
'borrowed' during and after the Japanese occupation. Mosquitoes bred in water in the basement, there was no power
for lights, electric lifts and refrigeration.

Things improved when battleships arrived with food—
bread, bacon, hams and eggs, a feast for former camp inmates.

The Peninsula's Roof Garden reopened on 19 December,
serving Chinese and European meals. But the hotel was still
requisitioned by the Hong Kong Government for office space
and quarters for civil servants. It was returned to the owners
the following year and life gradually returned to normal.

Industrialists, high society, business executives, and finan-
ciers flocked back. The spacious Lobby was the place to be
seen. As one drinker explained: 'If you stayed in the Lobby
long enough, you would see everyone who was anyone in
the colony.'

In the 1950s film stars including Clark Gable, James Stewart,
and Elizabeth Taylor and also Jennifer Jones and William

Holden on location for *Love Is A Many Splendoured Thing*, stayed at the hotel. One little boy asked Clark Gable for an autograph, thinking he was William Boyd, star of a cowboy movie series, *Hopalong Cassidy*. Told otherwise, he snatched back his autograph book, saying, 'No, I don't want you— I want Hopalong.'

The Emperor Haile Selassie of Ethiopia took over the entire sixth floor and insisted that European toilets be removed and replaced with Oriental squat-style ones. They were installed within two days.

The hotel had its share of eccentrics. One man came periodically for years at noon, ordered a pink gin, then marched up and down the Lobby clutching a book and umbrella. He then sat, sniffed his drink for a few minutes, then downed it in one gulp before leaving. He turned out to be a lawyer who adopted this ritual whenever he had an important case.

Another patron came in several times a week, ordered a drink, slept for an hour, then quickly swallowed it and left.

Author Ernest K. Gann, a fan of The Peninsula, immortalized the Lobby in the early 1950s in his novel, *Soldier of Fortune*:

'There is a division down the exact centre of the great room and though it is invisible, it is there as surely as if it were wrought of steel, for this barrier is a product of custom and expediency, and none of the habitués of the Peninsula Lobby would think of violating it.

'The division begins at the entrance door and runs straight across to the reception desk, bisecting a wide thoroughfare between the tables. The right side of the Lobby is almost invariably pure British and in the mornings is relatively unpopulated except for a few eccentrics who prefer eating their kippers and reading their *China Mail* in public rather than in the privacy of rooms.

'About noon and countinuing through the day, the space slowly accumulates life, for here the older and more solidly emplaced China hands meet to transact what crumbs of business there may be left for white men in Asia. Or they simply have a quiet tonic and talk about home. Their ladies, too, frequent this space. At late lunch and teatime they are most evident, sitting like wan pink flowers in bunches of four and five. They almost never join their men and are rarely to be

MENU

Breakfast
7.30 to 10.00 a.m.

1 Compote of Californian Raisin
2 Quaker Oats
3 Boiled Rice
4 Corn Flakes
5 Puffed Wheat

Special Breakfast Dishes
6 Poached Fillet of Fish, Capers Sauce
7 Assorted Cold Meat
8 Potato Salad
9 Scrambled Egg with Fresh Tomato

To Order
10 Grilled Bacon
11 Eggs any Style
12 Hot Rolls
13 Dry or Buttered Toast
14 Cinnamon Toast
15 Orange Marmalade
16 Strawberry Jam
17 Coffee, Tea or Cocoa

Peninsula Hotel

Tuesday, 15th August, 1939. $2.00
Dishes ordered not on this Menu will be charged à la carte.

Dinner

7.30 to 9.30 p.m.

1 Smoked Sprats and Ripe Olives
2 Consommé Madrilène (Hot or Cold)
3 Cream of Spinach
4 Poached Fillet of Garoupa Mexicaine
5 Roast Capon and Sausage
6 Baked Jacket Potatoes
7 American Succotash
8 Cold Roast Lamb (Mint Sauce)
9 Spanish Salad
10 Coupe Nid d'Abeille Biscuits
11 Munster or Cream Cheese
12 Fresh Local Fruit
13 Coffee

Peninsula Hotel

Saturday, 23rd September, 1939 $4.00
Dishes ordered not on this Menu will be charged à la carte.

seen after dark. The waiters on this side are all called 'boy' regardless of their age and by tacit agreement, the Chinese customers who frequent The Peninsula, both male and female, stay entirely away from it.

'The tables are the same on the other side of the barrier and the waiters are the same, but the patrons are of another planet. Some of them are seated at their favourite tables by ten o'clock in the morning where they remain all through the day and a large part of the night. These are the regulars and, though they live elsewhere, The Peninsula is their true home, their office, their club and their window on the passing world.

'The Chinese sit on this side of the barrier. The Australians and the Indians, the Siamese, the French and the Eurasians all maintain outposts here and mix without prejudice or rancour.'

In the 1960s the hotel underwent a twenty-six million-dollar renovation, attracting many royals (including Princess Margaret and Lord Snowden), heads of state and world celebrities. In 1975, after its reprieve from threatened demolition, it was given another multi-million-dollar face-lift.

In the eighties celebrities still arrive in one of the hotel's fleet of Silver Shadow Rolls Royces which meet guests at the airport. They sweep past the Chinese Lion statues flanking the door, are saluted by cherubic-looking page boys, and check in at the desk in the Lobby, becoming part of the hotel's fascinating, ongoing history.

THE ORIENTAL HOTEL, BANGKOK

THE grand old hotels with their old-world service, opulent surroundings and fascinating histories still attract the discerning traveller. They don't need to flaunt their charms, their reputation is spread by word of mouth.

The clients who flock to these charming hostelries are not those mass-market tourists who stay at international hotel chains, but the sophisticated travellers who enjoy their unique atmosphere and are prepared to pay for it.

The Oriental Hotel in Bangkok has a fascinating history. Somerset Maugham, Noël Coward and Tennessee Williams all loved it. Joseph Conrad rested from his voyages in its garden and dreamed up his novels which capture the romance of the East.

It is said that Maugham, recovering from a bout of malaria contracted up country in the late 1920s, sat on the terrace of the hotel watching sampans, barges and river boats on the River of Kings, and wrote up notes for *The Gentleman in the Parlour* (a record of his journey from Rangoon to Haiphong). In this book he recounted a charming fairy story, set in the Royal Court of a mythical Siam (the old name for Thailand), about the King and his two daughters, Night and Day.

Other famous guests have included Charlie Chaplin, Danny Kaye, Duke Ellington, writer Gore Vidal, millionaire Henry Ford II and his wife, Christine, not to mention princes, generals, adventurers and soldiers of fortune.

The hotel was once the palace of a prince and, during the Second World War, it became a billet for Japanese soldiers. After the war, American troops were billeted in it.

There are few records of the hotel before 1887 when it belonged to the prince. It had been a wooden shanty, owned by two sea captains who ran it as a hostelry.

In 1887 the hotel was a rambling colonial-type mansion, with lawns sweeping down to the river's edge. It became a hotel during the reign of the young Thai King Chulalongkorn, when Queen Victoria was on the British throne.

By the turn of the century, it was the focus for Bangkok's social life and a favourite spot for tourists who arrived by ship. When a foreign passenger ship berthed, the Oriental sent out a launch with an Indian on board to drum up business, as well as to collect the hotel's guests who had already booked.

They all boarded the boat which disembarked at the river landing alondside the hotel garden. The landing is still used today for boats which take passengers on trips to the floating market, the *klongs* (canals), and other tourist attractions.

History records that Louis Leonowens, son of the famous Anna, who wrote *Anna and the King of Siam*, was so thrilled with his new horse, that he rode the animal up the steps of the hotel and into the drawing room.

But the hotel's most glorious days were to come after the Second World War, when Bangkok was still a fascinating place with a gay, brilliant social life.

Many foreigners who found themselves in Bangkok during the war wanted to stay on when it ended. They included two American intelligence officers, Alexander MacDonald, who later founded the English-language newspaper, the *Bangkok Post*, and Jim Thompson, who was to become known as 'King' of the Thai Silk industry, because he revitalized the country's dying silk industry, making a fortune in the process.

But, in those days, Thompson was more interested in providing a hotel for the tourist he felt sure would flock to Bangkok. He and a Frenchwoman, a former war correspondent for a French news agency, Germaine Krulle, formed a company with a Thai prince, a local prominent lawyer, an American who had worked in the Free Thai Underground and a Thai general. They each put up US $250 and, although the sum of US $1500 was hardly sufficient to float the hotel, it was a start.

They took on a run-down, rambling, old-fashioned hotel with swinging wooden doors, endless halls, primitive kitchens, mosquito nets draped over beds and antique plumbing. Guests bathed by dipping cold water from huge pottery water jars. One enormous lady tourist mistakenly thinking the water jar was a bath, climbed in, became stuck fast, and had to be extricated by force.

Germaine Krulle, who became the manageress, described the place in her book, *Bangkok—Siam's City of Angels*. She wrote: 'It had a grimy little reception room and behind it a dirty dark room containing a huge built-in café with steel doors reaching from the floor to the ceiling.

'Opposite the staircase was a series of high, old-fashioned louvred doors. The old English-style lobby was lined with lovely teak panels which had been painted black to match the ceiling beams.

'All doors and window frames, as well as the open shutters, were black. Underneath the torn and rotting carpet, which covered the entire floor, were found attractive tiles. The most prominent pieces of furniture in the funereal sitting room were four big old-fashioned English club settees, which had seen better days.'

It was a challenge to restore such a dreary building, to put it mildly. Guests of today's elegant, luxurious hotel would find it difficult to recognize the hotel's shabby beginnings.

Jim Thompson, who had trained as an architect and designer, helped renovate it. But, unfortunately, he and Germaine fell out and Thompson withdrew from the project—fortunately for the Thai silk industry, which Thompson boosted into a top export industry.

Germaine opened the hotel. Thompson insisted on living there for a year or so. He avoided her and had great fun drumming up business by standing in the hotel foyer with his magnificent silks draped over his arm until guests asked where they could buy some.

The hotel has come a long way since then. Its Royal Suite, complete with precious antiques and marble bathroom, houses kings and millionaires. Armaments millionaire, Baron Arndt von Krupp and his mother, the Baroness Anne-Lise von Krupp, were staying there on my last visit to Bangkok. They gave parties for the staff every night on the cruiser, *Oriental Queen*.

Other important guests have included John Steinbeck, Peter Sellers, Tennessee Williams, Duke Ellington, Prince Albert of Belgium, Singapore's Prime Minister, Lee Kuan Yew, author Alec Waugh, film stars William Holden and Robert de Niro. The list seems endless: Danny Kaye, Lauren Bacall, Princess Grace of Monaco, Noël Coward, Somerset Maugham, President Nixon, President Franklin Delano Roosevelt. Conrad wrote a short story while a guest at the hotel, and called it 'The Shadow Line'. But the Oriental Hotel is not simply living on its past glories. It regularly makes the top forty hotels of the world (ratings are based on opinions of leading bankers) and has ranked first. Everything from room décor to food and service caters for the discriminating traveller, but for those with a taste for romance, its colourful past adds just that extra dimension.

THE MANILA HOTEL, MANILA

THE Manila Hotel, like so many of the world's grand old hotels, enshrines much of its country's romantic traditions and fascinating history.

Its memories range from lavish entertainment and glamorous occasions to wartime devastation; from spectacular fashion parades by the country's richest and prettiest women to frightened families sitting on their suitcases awaiting internment in Japanese prisoner-of-war camps.

The old-world atmosphere of Manila's Spanish past lives on in the hotel's vast lobby with its marble floors, soaring white pillars, colonial furnishings.

Its guest list ranges from the rich and famous to the ordinary traveller. The hotel has an amusing custom. It gives guests a list of illustrious predecessors, adding the new guest's name in a space left for that purpose. And so my name joined (at least for my visit) a rollcall which included novelist Joseph Conrad, General Douglas MacArthur, three American presidents—Lyndon Baines Johnson, Dwight D. Eisenhower and Richard Nixon, astronaut Neil Armstrong, entertainer John Lennon, writer James A. Michener, Bob Hope, the Duke of Windsor, Marlon Brando, William Holden, Dame Margot Fonteyn and Sammy Davis Jr.

The Philippines' most famous hotel had its grand opening on American Independence Day, 4 July 1912.

At that time there were few first-class hotels available in Manila—the Filipinos usually stayed with relatives when travelling. After more than 300 years of Spanish rule (1565-1898), the Americans had newly acquired the Philippines following victory in the Spanish-American War. By the turn of the nineteenth century about 16,000 Americans were stationed in the Philippines in military, government or business positions. They wanted somewhere classy for friends, relatives and business contacts to stay.

The Manila Hotel was built as an American hotel by an American architect, William Parsons, who decided to build a 'California Mission' style hotel with white-washed walls and steeply pitched green tile roof with wide eaves. Guests would arrive by car or carriage along a sweeping circular drive. The vast lobby would have graceful Doric columns of white plaster separated by arches and a double grand staircase.

The 149 guest rooms boasted private bath, telephones and pushbutton room service. The hotel had many firsts in Asia—the first intercom system, the first ice-making plant, the first electric elevators installed in a hotel. An additional annexe was soon built to accommodate another eighty guests.

Traditional Filipino materials were used—capiz shell set into wooden window frames replaced glass, local furniture was of rattan and bamboo, and parquet floors were of beautiful local narra mahogony. Peacock chairs of white-painted rattan were attractively grouped on the lobby's marble floors. The decor was a cool green and white, with lush tropical plants bringing the gardens indoors.

Silver, crystal, tea and coffee services were imported from England. Fresh fruit and vegetables were supplied from the hotel's own farm on the city outskirts.

In front of the circular drive two cannons from the Spanish-American War were placed. An American flag flew from the roof.

On the roof garden guests could relax, enjoying the cool breeze from the bay and being entertained by a musical or dance programme. The view of Manila's renowned flaming sunsets was spectacular.

The Luneta, Manila's most famous park, opposite the hotel, was the centre of social life, with beautiful women in graceful flowing dresses and men in white linen suits parading in horse-drawn carriages while a band played. In the park each morning, the American flag was raised, while the 'Star-Spangled Banner' was played and every Filipino had to salute the flag.

The hotel was designed by an American for Americans and Filipinos were at first discouraged from using it. The guest list for the grand opening consisted of prominent Americans, but no Filipinos.

It was a celebration to beat anything seen before in the nation's capital. Four hundred illustrious guests sipped champagne and feasted on American roast beef and Filipino lobster, dancing till dawn.

The spectacle opened with a parade of automobiles around the Luneta, led by Governor-General William Forbes and the Secretary of War Dickenson, while the Constabulary Band played and pretty girls showered the cars with flowers. After a band concert, fountains of fireworks burst across the sky over the old Spanish walled city of Intramuros.

At nine o'clock guests in magnificent evening clothes arrived in cars and carriages at the hotel while uninvited guests crammed the gardens, peering in windows. Many, emboldened by the festive air, took an uninvited tour inside.

The hotel management was totally American, while Filipinos occupied more lowly positions as waiters, waitresses, maids and bell boys. But gradually, prejudice broke down as Americans invited Filipino friends and business acquaintances to join them at dinner or drinks. The lobby became a favourite meeting place.

Celebrities began arriving. In 1922 the Prince of Wales arrived on the HMS *Renown* on a goodwill mission to Japan. He stopped in Manila for a few chukkas of polo and set feminine hearts a-flutter at a reception held at the Manila Hotel.

Lady Mountbatten, wife of the British Commander of the Pacific Fleet, was often seen at the hotel. Permanent guests included wealthy Americans who had made a fortune in timber, mining, pineapple or coconut plantations.

Douglas Fairbanks thrilled a crowded lobby when he nonchalantly vaulted the staircase with one hand.

The hotel's golden age was 1935 to 1941—from the time of the inauguration of the country's first president until the Japanese occupation.

There were lavish grand balls where Filipino beauties dressed in national costume—the delicate *terno* (or *mestiza*) dress, lavishly embroidered or beaded. The men wore *barong tagalog*—sheer embroidered shirts. Both were made from *pina* cloth (pineapple-plant fibre) or *jusi* (banana-plant fibre). 'Maria Clara' dresses of the same fabrics, Filipino versions of dresses worn by nineteenth century Spanish ladies, were also worn with the family's finest jewellery. Women spent a fortune on lavish creations by local designers such as Ramon Valera, trying to outdo each other in style.

The balls opened with the graceful, traditional ceremonial dance called the 'Rigodon de Honor' which dated back to the previous century. By the mid 1930s rhumbas, sambas, tangos, and pasa dobles were added to waltzes and formal court dances. This era also saw the great conventions and a tourist influx. Pan Am clippers had arrived, creating a faster link with the United States than sea voyages. Flights took five days, with stopovers for the night at Guam, Wake Island and Honolulu, while ships took twenty-five days.

The Manila Hotel became inextricably linked with General Douglas MacArthur in 1935, when President Quezon asked him to become his military adviser.

MacArthur had many links with the country. His father, General Arthur MacArthur, had headed the combined United States and Filipino army which drove the Spaniards out during the Spanish-American War, and had subsequently become the First American military governor. Douglas first came in 1903 as a young lieutenant to oversee defence fortifications including Corregidor (where he was to make his famous stand in the Second World War) and returned in 1922 to help plan defence.

General Douglas MacArthur was agreeable but demanded VIP treatment—a salary equal to that of former governors-general and accommodation in Malacanang Palace. He got the salary, but not the palace. Instead, Pedro Luna, son of one of the greatest Filipino painters, was commissioned by the Philippine government to design and build the general a penthouse on the top floor of the Manila Hotel.

For six years MacArthur and his family lived in what is now known as the MacArthur Suite. By all accounts it was a luxurious pad—seven bedrooms, a library to hold his 10,000 books on military history, a music room, formal dining room, bathrooms, kitchen, maids' rooms—and air-conditioned throughout.

His personal staff of five officers was headed by Major Dwight D. Eisenhower, who with wife, Mamie, was later to make a return visit.

Macarthur's accommodation charges were taken care of by making him chairman of the hotel's board and providing free rent in lieu of a retainer. The hotel provided him with a permanent household staff.

Some of the MacArthur family's most pleasant memories were linked to the hotel. MacArthur had married in 1937 in the United States a Jean Faircloth—she was thirty-six, he was fifty-seven—and had a magnificent wedding reception at the hotel. Their son, Arthur, born in 1938, was christened at the hotel. President Quezon and his wife Dona Aurora were godparents.

Following President Quezon's inauguration in 1935, leading Filipino families with fortunes from mining, timber, shipping and publishing flocked to the Manila Hotel for parties, balls, debutante launchings, formal dinners and weddings. The open-air Fiesta Pavilion became the 'in place' for dining, dancing and romancing to the hotel's orchestra. Blocks of ice were set around the edge of the pavilion with fans blowing on them to cool the dancers.

The band played and people danced and drank literally up to the day the Japanese invaded and occupied the city on 27 July 1941. American and European guests were ordered to pack only one suitcase each with three days' supply of food and some blankets and await further instructions. About 4000 ended up in an internment camp in the University of Santo Tomas. To add insult to injury, they were sent outstanding accounts for payment in cash, by the Japanese who had taken over the hotel. Those who could pay got the rest of their luggage back, others only the most necessary items.

The MacArthur family had left their penthouse with practically all their personal belongings shortly before the Japanese arrived, and dug in with troops on the fortress of Corregidor, a tiny rock island, a short distance from Manila.

The Japanese military took possession of the hotel which became military headquarters for the highest ranking army and navy officers. Visiting dignitaries from Tokyo included General Tomoyuki Yamashita, the 'Tiger of Malaya' and conqueror of Singapore, and Premier Hideki Tojo, who made two wartime visits.

MacArthur's penthouse was left intact for visiting Japanese VIPs, perhaps because he had left a pair of bronze vases at the entrance, gifts which had been inscribed to his father, General Arthur MacArthur, from the former Emperor of Japan. But, unfortunately, the suite did not survive the last great battle of Manila in 1944.

MacArthur and his allied forces had fought their way through the Philippines islands and the Japanese made a last stand in the city, more than eighty per cent of which was destroyed.

The Japanese withdrew into the old walled city, Intramuros, and the Manila Hotel, which had been converted into a fortress. The hotel saw bitter floor to floor and room to room fighting. The MacArthur suite was put to fire and personal effects (those which had not already been stolen) destroyed. The allied soldiers found a Japanese colonel dead on the penthouse threshold, the broken pieces of the Emperor's vases at his head and feet.

The hotel was devastated by war, but nothing could keep down its fighting spirit. MacArthur had returned as promised. It was time to get on with the business of living. The hotel's first job was to supply Chinese cooks to prepare meals in the prison camp for survivors. Its first post-war guests were soldiers garrisoned in its stark rooms.

A new MacArthur suite was built. MacArthur himself gave a joyful dinner for old friends in the ruined Fiesta Pavilion, its shattered plaster walls draped with parachute silk.

The great balls were resurrected and ladies appeared again in freshened-up pre-war embroidered gowns with fine jewellery (recovered from hiding places). They took once more to the dance floor with the graceful Rigodon de Honor. Charity balls were held to raise money to rebuild the city.

A new manager, a Swiss Filipino, Charles Holman, was appointed. A stylishly dressed and renowned sportsman, he determined to make the hotel the centre of social life again and also to attract less exclusive customers. The famous *merienda* afternoon teas were restored and a splendid Saturday lunch buffet—as much as you could eat for a few dollars—became an institution.

Nightclub acts, lively dance bands and singers (Benny Goodman and Buddy Greco performed), dance competitions, door prizes—even dancing lessons—attracted new customers, while famous balls continued to be showcases for rich society women who modelled gowns by famous designers.

In 1950 a new nightclub, the Winter Garden, opened.

But, amid all the gaiety, an ugly element—violence and corruption—had crept into Manila life, involving the hotel in some nasty incidents. An American investigator named Prescott was murdered in the hotel lobby. Two jeep-loads of hoodlums, armed with machine guns, shot him through the open door as he sat in an armchair reading a magazine. News had apparently got around that he was there to investigate corruption surrounding misappropriation of American surplus war supplies given to the Phillipine government.

A second shooting occurred following an argument over table reservations between two wealthy Filipino families. A young man of the Batangas family killed a son of the Malabon family while diners dived for cover under tables.

On another occasion, a room boy at the hotel shot one of the security guards as he slept in staff quarters, after the guard had reported him to management for stealing a bottle of whisky.

Even the luxurious MacArthur suite got a reputation for sinister goings on as corrupt politicians met there to talk over nefarious deals.

Like all great hotels, the Manila had its share of interesting and bizarre characters. A wealthy Canadian couple, for instance, ate everthing in sight including leftovers such as bread, cake and rolls, which they folded in their table napkins and consumed in private. Their gargantuan appetites caused such gross overweight that they had to dance side by side. Their vast bellies got in the way of face to face, let alone cheek to cheek,dancing.

A colourful 'nephew of the Nizam of Hyderabad' turned out to be an impoverished Englishman who was thrown out when he refused to pay his bill. A 'Prince Kamala of Hawaii' was prosecuted for swindle and deported after he ran up an enormous unpaid bill. An official Argentinian representative of Eva Peron was arrested after failing to pay hotel charges.

The eccentric 'Baroness Anna Jean von Hagen', who treated staff arrogantly and insisted on being called 'Princess', 'Baroness' or 'Your Highness', would tell anyone who listened that her five husbands had included a Hindu prince and a German nobleman. When her fortune was dissipated in lavish living, the hotel suggested she move on. She did—to other grand hotels in the East.

The hotel's most unusual 'guests' were 400 cats (the population had exploded from an original few cats kept to keep down rats in the kitchen) and twelve dogs, there for 'security reasons'.

By the 1950s the great hotel was in debt. Leading political figures had parties and had run up enormous bills without paying, the hotel was overstaffed, and competition from new hotels fierce. Pilfering had created a big loss as customers souvenired silver, towels, and linen.

The Government decided to offer the hotel for lease and eventual sale. In 1954 the Bayview Hotel Corporation took it over and renovated it.

VIPs began flocking to the charmingly restored hotel. They included Sir Anthony Eden, Senator Robert Kennedy, President Sukarno of Indonesia, and at various times film stars galore—John Wayne, Marlon Brando, Burgess Meredith, Van Heflin, Cornel Wilde, William Holden, Tyrone Power and wife Linda Christian. Twentieth Century Fox held a huge reception in the Winter Garden so that locals could meet some of the stars. Many a movie was being shot in the glamorous East.

The hotel also served as official residence for important government guests and was still used for government functions.

By the 1960s tourists (including war veterans) were flocking to Manila.

Then, in 1972, the now really shabby hotel was shut down for four years, following a rash of bombings in the capital, including one in the Manila Hotel where a Constitutional Convention was being held. After that came martial law.

Following complete refurbishing, it reopened officially in December 1976. Its graceful colonial characteristics had been restored and even surpassed. Local materials—capiz shell in chandeliers, brass, narra wood ceilings, marble floors, seashells, stones, handwoven textiles—added to its charm. The elegant formal dining room was christened the Champagne Room and the grand ballroom became the Fiesta Pavilion (the earlier pavilion was destroyed during bombing). Today it has 570 guest rooms and suites, three restaurants, three bars, a swimming pool and health club.

But the grandest suite of all is, of course, the MacArthur Suite, now with its master bedroom, dressing room, two bathrooms, formal dining room, sitting room and kitchen, and luxury furnishings. On the walls, portraits of the General looked back at me.

The hotel has seen its good times and its bad times—but today it basks in a reputation as one of the finest grand old hotels of the East.

TAWARAYA JAPANESE INN, KYOTO

KYOTO'S famous traditional Japanese inn, the Tawaraya, is located in a narrow little street bordered with typical wooden houses with lanterns hanging outside, in the heart of this historic city.

Tawaraya means 'rice bale' and the *ya* signifies a place of business. A rice merchant lived on the spot when the inn was founded over 300 years ago, the period in which it has been owned by the Okazaki family.

It was burnt down twice and the present building is about 150 years old. The manageress, an attractive young woman, Mrs Toshi Sato, is the eleventh generation of the Okazaki family to run the inn. Her husband is director of photography at Kyoto's School of Design and a former photographer for *Time/Life* magazine. The artistic photographs on the postcards in the lobby were taken by him.

The inn has a rich history. Signatures in old registers include those of Prince Ito, Japan's first prime minister, countless *daimyo* (feudal lords), and even members of the Imperial family.

Western celebrities who have been guests at the inn include writers such as William Faulkner, Arthur Miller and Arthur Koestler, philosopher Jean-Paul Sartre and his companion, Simone de Beauvoir, film makers Alfred Hitchcock and Michelangelo Antonioni, painter Willem de Kooning, composer and conductor Leonard Bernstein, Canadian Prime Minister Pierre Trudeau. John D. Rockefeller IV spent part of his honeymoon here.

The accent is on traditional service. Each room has its personal maid who attends to every want. Guests are welcomed by a row of kimono-clad servants. An old man takes guests' shoes, quickly burnishing them to a mirror finish before they are ready to leave the hotel.

Then you pad off in slippered feet to a room furnished in impeccable Japanese style—from the long low red lacquer table surrounded with cushions and richly brocaded arm rests, to the graceful ikebana flower arrangement and the tasteful brocade scroll on the wall.

A welcoming drink of seaweed tea—good for the health I was told—and thin rice biscuits await me while I fill in hotel registration forms in my room. A sliding screen reveals a small sitting room overlooking a tranquil private garden—Japanese style, down to the stone basin and bamboo scoop worshippers used outside temples to wash. A television set on the bedroom floor, beside a rice paper lantern, provides a modern touch.

When I return from exploring the city, I find the *futon* (bedding) laid out on the *tatami* (floor mats) with lots of warm blankets and pillows, a back rest and quilt provided. A *yukata* (Japanese bathrobe) is neatly folded on top. A jug of iced water, newspapers, a torch, and the lighted paper lamp are placed by the bed.

A steaming hot bath has been laid in the big square wooden bath with its three-hinged lid to keep the water scalding hot. A thermometer is provided to test the temperature.

You don't soap in the bath. The correct ritual is to sit on the little wooden stool, soap yourself, then rinse off with a basin of water (or under the shower in this case). The satiny cypress bath is for a long relaxing soak with water right up to your chin.

I am woken gently next morning when a bowing maid presents green tea and a neatly folded newspaper. Later, she returns to fold the bed linen and place it back in its cupboard. I opt for a Western-style breakfast of scrambled egg, toast, marmalade, fruit juice and tea as a change from traditional ones which include seaweed, rice with raw egg, and pickles.

I feel like royalty as the whole staff assemble and bow to farewell me. A stay at a *ryokan* (Japanese inn) is a wonderful boost to the ego.

THE AMERICAN COLONY HOTEL, JERUSALEM

GRAND old hotels, hotels with fascinating histories, or charming small hotels with friendly staff, always attract me on my travels.

The American Colony hotel in Jerusalem, for instance, is

unique. It used to be a Turkish pasha's mansion, with a harem of beautiful ladies secreted behind locked doors.

Today's lovely garden courtyard, with its splashing fountain and lemon and palm trees, was once part of the harem. Its tranquil atmosphere encourages you to linger, sip coffee and eat rich chocolate cake at little tables under gay umbrellas. One of the palm trees was a gift from Baron von Ustinov, grandfather of actor Peter Ustinov. From the courtyard you can see the minaret of the mosque next door and hear the muezzin's call to prayer.

The hotel is white-washed, covered in blue honeysuckle and lies within the Arab quarter, about a twenty-minute walk from the old walled city. It has stone floors, curved archways and old Arabian coffee pots, tables and trays of brass. Yet the simple, modern Swedish furniture fits in splendidly. There is a superb mosaic wall in the foyer, made of Persian blue tiles produced by the local Armenian tile factory in the 1920s. The factory, incidentally, is not far from the hotel and still produces lovely tiles.

Bedrooms are simple with white-washed walls, rugs on stone floors. Mine was cleaned by an Arab woman, in voluminous robes and head scarf who lurked around constantly (always in attendance when I left or returned to the hotel). I called her the 'Red Shadow' and discovered later that it was not devotion to duty which kept her there, but the fear guests would leave without tipping her.

The hotel was famous for its food, including its Arab dishes, and its enormous buffet breakfast. The swimming pool added a modern touch and a dip was always welcome after a long day sightseeing. I was lucky enough to meet a fellow guest, a professor of archaeology from America, awaiting his students who came on a yearly expedition to Caesarea. He was an ideal companion for walks in the Old City.

The hotel is a favourite haunt of journalists, writers, United Nations officials, painters, actors and archaeologists. Peter O'Toole, Sir Alec Guinness, Graham Greene, John le Carré, Leon Uris, Peter Ustinov, Malcolm Muggeridge have all stayed here. It was the location for a number of movies including *Ashanti* and *The Pay Off*. In the early days of the British occupation, Field Marshall Lord Allenby and T.E. Lawrence (Lawrence of Arabia) stayed here frequently.

The hotel played a significant part in the surrender of Jerusalem on 9 December 1917, when the Mayor of Jerusalem, Hussein el Husseini, used a sheet from the hotel as his white flag when he went to meet the British army which was advancing on Jerusalem from the west.

The hotel was actually built as a private house by a Turkish lawyer from Istanbul called Khaldi. When he died without children, the house was shared out among 140 relatives. It took the Spafford family, who now own it, fifty years to buy them all out. The family bought the hotel on the advice of Baron von Ustinov, who owned and managed the Park Hotel in the seaport of Jaffa, and who considered hotel accommodation in Jerusalem inadequate.

The story of the American Colony Hotel begins with a shipwreck on the night of 21 November 1873. An American couple from Chicago, Horatio and Anna Spafford, had planned a holiday in Europe with their four little daughters. Mr Spafford was delayed by business and his wife and the children went on ahead of him.

In mid-Atlantic their ship, the SS *Ville du Havre*, collided with another ship and sank. The four children were drowned and the mother alone was picked up unconscious. That night she had a religious experience which changed her life. It is not recorded exactly what that experience was.

Back in Chicago the Spaffords became dissatisfied with their lives and, with a group of friends, decided to go to Jerusalem.

Shortly after their arrival, Horatio Spafford died and his widow, with the two daughters born after the shipwreck, and the other members of the group, decided to stay in Jerusalem. They lived a simple communal life in a house inside the city walls.

Some years later, a group of Swedish farmers joined them. The story of their arrival and subsequent life in Jerusalem formed the basis of two novels by the Swedish writer, Selma Lagerlof, one called *Jerusalem*, the other *The Holy City*, for which she received the Nobel Prize.

In order to support themselves the group opened a souvenir shop at the Jaffa Gate and a photographic enterprise, which became famous for its archives of the Middle East, now in the Library of Congress in Washington. The Swedish farmers became the artisans of Jerusalem, its carpenters and mechanics.

About 1890 they started buying the buildings which now form the hotel. At that time pilgrims came in large numbers, frequently on foot. They arrived at Jaffa, on the coast, by ship and were met on board by the local tourist agent who had arranged their tours in the Holy Land. They were brought ashore to spend a night in a hotel in Jaffa, possibly the Park Hotel. Then they travelled the country on a horse, camping at sites of historic interest, and finally rejoining the ship in Jaffa, Haifa or Beirut.

The American Colony Hotel came into being in 1902 to cater for this type of tourist. It was so called because it was situated in the northern part of Jerusalem which, at that time, was known as the American Colony.

The same family still own it, although it is now managed by a Swiss company. Horatio Vester, a lawyer and grandchild of the original couple, managed it for fifteen years. When I met him and learnt the hotel's fascinating history, he was retired, but still living in the hotel.

The family's remarkable story is told in *Our Jerusalem— an American Family in the Holy City 1881–1949* by Bertha Spafford Vester.

Even as I wrote my notes, the muezzin's evening call from the nearby minaret conjured up visions of the harem beauties who once enjoyed the garden in which I sat sipping my coffee.

THE BEVERLY HILLS HOTEL

THE Beverly Hills Hotel on Sunset Boulevard symbolizes all the glamour of Hollywood in its heyday.

Film stars have always flocked to the luxury hotel they call the Pink Palace. Liz Taylor's father ran an art gallery in its shopping arcade and Liz spent a lot of her childhood here.

Guests at this home away from home for the rich and famous have always felt they could 'do their own thing'. Katherine Hepburn, for instance, clad in tennis gear, once leapt into the swimming pool for the hell of it.

Ventriloquist Edgar Bergen held a party for his dummy, Charlie McCarthy, in the ballroom which was transformed into an old-style music hall.

A fourteen-year old son of a Turkish *pasha* hid a bear cub in the bathroom.

Millionairess Barbara Hutton booked seven rooms, including one for her clothes. When John Lennon and Yoko Ono stayed in a garden bungalow, four armed guards were hired to protect it.

The Pink Palace itself has also starred in movies, including Neil Simon's *California Suite*.

The hotel has a fascinating history. It was built in 1912, a year before Beverly Hills became incorporated as a city, by Burton Green, president of the Rodeo Land and Water Company which had subdivided the area for development in 1907.

The company had started life as Amalgamated Oil and drilled for oil, but found water, a marketable commodity at the time. Green decided that a hotel would attract home buyers to an area which was largely deserted, apart from a few farmers.

He created a gracious, pseudo-Spanish mission-style stucco hotel with ochre tiles. Instead of the usual white, it was painted salmon pink. Its first manager, Mrs Margaret Anderson, was poached from the Hollywood Hotel with an offer of a lease and option to buy at a reasonable price.

As Green had hoped, wealthy people bought homes and Mrs Anderson bought the hotel. In the 1920s it became a popular country retreat and centre of social life with dances, parties, and concerts. Tennis, a pool, and free movies were other attractions.

Even then it attracted celebrities. Barbara Hutton, a rich child at the time, arrived with her chauffeur and bodyguard to enjoy the free games and entertainment the hotel provided for children on festive occasions.

As the roaring twenties got under way, the hotel changed its conservative image to a more jazzy one. The façade blazed with a battery of red, yellow and blue lights as flappers arrived to charleston. During prohibition Le Jardin (The Garden) Lounge—later to be renamed the Polo Lounge—served tea instead of alcohol.

Business confidence evaporated as the Wall Street crash ushered in the Depression years. The hotel was shabby and there was no money to refurbish. It closed in 1933, but managed to reopen the following year.

It became a favourite hangout for revellers such as John Barrymore, W. C. Fields, Darryl Zanuck, Errol Flynn and Charlie Chaplin. Writers who patronized it included F. Scott Fitzgerald and John Steinbeck. Writer and wit, Dorothy Parker, said waspishly at the time: 'This is the place where elephants go to die'. Perhaps she meant pink elephants as the gang were a convivial bunch.

By 1936 the hotel was in trouble again. It was saved when a group led by a flamboyant bank executive, Hernando Courtright, bought it.

Hernando became manager and determined to glamorize the Hotel's image. Each suite was individually designed by a fashionable designer. The gardens were replanted. An arcade of shops was added.

Film stars flocked to the hotel—Cary Grant, Constance and Joan Bennett, Katherine Hepburn. So did bankers, business tycoons, maharajas, millionaires, jet setters, royalty, heads of state. The swimming pool became an exclusive club with members owning the colourfully striped canvas cabanas surrounding it.

In 1943 Courtright and his friends, who included film stars Irene Dunne and Loretta Young and their husbands, Frank Griffin and Tom Lewis, bought the hotel, which became even more popular with film celebrities.

Then came the Second World War and the hotel became a popular hostelry for top military brass and aircraft executive.

Although alcohol supplies had dried up throughout America, the hotel still had the finest wines and champagnes, thanks to Courtright's foresight. He had done a pre-war tour of Europe's vineyards, stocking up the cellar.

After the war, the stars returned—Danny Kaye, Hedy Lamarr, Paulette Goddard, Liz Taylor. But rumours of the impending opening of the Beverly Hilton Hotel nearby scared the owners of the Pink Palace who sold it in 1954 to an investor, and real estate owner, Ben Silberstein, for $5.5 million. People thought him crazy to pay such a price (the land boom was still to come) but he saw the hotel's potential.

Today, the Beverly Hills Hotel still attracts royalty, business tycoons, television and film stars. As an old saying goes: 'If you want to make absolutely sure that everyone knows you are in town, stay at the Pink Palace.'

If you want to make a grand entrance, you can sweep up the palm-tree lined driveway in your chauffeur-driven Rolls Royce or Mercedes and proceed along the red carpet from the driveway to the lobby. But, unless you are a super celebrity, other guests are unlikely to notice. They have seen it all before.

Guests arriving with no luggage pose no problem. In the shopping arcade you can buy everything from a toothbrush to a glamorous nightie from exclusive shops. But, if you haven't booked well ahead, you stand little chance of finding accommodation. Even if you have, over-booking may mean you are referred to another hotel.

Once checked in, a bell boy conducts you from the lobby with its marble desk, mirrors, art deco murals, potted palm trees and enormous basket of flowers, to your suite. The corridors along the way are painted pink and lined with an incredible frieze of banana leaves, each individually cut from rolls of expensive wallpaper. The design was created by Don Loper, famous Hollywood couturier, in the late 1930s. It created such envy among female patrons that patches were souvenired from the ladies' room and the hotel had to put up a notice: 'If you really want this, contact our decorator.'

On the way to your suite you can ponder on the greats who stayed here. Royalty include King Olav of Norway, Queen Margrethe II of Denmark, the Emperor of Japan, Queen Juliana of the Netherlands, King Faisal. Famous include President Kennedy, Lindberg the flying ace, Groucho Marx, comedians Jack Benny and Jack Lemon.

Woolworth heiress Barbara Hutton lived in seclusion at the hotel for years. So did eccentric millionaire, Howard Hughes. Warren Beatty had his office here. Glenda Jackson, Peter Ustinov, George Segal, Gregory Peck, Sidney Poitier, and Paul Newman have sampled its luxury.

Your room will have thick, soft towels, scented monogrammed soap, a basket of flowers. Pick up the phone and the switch girl will answer with your name.

Once you've been a guest you name goes onto a guest card. The filing system goes like this: white cards for first timers, blue for second visitors, pink for VIPs. Your likes and dislikes will be noted—favourite drinks, preferred room locations, preference for a hard or soft mattress, food dislikes.

The hotel tries to please. Faye Dunaway got the fried chicken she requested in the middle of the night. Ethel Kennedy's children played chasing in the kitchen. Barbara Hutton received a constant supply of Coca-Cola. Lord Snowden got his French cigarettes specially flown in. Princess Margaret's favourite gin and tonic was supplied, instead of the champagne she dislikes. Liz Taylor's suite always had pistachio nuts on the table to nibble with her drinks.

One Texas oil millionaire asked for bear steak for breakfast as a joke. He got it on his next visit. It had been frozen and flown from Alaska, much to his astonishment.

The Duke and Duchess of Windsor ordered *filet mignons* from room service for their pampered pugs. Princess Margaret and Lord Snowden reserved an entire fourth floor and management redecorated it to please them.

Raquel Welch used to visit the hotel's beauty salon, the Duke of Windsor, Howard Hughes and Mike Todd the barber shop, while an array of stars—including Sophia Loren, Clark Gable, Ginger Rogers, Tyrone Power and Harpo Marx—patronized the coffee shop. Brigitte Bardot is reputed to have been turned away from the pukka Polo Lounge because she was bare footed.

With so many film-star guests, it is not surprising that the hotel has a private cinema including a 35 millimetre Cinemascope screen. Dean Martin, Sammy Davis junior, Elizabeth Taylor and other stars have rented it.

Apart from the main building, the hotel has twenty-one pink bungalows in the garden. These are popular with celebrities wanting privacy. Howard Hughes and Jean Peters, his wife, lived in adjoining bungalows for years. At one time he kept four bungalows, two suites and two rooms permanently, at a cost of more than $1000 a day (a fortune in those days). One bungalow was for his wife, another for eight Mormon bodyguards, other suites for guests, a fourth bungalow left empty, with no one allowed in. One inquisitive bell boy found piles of blueprints and records for his flying boat, the *Spruce Goose*, which he designed to help win the Second World War, but which only managed to fly one mile in 1947. It is now in a special museum at Long Beach. When Hughes left the bungalow the place was thick with dust and curtains crumbling.

Hughes would drive up in a panel van to evade people

and management were forbidden to speak to him. Two leased Cadillacs were kept in the garage but never used. In the grounds several cars and a station wagon waited just in case. He tipped garage staff $600 at Christmas just to keep his cars on standby.

When he couldn't sleep, the eccentric millionaire sometimes hired an orchestra to play all night.

One full-time employee was occupied solely in making roast beef sandwiches, wrapping them in wax paper and leaving them in a certain tree near the bungalow so that Hughes could secretly collect them.

Hughes once called a business meeting for 4 a.m. in the vast Crystal Room, refusing the management's suggested smaller room. He and his three associates sat at a small table under a crystal chandelier discussing business, secure, Hughes said, in the knowledge that no one could spy on them.

Liz Taylor stayed at Bungalow 5, the largest, when married to Burton—at other bungalows with other husbands. Marilyn Monroe and Arthur Miller once occupied No. 20, with Yves Montand and Simone Signoret next door in 21. Monroe and Miller were reputed to have had a grand affair here in the late 1950s. Clark Gable and Carol Lombard are also said to have had several secret meetings in the bungalows.

Driving up to the rose-pink-painted hotel in its nearly five hectares of lush gardens bordered with palm trees, I noticed on the right side of the hotel portal an inscription. It read: 'Bien Venido Amigo' (welcome). On the left another inscription read: 'Vaya Con Dios' (goodbye). It is a reminder of the tradition of Spanish mission hospitality.

In early Californian days, Spanish missions welcomed weary travellers. Friars seated them before a roaring fire, and gave them food and wine. The missions, built a day's journey apart, gave hospitality to wayfarers in the days before hotels served that purpose.

The flickering hearth fire in the lobby which never goes out, summer or winter, is another symbol of hospitality. Once it was a roaring log fire; now artificial logs and a gas flame occupy the fireplace.

In the grounds are championship tennis courts presided over by former Wimbledon champion and professional coach, Alex Olmedo. An Olympic-size heated swimming pool with a cluster of yellow and white striped cabanas alongside (reserved for members of a private pool club) is a popular spot for stars of film and television staying at the hotel to show off their tans.

But, if you want to spot celebrities, the Polo Lounge is the place to be. Over a gin and tonic in the lounge I saw Ginger Rogers paying her bill. Johnny Carson (American television star), Barbara Stanwyck, and writer Gore Vidal were staying at the hotel.

Dinner in the hotel's lavish restaurant can set you back $200 a couple, but you can have a light lunch in the Polo Lounge—spaghetti and salad, with ice tea, for instance—for about fourteen dollars, at a table set with shiny silver and a vase of fresh pink roses.

One of the most popular dishes is the McCarthy Salad, named after Neil McCarthy, Philanthropist, polo player and lawyer (one client was Mary Pickford) who patronized the lounge. It consisted of chicken, cheese, egg, bacon, beetroot, and chopped lettuce.

A drink in the Polo Lounge will set you back about as much as in a Sydney first-class hotel.

The Polo Lounge changed its name from Le Jardin Lounge in 1941 when polo players who gathered there, including actors John Barrymore and Will Rogers, and producers Darryl Zanuck and Walter Wanger, thought it sounded too sissy. The new name was clinched when a polo trophy was left there by a winning player.

Over lunch in the lounge, literary agents, film producers and investors do deals, sign contracts, interview job seekers. Everyone wants to be seen at the Polo Lounge—or at least make their presence felt by being summoned to the phone.

Diminutive (120 centimetre tall) page, Buddy Douglas, dressed in brass-buttoned jacket and red-striped pants, is a famous figure. Buddy will call your name, then bring the pink phone and plug it in to your table—that's if you are at one of the banquette tables, the most desirable ones. Otherwise you have to follow him to the phone. Buddy is rumoured to be rich from generous tips.

It is said that fading film stars have themselves paged by telephoning the hotel from afar, hoping to remind producers they are still around and in demand.

Many up and coming Australian film producers stay at the

Pink Palace because it's 'the place' to be seen and to sign contracts.

The rich and famous often drop by the Polo Lounge for a meal or drink. The cast of thousands has included Frank Sinatra, Princess Grace, Henry Kissinger, Paul Newman, Liza Minelli, Warren Beatty, Jack Nicholson, Joan Fontaine, Olivia de Havilland, Cary Grant, and Faye Dunaway.

Cocktail time—5 to 7.30 p.m.—is popular partly because of the delicious free guacamole dip, crackers, cheese and tortilla chips.

Today the Beverly Hills Hotel is a much-loved institution— part of the history of Hollywood's most glamorous heyday. Showbiz stars may fade, movie studios close, royals disappear into history, but the Pink Palace goes from strength to strength.